Echoes from Hawaiki

Echoes from Hawaiki

The origins and development of Māori and Moriori musical instruments

JENNIFER CATTERMOLE

OTAGO UNIVERSITY PRESS
Te Whare Tā o Te Wānanga o Ōtākou

Tukua te wairua kia rere ki ngā taumata
Hai ārahi i ā tātou mahi
Me tā tātou whai i ngā tikanga a rātou mā
Kia mau kia ita
Kia kore ai e ngaro
Kia pupuri
Kia whakamaua
Kia tina! Tina! Hui e! Tāiki e!

This book is dedicated to Shannon Mako, an incredibly generous, kind and spiritual man and gifted taonga pūoro maker and player, who made an indelible mark on all those lucky enough to meet him. It is also dedicated to my father, David Cattermole, who journeyed alongside me on te ara pūoro during the last few years of his life. The inclusion of many of his taonga in this book is a tribute to his mahi.

Kua hinga te tōtara i Te Waonui a Tāne.

Contents

Foreword

E muramura ahi ka ki uta
E muramura ahi ka ki tai
Ki tararava`i ra a te moana
Ki tini moutere ki tafiti

Me koragia o tadu ahi ka
Kia kitea e tadu noa

May our fires burn brightly inland
May they burn along our coasts
And across the seas
To distant lands far beyond

May the sparks of our bright fires
Be seen by us all

It was not long ago that bright fires were generated by our Polynesian ancestors. They lived with the environment, totally reliant on the natural world. The time available for activities like making music was limited by daylight hours, seasonal patterns and the need to prioritise essential pursuits for survival and daily living. This raises the question, 'How did our forebears succeed in creating a bountiful array of musical instruments using stone tools and natural materials?' This book answers that question in fine detail.

Making an instrument may have been as simple as plucking a leaf from a tree. Often it was more difficult, involving stone tools, fire, fibre, water, steam, sharkskin or sinew from birds and animals. These instruments might be decorated with feathers, flowers, shells, stones, dyes or anything else that came to hand. They provided voice, sound, rhythm, melody or vibration to accompany dance, art, craft, healing, rituals or other human efforts.

In more recent years, sparks from that older world have been rekindled to proudly take their place in our own hearths, as bright and vibrant fires that inspire our present generation to instigate quests for answers.

Within the pages of this book, we are invited to venture, in good faith, into our ancestors' world of musical instruments. Many taonga pūoro were nearly lost to mind but have been resurrected through in-depth and interactive research involving a protocol that prioritises the sharing of knowledge and expertise in conversations between writers, well-informed persons and 'the people of the place'.

It has been said that we place our names to remind us of our history and who we are. To place a name is a very special task and should not be undertaken lightly. It is pleasing to learn the reasoning behind indigenous naming processes associated with individual groups of instruments.

Jennifer Cattermole's observations show how our present generation is reviving indigenous culture and language, thereby sustaining our brightly burning fires. Modern machinery and advanced photography enable us to gaze and reason upon images with greater clarity and purpose. The photographs here that accompany the text are stunning, and beautifully support the narrative.

Individuals and organisations can take hold of and use the wealth of wisdom and information contained within this study. Protocols, skills, training, teaching, learning and experimentation become streams for further development and improvisation of our precious world of authentic Māori and Moriori musical instruments.

This publication will be a most worthy companion, an inspiration and a font of knowledge to anyone who turns its pages. At last, this book has found us a time to return the ancient sounds to the landscape.

Me enei rau o ro tonu tenei taoka nei, kia filifilia ra me aroha noa.
May these leaves within this treasure be truly rustled with loving care.

Heoi ano
So be it

Boua Huata Holmes
Kāitahu, Kāti Mamoe, Waitaha, Hāwea a Rapuwai ano
Kaumātua
November 2023

Preface

Everyone's journey along te ara pūoro, the pathway of sound, is unique. The catalyst for my own journey was a presentation made by Richard Nunns, a key member of the taonga pūoro revival, to a class I attended at the University of Otago. Richard laid a variety of taonga on a table covered with black velvet and demonstrated their uses and sounds. The instruments were indescribably beautiful and their voices resonated in my heart and soul. His stories captivated and touched me – particularly those about his experiences of using the taonga to communicate with whales and birds, and the instruments' profound connection to the spiritual realm. Taonga pūoro seemed the perfect combination of several things I was deeply interested in: Māori culture, whakairo (carving), the natural environment and music.

When I was young, carver Noel Gorton taught me to shape soapstone using saws, files and scrapers. I became interested in bone and pounamu carving and Māori carving styles and made a commitment to respectfully and safely engage in Māori creative practice informed by tikanga and mātauranga Māori.

In 2011 I was offered a job teaching ethnomusicology at the University of Otago. I was keen to learn more about taonga pūoro and integrate these into my creative practice and teaching. The head of music, Graeme Downes, was encouraging, and the department purchased a whānau of taonga pūoro made by Brian Flintoff, Clem Mellish (Ngāpuhi) and Warren Warbrick (Rangitāne, Te Arawa). I found myself kaitiaki of these incredible instruments and was conscious of the need to understand the appropriate tikanga for such profoundly tapu taonga. In 2012 Richard Nunns and Alistair Fraser visited Dunedin to record at Orokonui Ecosanctuary and run a wānanga at the University of Otago. They taught me key things about tapu and noa as these concepts relate to taonga pūoro, and this gave me sufficient knowledge to start engaging with the taonga, learning how to coax them to sing so that I could pass that knowledge on to others.

In my last conversation with Richard, he mentioned receiving knowledge about taonga pūoro in dreams. That's something we have in common. I'm humbled to also receive knowledge in dreams; this gives me a sense of validation and inclusion within the taonga pūoro community. I'm continually learning. I'm in awe of the healing abilities of these instruments and am constantly surprised when I hear new and unexpected facets of their voices, even after several years of playing. I love that every taonga is unique and that they all have their own distinctive wairua and, on occasion, a very definite will of their own. Every act of 'playing' is an act of partnership and co-creation. For me, these performances reinforce and help me better understand the Māori idea that everything (or, more appropriately, every*one*) is animate and possesses wairua.

There's something in my spirit that needs grounding in nature: getting dirt or sand on the soles of my feet and under my fingernails; listening to birdsong and the voices of wind and water; caressing bark, moss and leaves; smelling clean, cold air, tangy sea salt, rich and musty disturbed humus. All these things nurture and sustain me. Taonga pūoro have helped me better understand my place within Aotearoa and my relationships with te ao Māori and the natural world.

Taonga pūoro have also changed how I relate to my environment. My father, David Cattermole, made a nguru (flute) from stone sourced from Douglas Creek in South Westland and we returned there to seek the river's blessing on that taonga and to introduce the awa to that nguru's voice. The awa sang to us in a flute-like voice, and by sharing our hau (breath), the nguru and I sang right back to the awa. I've learnt to consciously and actively listen to my environment, and this has changed my sense of self when I play outdoors. I become purely a channeller and enabler of sound as I attune to my surroundings. When I'm concentrating solely on what I hear, I'm hyper-aware that I am only one sound in a vast and ever-changing soundscape, which is humbling. I experience a profound sense of connectivity, of being part of a whole. I also delight in finding those exceptional naturally occurring taonga whose special voice means they end up joining the whānau at home: shells and barnacles, stones with natural depressions or holes in them, pieces of wood or kelp.

This book aims to further the revival of Māori and Moriori musical instruments, and to consolidate and deepen how they are understood. In the 19th and early 20th centuries, the playing of taonga pūoro was suppressed during the drive to assimilate and Christianise Māori. By that time, the Moriori people had suffered such population loss and trauma that little was remembered about their instrument traditions. The voices of these instruments were almost completely silenced, but not forever. Ngāti Tarāwhai kaumātua and educator Joe Malcolm was instrumental in the taonga pūoro revival in the 1980s, and he shared his knowledge with Hirini Melbourne (Ngāi Tūhoe, Ngāti Kahungunu), Richard Nunns and Brian Flintoff, who later became central figures in the Haumanu collective of taonga pūoro players and makers. This collective is still going strong. Inspired by Haumanu's work in Aotearoa, since 2019 I and others have been contributing to the Hokotehi Moriori Trust's ongoing efforts to revitalise Moriori music.

Both Melbourne and Nunns became interested in taonga pūoro after hearing about or seeing instruments held at Auckland Museum Tāmaki Paenga Hira. Nunns described seeing an article in the *Auckland Weekly News* in the late 1950s, which described several objects of great beauty that museum staff thought could be Māori musical instruments. The article noted that no one knew how to play them, as the performance tradition had been broken. Melbourne recalled seeing some of these instruments on display. He pressed his nose against the glass and wondered about the sounds they would create – an experience poignantly remembered in his composition 'Taku pūtōrino'.[1] The members of Haumanu resurrected taonga pūoro performance by experimenting with instruments held in museum collections or with replicas and reconstructions based on them, in conjunction with information sourced from existing literature, oral histories and music recordings. It is thanks to them, and other culture bearers in the community, that these treasures sing today.

Melbourne used a whāriki – a woven mat – as a metaphor for Māori traditional knowledge, though given how precious this knowledge is perhaps tīenga, meaning an ornately patterned mat, is an even more appropriate metaphor.[2] A key aim of this book is to help Māori reconnect with the instrument traditions of their iwi in cases where the strands in that woven mat have become frayed or broken. This book teases out some of the key similarities between regional musical instrument practices across the motu in an effort to trace the iwi and rohe that innovation came from and to shed light on possible inter-iwi relationships. Which iwi maintained their ancestral musical traditions or created new ones? What was kept? What changed and why? While this discussion is far from comprehensive, I hope the information presented here might help iwi reconnect with aspects of their own tribal cultures where that knowledge has been otherwise lost.

Only one piece of research on Moriori music has been published to date, almost 20 years ago; poignantly, it is titled 'The Silent Echoes of Chatham Island'.[3] There is more to the story, however. This book investigates Moriori miheke oro (traditional musical instruments) in a comprehensive way for the first time. The timing of this work has been serendipitous, building on, contributing to, and sometimes coinciding with work being led by the Hokotehi Moriori Trust to restore and rejuvenate aspects of Moriori culture as part of the ongoing Moriori cultural revival. I hope that the information presented here, as well as the workshops and concerts myself and my colleagues have been involved with in recent years, will inspire Moriori in their revival journey.

If this book prompts recollections of your own about Māori or Moriori musical instruments, I encourage you to preserve that information by passing it on to whomever, and in whatever form, you feel is appropriate (if, indeed, it is appropriate to do so). As Māori language, literature and culture researcher John Moorfield notes: 'The first beneficiaries of indigenous knowledge must be the direct indigenous descendants of such knowledge. Indigenous peoples are the guardians of their customary knowledge and have the right to protect and control dissemination of that knowledge'.[4] In the spirit of the karakia that opened this book, what is most important is simply that this knowledge is passed on.

JENNIFER CATTERMOLE
November 2023

Introduction: Weaving new strands in the whāriki of knowledge

This book explores the way the peoples who became Māori and Moriori continued with their ancestral musical instrument types, playing techniques and uses, while also making innovative changes to them in response to the context, materials and ways of living in their new home. In tracing this continuity and change, the book attempts to identify the likely origins of some Māori and Moriori instruments, informed by knowledge from a range of scholarly fields. This discussion is important not only to Māori and Moriori, but also to scholars internationally who are interested in histories of Polynesian migration, trade and cultural development.

Echoes from Hawaiki was inspired by a conversation with Ian Barber, a University of Otago archaeologist with extensive Moriori research experience. He suggested studying the Māori and Moriori traditional musical instruments that we now call taonga pūoro and miheke oro, respectively, and using them as a lens through which to test current theories about the origins of Aotearoa's indigenous peoples.[1] Māori musical instruments and their forebears had previously been researched by anthropologist Te Rangi Hīroa (Sir Peter Buck) in the first half of the 20th century and by ethnomusicologist Mervyn McLean in the second half, but their work required updating in light of the large amount of research done more recently that helps answer the question of where the ancestors of Māori and Moriori voyaged from.[2] While much of McLean's later work concentrated on the origins of Polynesian peoples and their music, this book's focus is a little different: it concentrates instead on the immediate geographical origins of Aotearoa and Rēkohu's first settlers.

Both Māori and Moriori oral histories name Hawaiki as their ancestral place of origin (hence the title of this book), though other terms and their variants are sometimes used interchangeably with Hawaiki, including Tahiti, Rangiātea/Ra`iātea,

Rarotonga, Vavau, `Uporu, Manuka and Iva.[3] Spiritually, Hawaiki is the source of all life and also the place the spirits of the deceased return to.

Aotearoa and Rēkohu's first inhabitants retained knowledge about the general direction their ancestors had travelled from. This knowledge was used to ensure the souls of the dead were reunited with their ancestors. In Aotearoa, souls were believed to depart for Hawaiki from Te Rerenga Wairua (the Leaping-off Place of Spirits, or Cape Rēinga) at the northern tip of Te Ika a Māui (the North Island), the location in mainland Aotearoa nearest to tropical Polynesia. Hawaiki, as the source of all life, is located in the direction of the rising sun (the east) and, as the destination of departing spirits, in the direction of the setting sun (the west).[4]

The same concepts were also important to Moriori. Moriori souls departed for Hawaiki from the westernmost points of Rēkohu – Te Raki Point and Operau – indicating a belief that Hawaiki lies to the west of Rēkohu. This is consistent with Moriori having travelled to Rēkohu from Aotearoa.[5] Moriori ancestors may have also voyaged directly to Rēkohu from central East Polynesia.[6] The first Polynesians to arrive at Rēkohu 'called themselves Hiti, which possibly indicated "Eastern people" or people of the Sunrise and the Dawn'.[7] In line with this, Wairua, the island's easternmost point, is believed to be another point for departing or arriving spirits.

Hawaiki is a name given to places in the everyday physical realm, too, with more recently inhabited places 'named in memory of the older'.[8] Hawaiki and related names also refer more generically to distance. According to respected Kāi Tahu rangatira Teone Taare Tīkao (c. 1850–1927), for example, 'Tawhiti means distance, and is only a substitute name for those places used because our people cannot describe the exact position of those countries or islands.'[9] This means that placenames featured in oral histories cannot necessarily be taken as literal historical accounts of where Māori and Moriori ancestors voyaged from, though they may offer clues about population movements.[10]

This book looks at Hawaiki as it exists in both he ira atua (spiritual) and he ira tangata (everyday) realms. With respect to he ira atua, it looks at some of the sacred uses and meanings of instruments in relation to, for example, the beginning and ending of life. For he ira tangata, it asks: What can musical instruments tell us about the places that were the immediate departure points (or the most recent Hawaiki) for the first Polynesian voyagers to Aotearoa and Rēkohu?

The comparative study of musical instruments here supports the now widely accepted view that the ancestors of Māori and Moriori most likely originated from central East Polynesia, particularly the Society and Southern Cook Islands and possibly the Austral Islands. Moreover, it shows possible cultural influence from the Northern Cook Islands, though evidence from the Marquesas is inconclusive.

Similarities with instruments from Hawai`i may be explained as independent invention or may point to shared ancestral musical instrument traditions and knowledge between the ancestors of Hawaiians and Māori. Such traditions might previously have been shared across a wider expanse of Polynesia but preserved only in the marginal areas. West Polynesian influence on Māori musical traditions occurred post-Pākehā contact, though it is also possible a minor degree of influence from this region occurred before the cessation of long-distance voyaging to and from Aotearoa because of the Little Ice Age. Certain similarities between some Māori and Moriori musical instruments may be the result of common cultural origins in tropical Polynesia, which encompasses all of Polynesia except Aotearoa and Rēkohu, or the result of cultural exchange between the ancestors of Moriori and Māori in Aotearoa before Rēkohu was settled.

There are some notable similarities in instrument types, uses and even names between Māori and Moriori musical instrument traditions and those of peoples from Melanesia (particularly Papua New Guinea), Micronesia and the Polynesian outliers. This is remarkable, given that these tropical regions lie beyond the generally accepted 'Hawaiki zone' from which the ancestors of Māori and Moriori originated.

Parallels across musical instrument types and usages across Polynesia offer possible clues about ancestral interactions and travel. However, the sheer extent of creativity, innovation and adaptation evident in Māori and Moriori musical instruments is also noteworthy. These peoples developed innovative instrument traditions in response to the availability of new materials and their evolving cultural needs. Materials used to make instruments in tropical Polynesia were unavailable in Aotearoa and Rēkohu, resulting in some profound changes. In some cases, Māori found substitute materials: for example, harakeke (flax) and raupō (bulrush) replaced equivalent tropical Polynesian materials such as coconut or pandanus leaves, and wood was used instead of tropical fruits and nuts.

The absence of bamboo drove the biggest innovations, particularly in flutes and trumpets. Initially, the absence in Aotearoa and Rēkohu of naturally hollow long tubes meant that flutes had to be made shorter. Some of the earliest functional substitutes for bamboo in Aotearoa included human, kurī (dog) and bird bone; whale teeth; pithy tutu or poroporo branches or kōrari (flax-flower stems); or hollow materials such as hue (gourds) or kelp stipes. Material from kurī and hue would have required little work to make into instruments. Neither of these species was successfully introduced to Rēkohu.[11] Using wood and stone to create instruments likely came later, given they are harder to work. The use of wood as a material enabled the proliferation of a variety of innovative flute types and contributed to localised developments in making log gongs and trumpets.

So much information about Moriori musical instruments has been lost that, unfortunately, it is not possible to discuss Moriori tribal differences in instrument types, manufacturing technologies and methods, meanings and uses, or the instruments' evolution over time. There is, however, a wealth of information concerning Māori taonga pūoro, which display tremendous diversity in terms of locally distinctive instrument uses, names and manufacturing materials. This diversity highlights the vital role instruments have played in the representation and construction of iwi identities.

Some instrument types have a restricted geographical distribution – they are used only within one rohe (tribal area) – while others are particular to either Te Ika a Māui or to Te Wai Pounamu (the North and South islands of Aotearoa). In some cases, the same names are used to refer to very different instruments. As many traditional Māori instrument names have become quite standardised, it is important to people's iwitanga (tribal culture) to retain or reinstate these differences. Instrument makers sometimes used natural materials that were only available locally, which means that when examples made out these materials turn up elsewhere, this is indicative of trade or migration. Similarly, when comparatively rare instrument types are found in more than one locale, this points towards possible connections between those iwi.

The first two chapters of this book focus on the development of Māori and Moriori musical instruments. Chapter 1 examines the meanings of Māori instrument names, which shed light on their uses and playing techniques and the way Māori conceptualise the sonic world. Chapter 2 compares distinctive aspects of taonga pūoro – their types, materials, uses and names – from different rohe in Te Wai Pounamu and Te Ika a Māui. It highlights the importance of taonga pūoro in establishing and maintaining distinctive iwi identities and also suggests possible cultural influence resulting from inter-iwi relationships.

The following two chapters focus on differences and similarities between Māori and Moriori musical instruments and those from tropical Polynesia. Chapter 3 highlights Māori and Moriori ingenuity and creativity as they developed their own cultures, and explores factors that drove instrument innovation. Chapter 4 investigates the physical attributes, uses and names of the instruments in order to learn more about their possible ancestry and, thereby, the immediate geographical origins of Aotearoa and Rēkohu's early settlers.

A note on the text

For the purposes of this book, 'musical instruments' includes all tools that humans have used to intentionally and meaningfully create sound. The past tense is often used, but simply to indicate the historical nature of the information. It should by no means be taken as meaning that these instruments belong only to the past, as that is obviously not so.

Material on taonga pūoro in te reo Māori, whether published or unpublished, is outside the scope of this book. Body percussion is also not included. Although the human body is considered an instrument (a 'corpophone') – for instance, clapping, stamping or slapping skin – it remains unclear whether Māori historically considered body percussion as belonging to taonga pūoro. Body percussion is omitted from historical European accounts of Māori musical instruments, but that might simply be due to ethnocentric bias.

A note on audio files

A sound recording of the author playing a particular taonga pūoro is indicated by the ♪ symbol in the caption and accessable by scanning the QR code on page 228. A complete playlist of the recordings is available online at oup.nz/efh-audio

Chapter 1: Taonga pūoro names and whakapapa

Studying the names of musical instruments generates some important insights into their uses and playing techniques, and how Māori conceptualised them – all of which is crucial in understanding their development.

Taonga pūoro are regarded as the living descendants of ngā atua Māori – Māori deities and other beings responsible for originating and regulating aspects of the natural world – and this is often reflected in their names. Instrument names also hint at otherwise undocumented possibilities such as the use of shells as birdcallers and slats swung to disguise the human voice in sacred ceremonial rites. There is a degree of fluidity in Māori instrument naming practices, with instruments named according to one or more attributes: their use, sound, shape, motion, playing method or materials. Some instrument names are steeped in narratives of the past, while others show the use of metaphor or subtle wordplay. Small differences in pronunciation can profoundly change a term's meaning. This highlights the richness and complexity of te reo Māori and the often multilayered nuances of meaning Māori imbued their instrument names with. Some names defy straightforward definition.

For the exploration of instrument names and their meanings, I have relied heavily on Herbert W. Williams' *Dictionary of the Maori Language* (1844) and on ethnographic literature on taonga pūoro.[1] Williams' dictionary is the most significant Māori–English dictionary, and a vital resource for te reo Māori learners. Unless otherwise stated, all definitions in this book derive from this source. As I am a non-fluent speaker of te reo, some nuances of meaning may have eluded me and any misunderstandings and misapplications of definitions are entirely my own. Breaking te reo names into component parts can offer insights into the meanings and uses of taonga pūoro; I hope this approach may be of interest to others. Those who are fluent in te reo Māori or in particular iwi dialects, and other taonga pūoro players and knowledge bearers will have their own insights to add.

Unfortunately, it isn't possible to analyse original Moriori instrument names in the same depth as Māori names, as – with just two exceptions – they are undocumented.

Becoming taonga pūoro

We do not know if Māori historically grouped all musical instruments under a collective name. For a time, the term kōauau was used as a generic name for musical instruments, rather than as the name for a specific type of Māori flute, as it previously had been and is today. (Other instrument names were also reapplied more broadly.) According to taonga pūoro practitioner, researcher and revivalist Richard Nunns:

> Knowledge of instruments and the linguistic connections had so vanished from people's common understanding that when a pānui (advertisement) was sent around the East Coast calling for players of the kōauau, people arrived with a range of instruments including saxophones and guitars. Kōauau had become a collective noun for musical instruments in general.[2]

The current collective noun for traditional Māori musical instruments, taonga pūoro, is probably contemporary in origin – it does not appear in 19th-century dictionaries or the writings of early 20th-century ethnographers – though who coined this term and where or when it was first used, remains a mystery.[3]

In te reo Māori, taonga refers to anything 'highly prized' and pūoro to 'sound', so taonga pūoro translates as 'sounding treasures' or 'treasured sounds'. Puoro, without the tohutō to mark a long vowel, is sometimes used instead of pūoro; it means 'song, sing or rumble'. Although both puoro and pūoro are equally applicable to musical instruments, pūoro is used throughout this book because pū features in the names of many Māori musical instruments and because it relates to their sacredness.

Pū means 'to blow gently', 'pipe, tube or flute', as well as 'origin, source or root'. Pū is a generic name for wind instruments (by itself, it is also a name for long straight-bored flutes and shell trumpets): 'not only because it is the name of winds, but because music is a force like the wind – unseen but felt. In the Polynesian conception, winds carry messages: a wind brings the thoughts of a lover, another wind the premonition of a death or danger'.[4] The customary Māori use of taonga pūoro to channel verbal messages via the wind is an extension of this concept. Tāwhirimātea (god of the winds) carries sounds and their wairua to their destination, along with the mauri (life force) of the player; Hūruarangi (guardian of swung instruments) is the custodian of these types of communication. One kōrero mentions how 'Hine-aroaro-pari controls the southern winds and causes a sound to echo as it rides upon her fan'.[5] These ideas are exemplified in the Tūhoe belief that the sound made by swung slats (called pororohū in Te Urewera) is that of the player's wairua.[6]

Pū has particular resonance when viewed in relation to a creation story related by Kāi Tahu leader Matiaha Tiramōrehu in 1849, as presented by renowned taonga pūoro maker and scholar Brian Flintoff:

> 'Kei a te Pō te timatatanga o te waiatatanga mai a te Atua. Ko te Ao, ko te Ao mārama, ko te Ao tūroa' ... ('It was in the night, that the Gods sang the world into existence. From the world of light, into the world of music').[7]

In this telling, music was the means by which the universe was created. Sonic vibrations are a form of energy, and can therefore be viewed as an aspect of mauri; they act on, and resonate through, all matter. This principle of resonance is crucial to sound healing practices involving taonga pūoro.[8] When a person is healthy, their mauri is in a state of balance (mauri tau). Taonga pūoro can play a role in restoring balance and harmony when someone is ill. They enable people to become properly aligned with the energies of the universe.

The second component of the word pūoro, oro, means 'rumble or sound'. Among Ngāti Porou, oro is a continuous sound, such as that made by a waterfall or by rolling or sustained thunder.[9] Importantly, this definition relates to sounds that have the ihi (power) to inspire wehi (awe, fear, respect) due to their loud volume and low frequency. The continuous nature of the sounds makes them apt metaphors for the eternal. Oro is also used by Ngāti Porou and Tūhoe (Rūātoki) as a term for a fixed intoning note or durational tonic; a tone that can be described as the centre of gravity or a point of continual return for a song or chant.[10] This idea calls to mind Hawaiki, the place where, for Māori and Moriori, human souls originate and to which they return after death. Given these meanings and associations, it is easy to understand how oro, like pū, pertains to Māori spirituality.

In contemporary discourse, taonga pūoro practitioner Rangiiria Hedley (Ngāti Tūwharetoa) defines the term 'pūoro' metaphysically, using hand-clapping as an analogy: 'If I clap my hands, there's two things coming together that produce sound [claps her hands] and that's the clap. So the source – the pū – is my hands and the oro is the sound that it gives off.'[11] In other words, pū refers to the actions that activate the sound and oro to the sonic vibrations that result from those actions.

These conceptual and sacred meanings of pūoro are apt for instruments that are the living descendants of ngā atua Māori, as indicated in the materials of their bodies, in their voices and in the pūrākau (legends) concerning them. Their tapu nature and sacred functions (for example, as a means of communicating with atua and ancestors) derive from their whakapapa and the role of music in creation.[12] Like many beings in the Māori world, including humans, they originate from the spirit world, have divine lineage and are manifested in the world of the living.

Instruments can be divided into whānau according to their whakapapa. Two key components of music – rhythm and melody – are ascribed to the primeval parents. Rhythm is the heartbeat of Papatūānuku (Earth Mother) or is ascribed to both Papatūānuku and her unborn child Rūaumoko. Rūaumoko, as the originator of creativity, is also the deity that lies at the heart of singing and playing musical instruments. Melody belongs to Ranginui (Sky Father). Rhythm and melody are traits that have been passed down to all of Rangi and Papa's descendants. One of their progeny, Tāwhirimātea, is responsible for wind and breath and is the bearer of sound.

The descendants of Rangi and Papa are the ancestors of a variety of taonga pūoro. Shell instruments belong to Hinemoana (mother of shellfish) or are regarded as the children of both Tangaroa (god of the ocean) and Hinemoana, while words and movement are attributed to Tangaroa.

Poi (swung balls that strike the body percussively) featuring the use of raupō trace their whakapapa back to Tāne (god of the forests) and Hineiterepo (the swamp maiden). As a women's art form, poi is also connected to Hineteiwaiwa (goddess of women's arts). She was a child of Tāne and Hinerauāmoa, the goddess of anything pertaining to women, including weaving, which is salient to poi making. Flax oboes are the descendants of Tāne and Pakoti (mother of harakeke).

Tāne was responsible for bringing certain birds and insects to earth, and instruments that have bird or insect voices (lamellaphones, mouth bows and birdcallers) relate to him.

Stone instruments lie within the whānau of Papatūānuku or Tāne, although tumutumu (hand-held percussion instruments, sometimes made from stone) vary in their lineage depending on where the stones were sourced: river stones whakapapa to Parawhenuamea, mountain stones to Hine Tūparimaunga, and ocean stones to Rakahore. Clay instruments whakapapa to Hineukurangi.

Hinepūtehue, another daughter of Tāne and Hinerauāmoa, is the guardian of all instruments made from hue. When Tāne separated Rangi and Papa, there were divisions and fighting between Tangaroa and Tāwhirimātea, until Hinepūtehue drew that anger into herself and gave out a song of peace, using her body as a sounding vessel. Hue also belong to the domain of Rongomātāne, god of cultivated plants and peace.[13]

As descendants of the gods, and closely associated with their various divine responsibilities and physical manifestations, taonga pūoro bind tangata whenua in an enduring, complex relationship with both the material and spiritual worlds. For all these reasons, taonga pūoro is an apt umbrella term for these musical instruments.

Instruments named according to their use

In Māori vocal and instrumental music, intention and function are of paramount importance, so it is unsurprising that instruments are sometimes named according to their use. Some of the key roles taonga pūoro play in Māori society relate to fertility (childbirth and raising crops), health, education, hunting, warfare, spiritual practices and death.

SACRED USES

Several instrument names indicate their sacred uses and meanings. For example, the te reo word pure is a component of the name pūrerehua (swung slat or bullroarer). Pure was a ritual that could provide spiritual protection (adding power to one's personal spiritual forcefield or tapu) to people engaging in activities involving tremendous mana, such as going into battle or undertaking esoteric learning. It could bring one's tapu back to its normal state after engaging in such activities (i.e. acting as a whakanoa or freer of tapu) or rejuvenate and restore one's tapu if it was damaged or destroyed through physical or mental illness. Tapu restrictions protected individuals and their communities from the potency of mana. Breaching tapu would invoke the wrath of atua kahu (the spirits of stillborn children), causing illness. Illness could also result from being subject to the malignant spiritual powers of mākutu (witchcraft). Pure would restore balance, banish negative powers, disperse evil spirits and invoke beneficent atua.

Pūrerehua may have been used historically to open pure ceremonies.[14] According to creation narratives, pure was performed to purify Tāne when he ascended to the highest heaven to obtain the three baskets of knowledge (ngā kete o te wānanga) for humankind. Rehua, the second component of this instrument's name, is the name of a whatukura (male messenger of Io, the supreme deity) who cleansed Tāne with the Wai o Rongo (waters of Rongo; also known as Wai o Rongomai) before being admitted to Io's presence while undertaking this task.[15]

One ritual cleansing ceremony:

> deals with binding and destroying any harmful atua, which include bad spirits such as ghosts and demons. To catch a bad atua the purerehua is employed. Karakia are said by the tohunga to draw the spirit out from its hiding place. The purerehua is swung around, making its roaring noise. Its song vibrates through the air, drawing out the atua in the form of a lizard. When an atua manifests in the form of a lizard the reptile is the aria or 'manifestation' of the atua, hence it must be destroyed ... Such lizards are green in colour and about 1 m (3 ft) in length. To destroy the atua the lizard must be captured and killed, and it is later cooked to destroy its wairua.[16]

In Murihiku (the region of Te Wai Pounamu south of the Waitaki River), names for this instrument are connected to this ritual use. These names include `gārara, which derives from ngārara (reptile), and hamumu ira ngā ngārara (or hamumu ina gārara or hamumu ira karaka), the sound that stirs the lizards to life.[17] Tūtangatakino is a spiritual reptile that crawls into people's mouths while they are asleep, gnawing on their stomachs and causing illness.[18] Here, the negative atua was drawn out of the body of the afflicted person and pulled into the vortex of the swung instrument through its centrifugal force – thereby curing their illness.

Pure or pūre also features in names for spinning discs (pūrēhua, pūrerehua). Like swung slats, spinning discs were also used for healing.

Rehua was one of the whatukura responsible for communication between Io and the atua descended from Rangi and Papa. Pūrerehua played a role in communication between their realms, forming a pathway or conduit between them. Rehua has the authority to open the pūmotomoto or gateway leading to the highest heaven, and therefore regulates access to mātauranga (knowledge). The apa – the messengers and attendants of the whatukura – are sometimes symbolically represented by whirlwinds, which relates to the motion of pūrerehua when they are in use.[19] When swung, above the head, the pūrerehua alternates between two flight patterns: it flies upwards, spiralling in a V-shaped cone formation above the hand that is holding the string, and then downwards in an inverted cone formation, below the level of the player's hand at approximately head height. Each movement feels very different: the former is joyous, uplifting and liberating; the latter creates a sense of being enclosed, enfolded and protected. A player can feel they are a balance point between the realms above and those below; a mediator channelling two complementary and interrelated energies: those of the masculine (Rangi) and the feminine (Papa); those of the heights and the depths, of the heavens (ngā rangi tuhaha) and the underworld (Rarohenga); and those of he ira atua and he ira tangata. This instrument relates very much to ideas of balance, the complementarity of powerful forces, and the constant and pervasive presence of he ira atua in he ira tangata – all of which are important in Māori culture.

Other instruments act as voice modifiers or disguisers for spiritual purposes, and this use is reflected in their names. For example, tararī and rōria are lamellaphones. These terms contain rī (screen) and ria (screening), respectively. Some recited chants were intended to be heard only by ngā atua, so lamellaphones and spinning discs were used to mask the kupu (words) from human ears. Similarly, hua – found in names for spinning discs (kōrerohua and pūrerehua) and swung slats (purēhua and pūrerehua) – also refers to the idea of screening. Spinning discs had a sacred function associated with chanting karakia (invocations) and with rongoā (healing). A name

PŪREREHUA *made from kānuka wood with pāua shell inlay. Descendant of Tāwhirimātea; wind instrument. Measures 24.5cms long. Made by David Cattermole.* ♪

given to spinning discs, 'Te Reo o Ng[ā] Atua (the voice of the gods)', indicates that their voice is tapu.[20] The continuous, deep sound of spinning discs and swung slats (particularly large ones) relates to the definition of pū discussed earlier: 'a powerful roar particularly associated with the gods'.[21]

Tararī is also a term for swung slats, which may indicate that these instruments were used as voice disguisers. Unlike lamellaphones and spinning discs, swung slats cannot be played in close proximity to the mouth, but they are loud enough to effectively mask the chanted words of karakia. There is no historical record of these instruments being used in this way, but the name tararī, as well as documented sacred uses of swung slats by tohunga (experts in spiritual matters), suggests the possibility.

The pūtōrino (flute) is another instrument associated with sacred practices. Tōrino, a component of pūtōrino and another name for this instrument on its own, is also a term for eardrum; 'when the environment, the forest and the ocean, were not responding with the kind of oral stimulation the tohunga needed, the pūtōrino was used to give him the information that he wanted'.[22] Pūtōrino are 'forest amplifiers'; tohunga trained birds to vocalise into these instruments during sports games (ngā tākaro).[23] The rua (cavities) of pūtōrino are the receivers of sonic tohu (signs) that tohunga interpret. Tōrino is also the name for a hole dug at the tūāhu – a sacred place that was used for divination and other mystic rites. Another name for that hole is rua tōrino. There is no text-based evidence that pūtōrino were used in rituals that took place at tūāhu, but this is not surprising given the secrecy surrounding such sacred rituals. If they were, though, perhaps the concept of rua tōrino provided an impetus for creating pūtōrino with two (rua) bores rather than just one. Doubling the bores may have increased the instrument's ability to amplify tohu, and is also a clever play on the two meanings of the term rua.[24]

LURING AND HUNTING

Some instruments were employed by tohunga to lure birds so that they could use them to communicate messages to ngā atua and ngā tūpuna (ancestors).[25] Birds, particularly ruru (owls), could be incarnations or visible representations of gods (ariā). They 'functioned as temporary hosts for the gods who took possession when they had something to communicate or were called on for consultation by their priests on ritual occasions'.[26] Birds who could mimic humans or whose song sounded like human speech were highly valued. One informant from Rāpaki reported a tame kākā 'playing' the kōauau, conceivably by holding the flute to its beak and mimicking its sounds.[27]

This use of instruments as bird lures is reflected in their names. For example, the generic name for birdcallers, karanga manu, breaks down into karanga, meaning 'call or summon', and manu, referring to birds and other winged creatures. Another name for such whistles, specifically ones made from leaves, is pepe, meaning 'to attract birds by imitating their cry', 'to use a leaf for this purpose' and 'the leaf used for this purpose'. The same instruments that were used to attract birds to communicate with them spiritually could also be used to lure them so they could be killed for food.

In another variation of hunting with sound, rattles – called patete or rore – were tied around hunting dogs' necks to attract or frighten and flush out game, as well as to enable hunters to locate the dogs and their prey. These instruments' function is reflected in their names: patete means 'move along' or 'irritate', and rore means 'ensnare' or 'trap'.

FERTILITY, BIRTH AND DEATH

Various taonga pūoro played important roles connected to the creation of new life. For example, toa (a term for poi with one-metre-long strings) means 'virile'. Poi are highly symbolic of both men's and women's fertility and reproduction. They can represent the penis and scrotum, symbolising strength and fertility, or Tāne, the fertile male progenitor of many species, with the ball representing his head and the cord his feet. Poi can also represent ovaries and fallopian tubes, as well as the placenta and the umbilical cord.[28]

There are Te Ika a Māui accounts of poi being used in courtship. For example, at Maungawhau (Mount Eden), poi accompanied songs that complimented young women on their appearance and alluded to the irresistible charms of young men.[29] At Ōtaki, poi was 'originally a moonlight dance performed by the riverside or stream. The young men eyed the women in their dancing and selected the one they fancied. At the end of the dance the maidens dived into the water, and the men pursued the woman of their choice. A romantic tryst was then held where the steeplejack tree grew overshadowing the water.'[30] A man could secretly send a poi to a woman. If she rejected him, she would throw the poi away; if she favoured him, she would use it 'on all favourable occasions'.[31] One definition of poi, 'bewitch', alludes to poi having ātahu (love charms/spells) spoken over them to make an unwilling young woman infatuated with her suitor.[32] Poi are also associated with birth and babies. For example, in South Taranaki, poi karakia are an adaptation of karakia used for the birth ritual.[33] A common practice performed by childless women involved nursing and singing to a stone, which was seen as a surrogate for a baby. A Tūhoe rangi poi (poi tune), which is also an oriori (a lullaby), was composed by Hineitūrama to sing to her child, who was a stone.[34]

Pūrerehua were linked to fertility and reproduction in relation to crop growth. Among its various meanings, the term rere (a component of pūrerehua) refers both to a fall of rain and to planting. Ngāti Porou swung slats (huhū, tūrorohū, tarari) were used in conjunction with the recitation of karakia to summon a gentle,

KARANGA MANU
made from pounamu. Descendant of Tāne; wind instrument. Measures 5.5cms long. Made by David Cattermole.

continuous rain – almost a fine drizzle – at the time of kūmara planting.[35] In the evening or at night, the player cast a handful of ashes to the south (the direction of the prevailing rain) and then turned his back to that direction so the south would be angered and send rain. A similar ritual is described as follows:

> a tohunga used the roaring sound of the purerehua with a rattle to invoke rain. The purerehua is said to bind together the scattered clouds and the rattle was used to make the sound of rain. This ritual used an ahua or 'image' of the land. Seeds were thrown over the make-believe area, duplicating the rain that would fall, and this was accompanied by several karakia and a rod for the atua.[36]

Pūrerehua create a vortex like a whirlwind when they are swung, drawing in rain. Some instruments are famed rainmakers, causing tears of love to fall from Rangi on to Papa.[37] For this reason, a generic name for these instruments is te reo o te whaea (the voice of the mother), which fits with the way the shape of this taonga resembles the vulva.[38] The vulva is the gateway to Te Ao Mārama (the world of light). Female genitalia also feature in pūrākau concerning the creation of the first human being: Hineahuone was created from earth at Kurawaka, the puke (pubic mound) of Papatūānuku. Instruments which form a shape relating to female genitalia, such as pūrerehua, played an important role in connection with fertility and reproduction. This instrument's association with new life also relates to the whatukura Rehua (a component of this instrument's name), who is believed to have the power to revive the dead.[39]

The survival of all things is dependent on water; without it, nothing can flourish. Yet, while water is essential to life, water can also take life. This highlights the importance of balancing forces according to te ao Māori. Mamae, meaning 'pain or distress', features in the swung slat names mamae and pūmamae. These instruments were used during the lying-in-state of a chief to summon tears to farewell the dead and to disperse evil spirits (similar to the role they may have played in the pure ritual, discussed above).[40]

There are many associations contained in the name pūrerehua. As well as being a messenger of Io, Rehua is sometimes figured as the god of the sun, the solar fire. Rehua is also identified with certain stars – Betelgeuse, Sirius or Antares. (The latter, for Tūhoe, was the star that signals the start of summer.)[41] Rere, another component of the name, has similar meanings, referring to rising and setting (for example, of heavenly bodies). Summer was a time of war, hence the whakataukī (proverb) 'Rehua kai tangata' (Rehua the consumer of men); Rehua is said to have an enervating influence, draining people of their vitality. There are, therefore, further connections between this instrument's name and death. Its vulva shape can be linked to the pūrākau of the demigod Māui attempting to gain immortality for mankind from

Hinenuitepō (the goddess of night, who receives and protects a person's spirit upon their death). Māui attempted to enter her vagina while she slept, but she woke and crushed him to death.[42] This is the origin of one name for vagina: te whare o aituā (house of misfortune).

Names for clay vessel flutes (ukutangi, pūtangitangi, ipūtangi, būdagidagi) also relate to death. Tangi means crying or 'a cry', and here refers to a wailing sound 'and also the breathing styles that can be used to imitate the feeling of sobbing'.[43] These taonga were made and played primarily by women during times of mourning, to bring on tears and help the player express the emotions they had been holding in. These outpourings of grief appease Aituā, god of misfortune and death.

WARFARE

Like the pūrerehua and its link via Rehua to the summer warfare season, several other instrument names pertain to war. For instance, hoariri, used in the instrument name kōauau hoariri, means 'angry friend' – someone you fight but whose mana you respect.[44] Historically, one means of demeaning a defeated enemy was to use bone from their femur (thigh), tibia (lower leg) or humerus (upper arm) to make a kōauau.[45] Such an act was seen as a desecration; an act of utu (in this case meaning 'revenge', a way of evening up a score and achieving restitution) that bolstered the mana of the victorious warrior.

Most Māori trumpet names relate to warfare, which is appropriate given their various wartime uses: as an alarm to alert people to an enemy's approach (or to any other impending danger); to keep people awake and alert in case of surprise attack; to gather scattered warriors and direct them during battle; and to intimidate the enemy and rally one's own warriors.[46] Several instrument names contain tara, which means 'courage': pūpūtara, pūtara pūtara, pūtara, pūtaratara, pūtātara and tātara.[47]

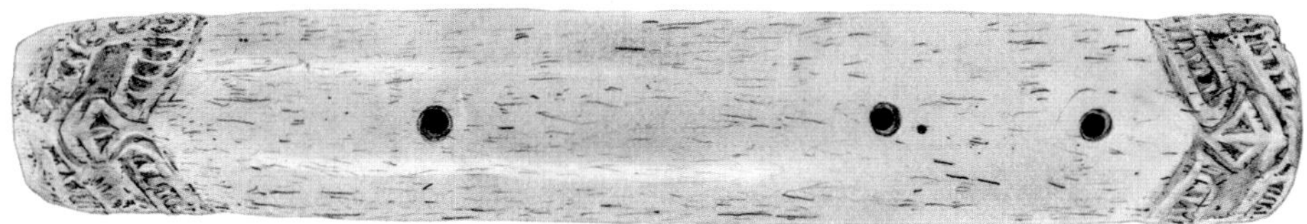

KŌAUAU NAMED MURIRANGARANGA *made from human bone, held in Rotorua Museum (catalogue number L1993.16.1). Descendant of Hine Raukatauri; wind instrument. Measures 13.4cms long. Drawing by Jennifer Cattermole.*

Meanings of tā, used in the latter two terms, include 'aim a blow at, strike, beat, cut, overcome'. Pakapaka, a component of the instrument name pūpakapaka, means 'quarrelsome'. Toto, used in the name pūtoto, means 'blood'. The names pūhāureroa/pūwhāureroa may relate to whāura (ruddy, fierce) and/or hau (breath; resound).[48] Tūteure, a large fusiform shell sometimes made into a trumpet, may have tūtei (sentry) at its root. Pūkihi, a name for a long flax oboe, contains kihi, meaning 'to destroy completely'. Another name for this instrument, pūpatea, refers to pātea, a breastplate made from thickly woven flax. The long wooden trumpet pūtahoro relates to tāhoro, meaning 'to cause to crumble or throw down a structure'. The meanings behind the terms pūkihi and pūtahoro suggest that the instruments were likely perceived as playing an important role in defeating one's enemies.

Kāeaea and its cognates (words that have the same linguistic origin) are used in several instrument names: the conch trumpet kāeaea; long wooden trumpets kāea and koea; and pūkāea – a name for both long wooden trumpets and flax oboes.[49] Kāeaea means 'to act like a hawk/falcon; look rapaciously'.[50] An alternative spelling for pūkāea, pūkaea, is sometimes used.[51] Kaea is appropriate for the peacetime functions of these instruments. For example, one definition of kaea is 'to wander', and these instruments were sometimes used to signal the arrival and departure of a group or a high-ranking man. As well as relating to this sort of travel, kaea may also refer to the carrying power of the instruments' sound.[52] These instruments were also connected with chiefs and their roles and duties, which aligns in a symbolic sense with another definition of kaea: the 'leader of a flight of kākā (parrots)'.[53] With a subtle alteration in pronunciation, the similar-sounding terms pūkāea and pūkaea thus encapsulate a range of uses for these multifunctional instruments and again highlight the importance of balance and complementarity in Māori culture – in this case, between times of warfare and peace.

LEARNING

In a society that transmitted much information orally, instruments were used to help learners memorise knowledge. One hand-held percussion instrument, tumutumu, was used as a learning aid. Tumu means 'foundation or bed (as in shell bed)' and whakatumutumu 'heaped up'. These terms metaphorically describe the instrument's use in establishing and increasing a student's knowledge.[54]

Pūmotomoto is the name for the gateway or entrance to the uppermost heaven, the place where all knowledge and wisdom ultimately originates (as is related in the pūrākau of Tāne obtaining the baskets of knowledge).[55] It is also the term for the fontanelle – the soft spot on an infant's skull where the bone sutures intersect – and the name of a flute used by Tūhoe to impart wisdom, knowledge and enlightenment to an infant. The pūmotomoto was traditionally played over the belly of a wahine hapū (pregnant woman) or over the fontanelle of a newborn baby to implant mōteatea, whakapapa, karakia and pūrākau/pakiwaitara directly into the infant's subconscious. The instrument, therefore, acts as a bridge between two gateways, behind which lie repositories of knowledge: the pūmotomoto of the highest heaven and the pūmotomoto of the baby.

Instruments named for their sound

A variety of instrument names relate not to their use but to their sound – though, in turn, the associations evoked by the sound may have influenced how they came to be used. For example, whēorooro, a term for swung slats, means 'rumble or reverberate'.[56] Huhū, a name for both spinning discs and swung slats, and also found in a name for humming tops, pōtaka huhū, means 'hiss, whizz, buzz'. Hūkeke (spinning disc) breaks down into hū (hiss) and keke (obstinate, stubborn), which refers to the persistent, repetitive sound of this instrument. The names kōrorohū, pīrorohū, pororohū, pūrorohū, tūrorohū refer to spinning discs or swung slats and can also be broken down into their component parts: kō (wind), pī (flow, for example, of the tide), pū (to blow gently) and tū (persistent, continuous); rorohū means 'whizz, buzz' and also refers to a 'squall of wind'.[57] Pūrorohū also means 'accompanied with a whizzing or whistling noise'.

Kaihōtaka (whipped tops) are not typically described as sound-producers in the historical literature, except in a 19th-century account from Te Ika a Māui rangatira Kōwhai Ngutu Kākā: 'The kaihotaka (humming top) was a great amusement to all, and the different tones sounded by these tops as they flew off the ground and bounded in the air from the lash of the muka (dressed harakeke) whips, sounded like the string of a harp when one of them is struck singly.'[58] This description, as well as the name component ho, which means to 'buzz', confirms the noises these tops customarily made.

When in motion, all these instruments sound like waves approaching then receding on a beach, as if they are the inhalations and exhalations of the great ocean taniwha Parata, as the Māori conception of the tides has it – or like the wind, or a person inhaling and exhaling. All these ideas are in line with what the components of their names mean. They are the sounds of breath. Breath is significant in Māori creation narratives, as it was breath that animated the first human being, Hineahuone.[59] Breath animated life and signifies life; it is essential to vitality and is vital essence and power. Lack of breath signifies death.

Further to the discussion of the pure ritual above, it is not only the swung slat's movement that lures lizards but also its sound, which closely resembles that of their prey: insects. This insect connection is reflected in different names for swung slats and spinning discs: ngārara, a kupu that can refer to insects as well as lizards; pūrēhua and pūrerehua, referring to 'moth, butterfly'; and rangorango and tīrango, referring to 'blowfly'. The use of instruments to lure particular bird species by imitating their calls is also reflected in some names, for example, karanga weka (woodhen), kōauau pūtangitangi (paradise shelduck), or poi āwhiowhio and whio rōria (blue duck).[60]

The names of short, straight-bored flutes and bird lures often contain terms that have sonic meanings. For instance, some instrument names feature whio, meaning 'to whistle' (such as the flute whio, and bird lures poi āwhiowhio and whio rōria). Similarly, the names of birdcallers whakahihī and korowhiti refer to 'whistling with a finger bent in the mouth'.[61] According to ethnologist Augustus Hamilton, who lived in Hawke's Bay and Te Wai Pounamu and was writing in the late 1890s,

> a Maori rarely or never whistled, and generally objected to Europeans whistling when in their company. Maoris of the older generation always felt uncomfortable at hearing Europeans, boys and men, whistling. Possibly this aversion to the sound was connected with the idea that a demon or atua manifested his presence by a sound somewhat resembling a long drawn whistle.[62]

Kaipara people likewise associate a whistling sound with atua; while whiowhio is a general term that means 'to speak in the whistling voice used by a priest when the medium of a deity; ventriloquial'.[63] Communications from ngā atua are sometimes described as half whistling, half whispering, or as a low-pitched whistle.[64] This association between whistling and the voices of several taonga pūoro highlights their nature as the living descendants of atua, their use in communicating with and receiving communications from the gods, and the spiritual nature, power and efficacy of their voices.

Taonga pūoro scholar Jo'el Komene (Ngāpuhi, Tainui, Tapuika) notes: 'People listened carefully to the many sounds in everyday life to discern the presence of atua, which might be conveyed through forest noises, the calls of birds, sounds that result from changes in the weather, including sounds created by the blowing of the wind, especially whistling sounds.'[65] Such sounds include dogs howling, pūpūrangi (kauri snails) angling their shells into the wind, and other land snails or marine molluscs being frightened and withdrawing suddenly into their shells. All these sounds are significant with respect to taonga pūoro.

KARANGA WEKA
made from mataī wood.
Descendant of Tāne;
wind instrument.
Measures 10cms long.
Made by Brian Flintoff.

As we saw earlier, some instrument names – for example, the birdcallers kōauau pūtangitangi and whakataki – contain the term tangi, which refers to a sound or cry.[66] Sonic references in the names of shells and birds point towards shells possibly being used as instruments that mimic bird calls. For example, toitoi is a name for the Cook's turban shell and both the pied tit and the brown creeper; another name for this shell, karikawa, also pertains to 'a bird'. Karoro is a term used for both cockle and the black-backed gull. The cockle is played by directing air across the fan-shaped base of the shell in a technique known as oblique embouchure or cross-blowing. The resulting sound closely resembles the cry of a gull. Barnacles can also be played using the oblique embouchure. Tio means both 'barnacle' and 'cry, call', while tiotio is 'a bird'.[67]

Birds and shelled creatures could be recognised as ariā of gods or other kaitiaki when their voices warned of an impending attack, helping to ensure the safety and survival of the tribe. This makes their voices spiritually important. For example, a small whelk played as a flute is called hoputea. Hopu can mean 'surprise', and teatea has a related meaning: 'apprehensive, afraid'.[68] Another example is pūpū harakeke, also known as pūpū whakarongo taua (flax snail shells). For Ngāti Kuri, the sounds the snails 'made as they hastily retreated into their shells when disturbed in the dark of night once alerted people to an approaching invader and saved their lives. Nowadays the empty shells are blown like a kōauau to create a special song.'[69]

Kōauau (sometimes abbreviated to kōau in the Murihiku rohe) is another name that relates to sound. The name of this short, straight-bored flute breaks down into kō (sing – as in birdsong, resound, wind) and auau.[70] One meaning of auau is 'frequently repeated', which may refer to vibrato.[71] This effect imitates the tremolo used at cadence points that was characteristic of certain vocal music genres in Aotearoa, as well as in the Tuamotus and possibly Tahiti.[72] Another way to achieve frequently repeated sounds is by using flutter tongue or a series of rapid glottal stops. There is no evidence Māori used these playing techniques historically, although they would have been appropriate given the sounds resemble the song of the tarakihi or kihikihi (cicada), an insect that personifies Raukatauri, goddess of flutes.[73] Similarly, pererau, possibly a Ngāpuhi term for a type of one-holed flute, may relate to pererū, meaning 'making a whirring, fluttering noise' – a definition that seems more apt for a swung slat, leaf whizzer or spinning disc than a flute, unless the possible use of flutter tongue is considered.

The term kōauau is also linked to kurī. The howling of dogs sounds like 'auau'. The reo Māori onomatopoeic terms used to denote howling are au and ao. (Similar terms for the barking or howling of dogs are used in Rarotonga and the Tuamotus and Ra`ivavae.) Dogs' howling was spiritually important. Northern Māori, for instance, believed 'that the wairua of men and women on their way to the underworld sing a last song of farewell before leaping down, and that the wairua of dogs howl a chorus at the end of each verse'.[74] If dogs' howling was associated with death, death was in turn connected to flute playing. According to one pūrākau, the very first death – that of Māuimua – followed his playing a flute in the presence of Hinenuitepō. In this pūrākau, as in the one in which Māui attempts to gain immortality for mankind from Hinenuitepō by entering her vagina while she sleeps, Hinenuitepō crushes the protagonist to death.[75] Like the pūrerehua discussed earlier, some kōauau are shaped like the female vulva, which was associated with both birth and death. Their voice, that of Raukatauri, was regarded as 'He reo whakamomori, mōteatea; he reo hotuhotu, mokemoke' (a pining voice, grief; a sobbing voice, lonely).[76] Given these associations, it's unsurprising that kōauau (and other flutes) were often played in connection with the return of a deceased person's spirit to their ancestors or gods.[77]

Intriguingly, one of only two names we have for Moriori miheke oro – pauawau – sounds very similar phonetically to kōauau, even though the instrument itself is physically dissimilar. This name, recorded in the Bernice Pauahi Bishop Museum's ethnology catalogue, describes an albatross-wing-bone flute that is around 25 centimetres long and has a single slightly rectangular-shaped hole in the centre of the bore.[78] It is possible that the uawau component of this name shares meanings with 'auau' noted above, though there is no documented linguistic evidence that supports this. The prefix pa in this instrument's name is also deserving of comment. In ta rē Moriori, pa means 'explode', which is consistent with its Polynesian protoform *paa(-kia), meaning 'strike against, hit'.[79] In Aotearoa as well as elsewhere in

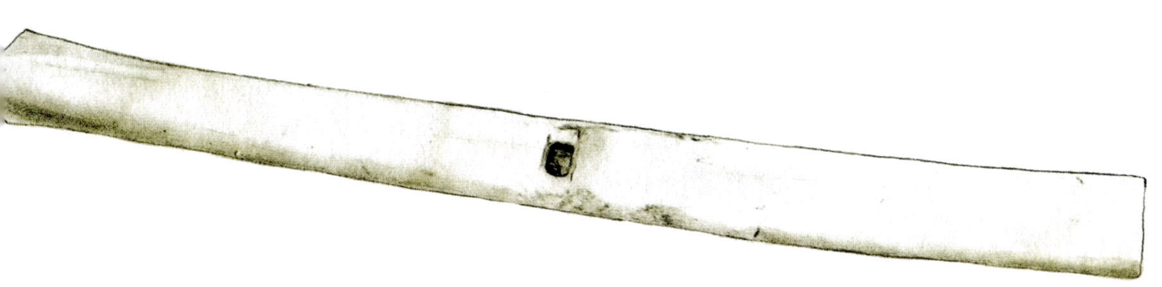

SINGLE-HOLED MORIORI FLUTE NAMED PAUAWAU, *likely made from albatross (hopo) bone, held by the Bernice Pauahi Bishop Museum, Hawai`i (catalogue number 08617) and acquired in 1899. Wind instrument. Measures 25.1cms long. Drawing by Jennifer Cattermole.*

Polynesia, pa is typically used as a prefix for percussion instrument names, making its use as a prefix for a flute name highly unusual (assuming that the name was recorded correctly). Pū would make more sense than pa as a prefix for this instrument but is not a documented Moriori term.

Like kōauau, nguru, a short flute with a semi-closed bore, also has sonic references in its name.[80] Meanings for this term include: to 'utter a suppressed groan, sigh or grunt; murmur; and rumble', of which 'murmur' most aptly fits its voice.[81] One description of a nguru, for example, notes that it was 'softly crooned into'.[82]

The name ororuarangi, used for a long, straight-bored flute, also refers to sound. Ororua is related to the idea of spirit voices (irirangi or rangirua).[83] The instrument is capable of producing harmonics, and these soft whistling sounds likely gave rise to the name. There is another possible explanation of this name's etymology when the term is broken down: oro meaning 'rumble' or 'sound'; rua meaning either 'two' or 'hole/cavity'; and rangi meaning 'tune'. The instrument typically has two fingerholes side by side in the middle of the instrument (though they can be joined to form one hole), which means there are two principal pitches. As Brian Flintoff notes: 'Their name echoes a remembered ability to jump between two sound pitches.'[84]

Hoho, a term for a type of Te Ika a Māui flute (also found in cognate terms for the same instrument, pūhoho or pū hoho hō), means 'an inarticulate call, a sort of trill, to call attention', while hō means 'shout'.[85] The term pū hoho hō thus refers to both its female flute voice (te waiata a te wāhine) and male trumpet voice (te kōkiri a te tāne).[86] As with the pūkāea/pūkaea example mentioned above, hoho and hō sound very similar but in fact have opposing though complementary meanings. Both are examples of subtle, clever wordplay, and again indicate the importance of balance and complementarity in Māori culture.

Anthropologist Te Rangi Hīroa suggested that the name pū hoho hō is onomatopoeic, derived from a particular sound made at the end of the verse of a song performed with this instrument. He described that sound as follows: 'The right hand held the middle of the instrument, and the fingers were placed over the figure-of-eight hole to modify the sound ... the hoho ho effect was caused by moving the fingers up and down.'[87] Ngāti Porou kaumātua Iehu Nukunuku, whose flute playing was recorded by ethnographer Elsdon Best in 1923, described the same sound, noting that this instrument made a deep booming or murmuring sound that trembled as the player's finger was moved, not lifted, over the central hole.

A saying pertaining to the hoho is: 'Me te wai e utuutu ana'; meaning it sounds like water bubbling into a gourd held underwater in a creek.[88] Another Te Ika a Māui name for this instrument, pōrutu (also a name for straight-bored flutes in Te Wai Pounamu), has similar meanings. As well as being an instrument name, the kupu can refer to the action of waves breaking on the shore or water splashing; rutu itself means 'to pour out (as in water)' or 'to fall in drops, drip'. This kind of sound occurs when a hoho player uses the technique described above, and is particularly noticeable when they vocalise into the bore.

Other names for this instrument (and other kinds of flute), tōrino and pūtōrino, also relate to sound. As well as the 'eardrum' meaning discussed above, tōrino means 'dulcet, soft-sounding' or 'flowing or gliding smoothly'. These terms refer to water but may also refer to the sound of the air spiralling down the bore and oscillating.[89]

Pūtōrino played an important role during childbirth, so meanings relating to water are significant. The waters breaking heralds the approaching birth of a baby. This physical act mirrors creation narratives in which water was the first physical substance to be created. This instrument's names also connect with a belief that the souls of newborns come from a lake called Te Wai a Tāne (also called Te Waiora a Tāne), passing over to their bodies when they draw their first breath. The voices of pūtōrino call back to Te Kore (the realm of unlimited potentiality), guiding newborns safely to Te Ao Mārama. Their voices act in some ways like an umbilical cord and like Te Aka (the vine of the heavens), which bridges these realms, spanning the development of human beings and all of creation.[90]

As noted above, flutes played an important role in death as well. The water-like voices of these flutes called forth tears from those who were grieving and eased the passage of the tūpāpaku (deceased's) wairua as they voyaged along the seabed on their journey to Hawaiki.

Rattling sounds are also indicated in instrument names. The term tara appears in names such as tarakimere (leaf whistle) and tātara (dog rattle).[91] It means to 'make a buzzing, rattling or other inarticulate sound'. Tarakimere may be a contraction of tātarakihi rau maire, referring to the cicada-like chirping that results when a maire leaf is played.[92] Another instrument, hue rarā (gourd rattle), contains the term rarā, meaning to 'make a continued (dull) sound'.

Lamellaphones and mouth bows, both forms of mouth percussion, are similarly named for their sonic qualities. Rōria (lamellaphone; also part of the name for the birdcallers tuarōria and whio rōria) means to 'make a droning noise'. Tua may pertain to tū, meaning 'persistent, continuous', followed by the conjunctive ā, which refers to a long duration; and/or to tūtū, 'summon', a meaning that relates to the instrument's use in hunting birds.[93] Kū, used in the terms kūkau (lamellaphone) and kūkau/kū (mouth bow), means to 'make a low inarticulate sound', which is apt given the quietness and intimacy of these instruments.

Tapping rods, clappers/castanets and gongs also all have names that relate to their sound. One of the names for tapping rods and other forms of percussion instrument, pākuru, means 'knock or to make a knocking noise' or 'to hit a light piece of wood out of which the pith had been extracted'. In other names for this instrument (panguru and panguru whakatangi), panguru means 'bass, gruff'; nguru in this context may mean 'rumble'.

The Ngāti Porou terms for different types of clapper (pākēkē and pākōkō) also relate to sounds made by these instruments.[94] Pākēkē means 'crackle, scrape' and pakē 'crack'; pākōkō means to 'make a loud sudden sound'. Another term for clappers, tokerangi, relates to kērangi, meaning a 'sharp, abrupt sound' and 'crack, snap', while kere (used in the term tōkere) is 'used with words of breaking'. Pahu, a term for various kinds of gong, relates to pahū, meaning 'burst, explode', which is appropriate given the loudness of these instruments. Other terms for gong have a similar meaning: pakū meaning to 'make a sudden sound, resound, beat, or knock'; patō meaning 'crack, snap, emit a sharp sudden sound, break, knock'; and rarī meaning to 'make an uproar or disturbance'.

Instruments named for their physical attributes

Instrument names sometimes relate to their physical attributes: for example, porotiti and porotītiti, both terms for spinning discs, mean 'disc' and 'revolving'. Poro means 'a piece of anything cut or broken off short', and titi refers to a peg or pin. Porotītiti is a particularly apt name for instruments made from a piece of gourd rind cut into a disc, with a wooden peg inserted in the centre that the player twirls between their thumb and forefinger.[95] (Other versions of this instrument comprise a disc with two holes drilled a short distance on either side of the centre point, through which a string is looped before being twisted, pulled and released to produce sound.) Another instrument name that uses poro in this sense is pororua (a short, straight-bored flute). In this case, rua (two or hole) is a wordplay involving both meanings to indicate that the flute has two fingerholes. An instrument that uses poro in a different sense is pōtaka (humming top). If pō can be taken as an abbreviation of poro, the original term for this instrument would have been porotaka, meaning 'round'.[96]

The 'peg' or 'pin' meanings of titi are also apt in the name of a long wooden trumpet, titi matai. There the term refers to the instrument's tohe or tohetohe (tonsil), which is located inside the instrument's bore. Another name for this instrument, wharawhara, refers to its bell-shaped mouth (whara).[97]

Meanings for the term tētere, used for the long wooden trumpet and flax oboe and also found in the term pūtētere (a conch trumpet), include 'large, stout, swollen', which aptly describe the size of these instruments.[98] A similar name, tere, was used

PĀKURU *made from matai wood. Descendant of Papatūānuku; percussion instrument. Body (left) measures 36.5cms long; striker (right) measures 42.8cms long. Made by Brian Flintoff.* ♪

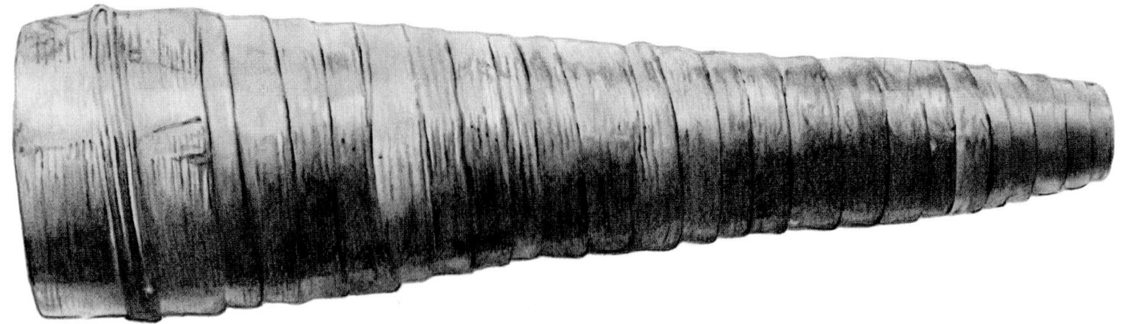

TĒTERE *made from harakeke leaves. Descendant of Hine Raukatauri; wind instrument. Drawing by Jennifer Cattermole from a photograph in Andersen,* Maori Music, *fig. 71.*

on Rēkohu to refer to a type of trumpet, according to the lyrics of a rongo (song) documented in a series of letters written by Moriori elders to George Grey in 1862.[99] As noted above, it and pauawau are the only two names of Moriori miheke oro that we know of.

A range of other instrument names also pertain to their shape. Several instruments feature the name poi, which means 'ball' (for example, poi, poi awe, poi kōkau, poi piu, poi āwhiowhio, poi waeroa). Another definition of the term poro, found in kīkīporo (tapping rods), is 'block'. Ngutu rakiraki refers to clappers made by splitting the woody end of a harakeke leaf and bending half back. Ngutu means 'beak or lip', which are similes for the physical shape of this instrument. Raki (or rangirangi) means 'dry, dried up', which indicates that dried harakeke was used to make the instrument. The term pū, as we have seen, has several meanings, including 'pipe' and 'tube', which could be applied to anything in the form of a hollow cylinder.[100] Pū is found in the names of a birdcaller, and a variety of flutes, trumpets and flax oboes – all of which feature hollow tubes.

Instruments named for their movement

Instrument names sometimes relate to their motion when they are played. This is evident, for example, in the names given to spinning discs. Pīrori means 'twirl round', and takawairore to 'be in a state of agitation'. The related term takawairori breaks down into taka (revolve) and wairori (turn around, twist).[101] Similarly, tara (used in taraere and tararī, the latter also used to denote lamellaphones and swung slats) means 'brisk', which describes the pace of these instruments when played.[102]

Many of the terms for humming tops also refer to their spinning movement. For example, taka (in pōtaka) means to 'turn on a pivot, revolve' as well as 'undergo a change of direction, veer' and 'range, roam at large'. Kukume (used in pōtaka kukume) means 'pull, drag, pull away, stretch', while whitireia can be broken down into whiti, meaning 'cross over, change, turn, spring, leap', and reia, meaning 'leaping, rushing and being run after'.[103]

Swung instruments are also named for their motion. For example, āwhiowhio, a component of the term for the bird lure poi āwhiowhio, means 'circuitous' or 'whirlwind, whirlpool'; āwhio means 'roundabout'. Two key attributes of whirlwinds are that they draw things into their vortex and they lift things upwards. Both of these attributes feature in Māori creation narratives. In one version of these narratives, a whirlwind (Ko-awhiowhio-rangi) is the force that Io used to draw the primeval parents Rangi and Papa together into their loving embrace, causing their unification.[104] The force of attraction between lovers is comparable to a whirlwind's power to draw things in, to lure and attract. Whirlwinds also feature in narratives concerning Tāne's ascent through the heavens to obtain ngā kete o te wānanga for humankind, resulting in humanity's enlightenment. Both these associations are connected with how poi āwhiwhio are used: to convey messages of love, and to summon birds so they can communicate messages for tohunga.[105]

Names for swung slats also relate to their movement. If po is taken as an abbreviation of poro with respect to pororohū (swung slat), then the term refers to 'round', describing the circular motion of the taonga as it is swung through the air. Swung slats are similar to poi āwhiowhio in that they, too, summon or draw things into their vortex (such as the cause of illness, rain, tears); they were also used for communicating with ancestors and atua, and therefore for seeking spiritual enlightenment. Rere, found in pūrerehua (swung slat), can mean 'fly' and 'be carried on the wind' (among many other meanings); it also means 'rush, run, hasten', referring to the speed at which these instruments are swung.

Instruments named for their playing method

Some instruments are named for their playing method. For instance, tarau (lamellaphone) means 'beat, pound'. Pākuru (tapping rods) and pākēkē and pākōkō (clappers), have the prefix pā, meaning 'strike, be struck'.[106] This forms the basis of many other percussion instrument names, such as those for tapping rods (pakakau, pakure, panguru and panguru whakatangi) and gongs (pahu, pakū and patō).

Another instrument, pōtaka tākiri (humming top), gets its name from a piece of wood called a papa tākiri, which was held against the top's upright spindle. The player's left hand kept it and the top in position, while the right hand pulled the string wound around the spindle.[107] Papa refers to 'anything broad, flat and hard', tākiri means 'draw away suddenly'.[108]

Some names refer to how blown instruments are played. A birdcaller and a variety of flutes, trumpets and flax oboes all feature the prefix pū, which can mean 'to blow softly'.[109] Papaki, used in harakeke papaki (birdcaller), has an almost identical meaning: to 'blow gently upon'. In a version of the tale of Tinirau and Kae told by Ngāti Toa rangatira Te Rangihaeata (c. 1780s–1855), the name appears to refer to a spinning disc.[110] The latter instrument can be blown upon while being played to alter the sound, so this naming would be appropriate. Some names indicate whether the instrument is to be played with the nose – for instance, kōauau pongā ihu, pongā ihu and kōauau whakatangi ihu; with ihu meaning 'nose' and pongā ihu 'nostril' – or the mouth (as in kōauau waha; with waha meaning 'mouth').

Instrument names sometimes refer to their performance in conjunction with human vocalisation. For example, ipu kōrero, a type of poi, may have been struck against the body as a memory aid or punctuation device during the recitation of whakapapa or storytelling.[111] Kōrero refers to 'speech' and ipu to 'vessel'. Ipu kōrero is also used as an honorific for a person who is a holder of stories.[112] One of the terms for spinning disc, kōrorohū, is modified to kōrerohua when the instrument is blown on, perhaps while being spoken, sung or chanted over while being played.[113]

Similarly, the name kīkīporo (tapping rods) features kīki, meaning 'speak', which is apt given that players often sing or hum while playing. The changing shape of the mouth creates different resonances, which may be perceived as different words, messages, songs or perhaps karakia. Esteemed players enunciate the words of waiata (songs), karakia and messages into various types of flute. This mode of performance may be reflected in the name rehu. Rehu (like kō in kōauau) means 'flute' and also 'sing, chant'. One type of rehu had words sung into it from one end, the player inserting their forefinger into the bore at the other end to alter the pitch.[114]

With respect to tīrango (spinning disc; leaf whizzer), tī relates to the terms tīngia and tīnia (thrown, cast), and therefore to their playing method. Tīrango are spun or swung on strings. Similarly, in the name poi piu (flax poi), piu refers to 'throw or swing'.

Instruments named for their construction materials

Instrument names sometimes mention the materials used in their manufacture. Several refer to plants. For example, tōtara wera (spinning disc) features the name of the tōtara wood used in this instrument's construction.[115] Titi mataī (long wooden trumpet) refers to the mataī wood often used in its manufacture. Māpara (clappers) refers to the material used in their making: the resinous heartwood of kahikatea or rimu. Kau, used in kūkau (lamellaphone and mouth bow), means 'plant stalk', which is a reference to the kareao vine used to make such instruments. Kakau, used in the names pakakau (tapping rods) and pūtōrino kakau rua (a type of pūtōrino that has two bores that join into one at the top and bottom), also refers to plant stalks.[116] Tō, found in tokerangi and tōkere (both clappers), also relates to plant stems, while mere (used in the term tarakimere, leaf whistle) means 'bush, shrub'.[117] Some instrument names (the birdcaller harakeke papaki, and flax oboes kōrari and pūharakeke) refer to the flax used in their making. Tī, in the name tīrango (leaf whizzer; spinning disc), pertains to various species of *Cordyline* (cabbage tree) and points toward these instruments originally being made from their leaves. While there are no documented historical accounts of this practice, pīrori (spinning discs) are made from harakeke, which is a similar material. Several instrument names feature hue, indicating the gourd material they are made from: pōtaka hue (gourd humming top), pūhue (gourd trumpet), hue rarā (gourd rattle). Finally, sometimes the naming practices worked in the opposite direction, with the name of an instrument coming to be applied to a plant material – as will be seen the discussions of flutes made from kelp or seaweed in Chapter 2.

Instrument names also sometimes derive from animals. For instance, awe, used in the instrument name poi awe, refers to poi decorated with the long white hairs from the tail and rump of kurī. Likewise, in poi waeroa, waeroa refers to waero (dog tail hair) decoration. These contrast with poi kōkau, with kōkau meaning 'unadorned'. The term pūkaea iwi refers to the use of bone (iwi) in that instrument's construction.

Several shell instruments take their name from the material they are made from. For example, bubu (the southern form of pūpū) refers to shells played as flutes. Pūmoana (conch trumpet) relates to moana (sea), and several names for this instrument are also the names for shells used in their manufacture: pūpūtara, pūtara, pūtaratara and pūtātara.[118] Kākara, another term for shell trumpets, refers not to conch shells but to various other shellfish: *Lepsia haustrum* (whelk), *Cookia sulcata* and *Austrofusus glans* (both univalve molluscs), of which only the *Cookia sulcata* shell is large enough to use as a trumpet. A shell rattle called kī pāua is made by placing shells, sand or pebbles inside two pāua shells and binding them together;

often a flax cover is wound around this instrument. The sounds made by the contents of the shell convey particular messages. Kī pāua can be used to provide percussive accompaniment to games (such as kītē);[119] they can also be swung like pūrerehua or suspended from kites or trees. The term kī refers generally to 'any type of small ball'.[120]

Stone is also used to make taonga pūoro. The name pahu pounamu, for example, derives from the pounamu (nephrite) used in its making. Kōhatu (stone) is an alternative Kāi Tahu name for tumutumu, a hand-held percussion instrument that can be made from stone.[121] Clay instruments such as ukutangi take their name from the uku (clay) used to make them.

As noted earlier, kō – in kōauau – means 'sing' (as in birdsong, resound, wind). Kō may, however, also have meanings that relate to its construction materials, and these meanings offer possible clues as to the instrument's origins. The etymology of the term supports a connection back to central East Polynesia if kō was an abbreviation of the central East Polynesian names for bamboo, a material for nose flutes, used in Tahiti, Cook Islands, Tuamotus, Rapa and Ra`ivavae.[122]

Kō could, alternatively, be an abbreviation of kōiwi (bone), in which case it might point towards the use of bone as a functional substitute for bamboo by Aotearoa's first peoples. Māori regard bones as sacred. They are important for giving strength and form, physically and spiritually, and denote being and belonging – as is illustrated by the connection between the terms kōiwi and iwi (tribe). A kōauau made from the kōiwi of a cherished ancestor or a friend could provide its player with mental and physical strength and endurance, and was especially effective in relieving pain when played during childbirth or the application of tā moko.[123] It could also allow a whānau pani (bereaved family) to gather strength to poroporoaki (farewell) their deceased, show them respect and express grief.[124] The kōiwi used to make such flutes belonged to people of importance, people who were loved and respected. This ensured their mana lived on after their death and provided loved ones with a spiritual and physical connection to them.[125]

The idea that kō may be an abbreviation of kōiwi is supported by a pūrākau where Māui turned his brother-in-law Irawaru into the first kurī as punishment for his laziness, and made a kōauau kōiwi from his remains after his death.[126] Perhaps the first kōauau in Aotearoa were made from kōiwi kurī. Dog bone was available in tropical Polynesia, but no dog bone flutes have been reported from archaeological sites there, though they are found in Aotearoa. No other flutes in Oceania have names sounding like kōauau or have origin stories connected with kurī.

Instrument name transference

As can be seen from this discussion of taonga pūoro naming practices, the terms Māori used to refer to instruments are various and were subject to change based on conditions, use, associations, materials, and language play and evolution. There is also one final broad change worth mentioning: sometimes the same instrument names are applied to different instruments in different parts of the motu. Linguist Ray Harlow suggests that the names of many instruments originated in Te Ika a Māui and then spread to Te Wai Pounamu, where they were applied to different instruments.[127] Acknowledging these differences in naming is a step towards restoring the iwitanga around these taonga in cases where Te Ika a Māui instrument names have become dominant, something that is of particular importance to southern peoples.

An example of name transference is pūkaea. Throughout Te Ika a Māui, this term is commonly applied to long wooden trumpets.[128] In Te Wai Pounamu, however, pūkaea is the term used for flax oboes.[129]

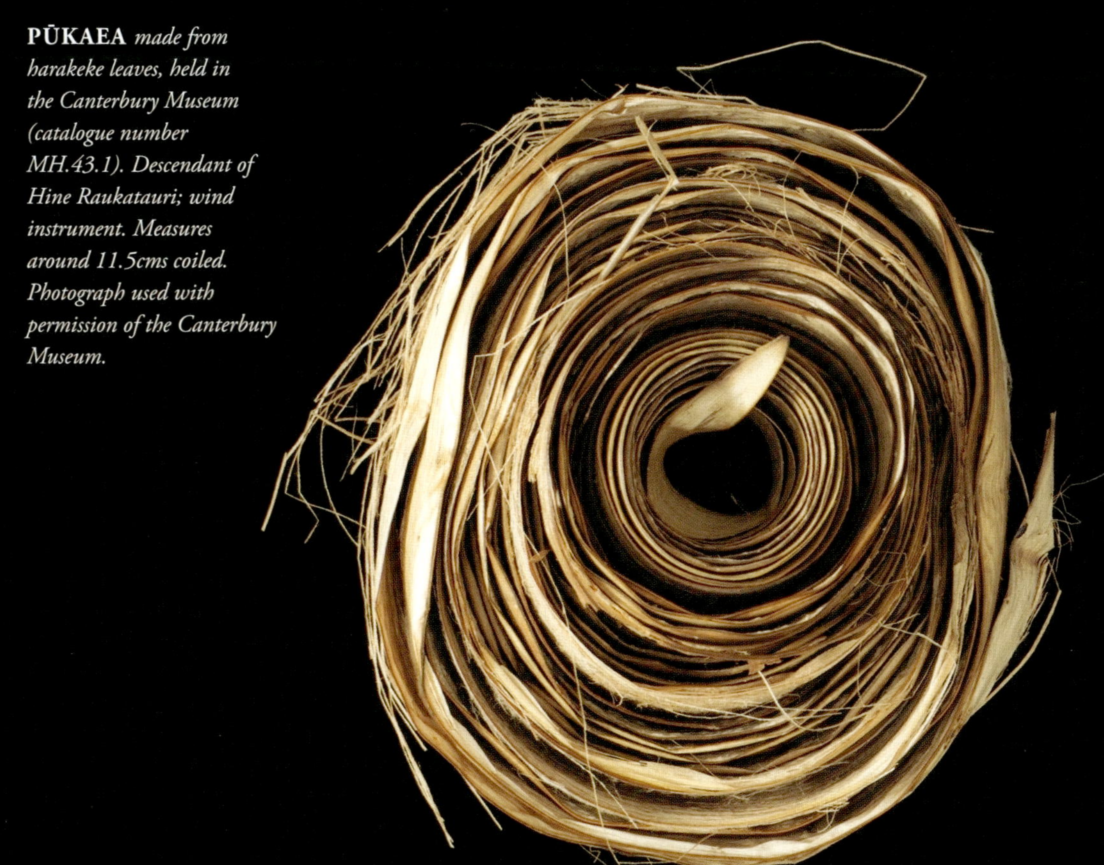

PŪKAEA *made from harakeke leaves, held in the Canterbury Museum (catalogue number MH.43.1). Descendant of Hine Raukatauri; wind instrument. Measures around 11.5cms coiled. Photograph used with permission of the Canterbury Museum.*

Pōrutu is another example. In Tainui, the term pōrutu is sometimes used for a kind of transverse flute (also called rehu) somewhat similar to Western flutes.[130] Throughout Te Wai Pounamu, however, the kupu is applied to a completely different kind of flute. A longer version of the kōauau, pōrutu were the most common flutes in the south. They have four to six fingerholes (termed rua or puta), are long ('almost as long as the Pakeha flute'), usually made from tutu (though mako or koari/kōrari could also be used), and are mouth-blown. In Murihiku, these flutes were used historically to accompany singing, and a short song was often sung into the bore.[131]

Similar name transference occurred with rehu and whio. In Te Ika a Māui, both terms were used to describe long flutes. Rehu were closed at the end nearest the player's face, and had three fingerholes plus a blowing hole; whereas whio were typically made from two pieces of mataī wood, each piece hollowed out then lashed together using kiekie, with two to three holes bored on the upper side and one on the lower.[132] Rehu was also a name for gourd trumpets in Taranaki. In Te Wai Pounamu, however, both names were used for short flutes made from the wing bones of seabirds or hollow tutu stems.[133]

Similarly, in Te Ika a Māui, the term pūtōrino typically describes a wooden instrument made in two halves and then bound, with a tapering shape and a large central māngai or waha (mouth) – though there were some regional variants. In Te Wai Pounamu, however, this name applies to a variety of different flutes. The various instruments this name applied to will be discussed in Chapter 2.

These name transferences almost certainly resulted from the migrations of northern peoples to Te Wai Pounamu. The application of these names to different, presumably pre-existing, instruments provides evidence of the intermingling between northern and southern peoples and of the adaptation to iwitanga that occurred as a result. As we will see in the next chapter, they are one instance of the remarkable diversity and creative development of musical instruments in Māori life that can be traced by language, whakapapa and geography.

CHAPTER 2: The iwitanga and rohe differences of taonga pūoro

ONE OF THE MOST REMARKABLE THINGS about Māori musical instruments is their sheer diversity, which is a testament to the ingenuity, skill, curiosity and creativity of their makers. This chapter compares taonga pūoro traditional practices from different rohe within Te Wai Pounamu and Te Ika a Māui, looking at aspects such as instrument types, materials and usages. Some of these aspects were unique to particular iwi, highlighting the importance of taonga pūoro for expressing group identity and mana.[1] In cases where aspects were shared between iwi – particularly iwi from neighbouring or nearby rohe – the similarities suggest cultural influence, perhaps through migration and trade. Instrument names specific to particular rohe are used wherever known.

The chapter will look first at unique Māori taonga found only in specific localised areas, then those that originated in Te Ika a Māui, followed by a selection of more widespread instruments. In regards to Rēkohu, while we have hints at various unique musical practices, we have little information on Moriori musical instruments and, as noted, retain the name of only one flute and one trumpet. For this reason Moriori instrumentation will be discussed in a later chapter. Finally, the closing section of the chapter covers some instrument materials and uses that vary by rohe.

Taonga pūoro associated with specific areas

We will likely never know the full story of the iwitanga of taonga pūoro. As Richard Nunns noted: 'many uses of, and stories about, the instruments vary from tribe to tribe. No single tribe has retained a complete body of knowledge about them'.[2]

Tai Tokerau

Mataatua

Tainui

TE IKA A MĀUI

Tairāwhiti

Taranaki

Arawa

Whanganui

Tākitimu

Manawatū

Te Tau Ihu o Te Waka

Te Upoko o Te Ika

Waitaha

TE WAI POUNAMU

Murihiku

While there is information documented in historical records, these references are fragmentary. Due to the disruption caused by colonisation, oral histories about these instruments are incomplete, and written records were often made by Europeans and are therefore subject to ethnocentric bias.[3] Additionally, taonga pūoro made from perishable materials have not survived in the archaeological record, and the provenance of most taonga pūoro held in museum collections does not include information about where the instruments were made or found.

However, despite these limitations, it is possible to identify the specific geographical distribution of some taonga pūoro within Aotearoa.

MURIHIKU

Tumutumu – hand-held percussion instruments made from stone, bone or wood – originated in Murihiku. Tumutumu were used as learning aids and provided a constant metronomic voice in the whare pūrākau (house of stories). Their sharp percussive sounds accompanied the kōrero kākāriki, or recitation of the students' learnings, to cement knowledge of long texts and genealogies.[4] As one account tells us:

> Stone was banged against stone at a regular rhythm in the background in order to regulate the chants taught inside the tohunga school and to give pace to the oral lessons. Its sound echoed all through the night and this is the rhythm of creation, which marks the pace in which the chants are recited. On the spiritual level it invokes the well-being of all those who attend the whare-kura [the first of three schools of sacred knowledge]. In chants it also demonstrates when sound became part of creation, even before forms of thought in the creation genealogy.[5]

TUMUTUMU PAKOHE. *Descendant of Papatūānuku; concussion instrument. The larger stone measures 8.6cms long and the smaller one 6.3cms long. Found by Brian Flintoff in the Nelson-Marlborough area.* ♪

Spinning discs made of flax, called pīrori, were also unique to Murihiku – in Te Ika a Māui, discs were made from wood. One form of pīrori, called pepepe, was used as a spinning toy to amuse children; the disc would be hung so that it revolved in the wind.[6]

Murihiku also offers us the only examples we have of birdcallers made from durable materials. For example, a seal tooth with an edge that had been ground flat found at Te Raka a Hineatea (Katiki Point) was 'probably for use as a bird call'.[7] Another seal tooth example was found at Pūrākaunui.[8] Birdcallers from this rohe were also made from bird bone or steatite (soapstone).[9]

Finally, two types of flax wind instruments are only found in this region: pūpatea (flax-leaf oboes) and pūkaea iwi (flax trumpets with a bone mouthpiece). Pūpatea are larger than other flax oboes. They are constructed using several layers of harakeke strips wound around the greased handle of a hoe (canoe paddle). A mixture of hinu (fat) and pia (flax gum) is applied between each layer, and the completed instrument is carefully slid off the handle.[10] Pūpatea are loud, which made them useful as signalling instruments.

As we have seen, the name pūkaea refers to a wooden trumpet in Te Ika a Māui and a flax one in Te Wai Pounamu. The Murihiku pūkaea iwi is different again, with the mouthpiece made from bone (possibly whalebone) and the long bell from flax. In the past, a lookout stationed on the taumata (platform) of a pā would blow into a pūkaea iwi to signal the approach of an enemy.[11]

STEATITE KARANGA MANU *held in Tūhura Otago Museum (catalogue number D31.760). Descendant of Tāne; wind instrument. Measures 6.1cms long. Photograph used with permission of Tūhura Otago Museum.*

WAITAHA

Two instruments found in the Waitaha region may have been particular to that rohe. Ethnographer James Beattie noted that they were unfamiliar to his informants further south in Murihiku.[12]

The first is a percussion instrument, called a pākuru, made from a thick hollowed stem of tutu rākau around one metre long, plugged at each end. It was played with either a 60-centimetre-long wooden beater or a softer one made of aruhe (pigfern stalk), sharkskin or whītau (dressed harakeke fibre).[13] This instrument was beaten as a signal for people to gather together and could also be played at tangi and kōrero.[14]

The second is an unusual, possibly unique type of instrument that was dimly remembered by Kāi Tahu scholar and leader Teone Taare Tīkao from Rāpaki pā at Horomaka Banks Peninsula.[15] This instrument was described as a type of trumpet that consisted of two sliding tubes, the larger one overlapping the smaller.[16] It was made from tutu or mako (wineberry) wood and 'packed with delicate flax tubing'.[17]

TE ARAWA

The Te Arawa rohe is home to a percussive instrument that is specifically associated with healing. Mahi rongoā kōhatu (healing with stones) was practised in Te Arawa. Tohunga rongoā (expert healers) involved in the traditional schools of healing would select a porous stone similar in size and shape to an afflicted organ or joint. This stone was placed on the afflicted area and tapped with a stone rod or a small stone hammer with a wooden handle. Its position was adjusted according to its sound and with feedback from the ill person. Once it was in place, appropriate karakia were recited and the stone would draw out the illness.[18]

The mouth bow instrument is a curved frame spanned with a taut string, played by tapping the string with a rod or the player's knuckles, or plucking with a finger. The player's mouth acts as a resonating chamber – their lips surround but do not touch the string, typically at the point where one end meets the bow.[19] They are called kū or kūkau in historical and contemporary literature. Te Arawa is the one place specified in the literature as having mouth bows (though it is unclear whether or not those names were used in this rohe);[20] there, they were described as one-stringed, made in the shape of a bow and about 25 centimetres long. Among Te Arawa, mouth bows were played by women and used to rehearse mōteatea (chants), to accompany karakia, and as a toy. One is said to have been given to Hinemoa by her lover Tūtānekai, though she could not play it.[21]

Mataī wood was used for the bow, which was strung with whītau, human hair, bird gut or, rarely, dog intestines.[22] Kurī were very highly valued by their owners. If a dog's intestines were used, the instrument was considered exceptional and was named after the dog.

KŪ *made from supplejack vine (the bow), synthetic cord (the string) and albatross wing bone (the striker). Descendant of Tāne; percussion instrument. Kū measures 73.5cms long when strung; striker measures 31.3cms long. Made by Brian Flintoff.*

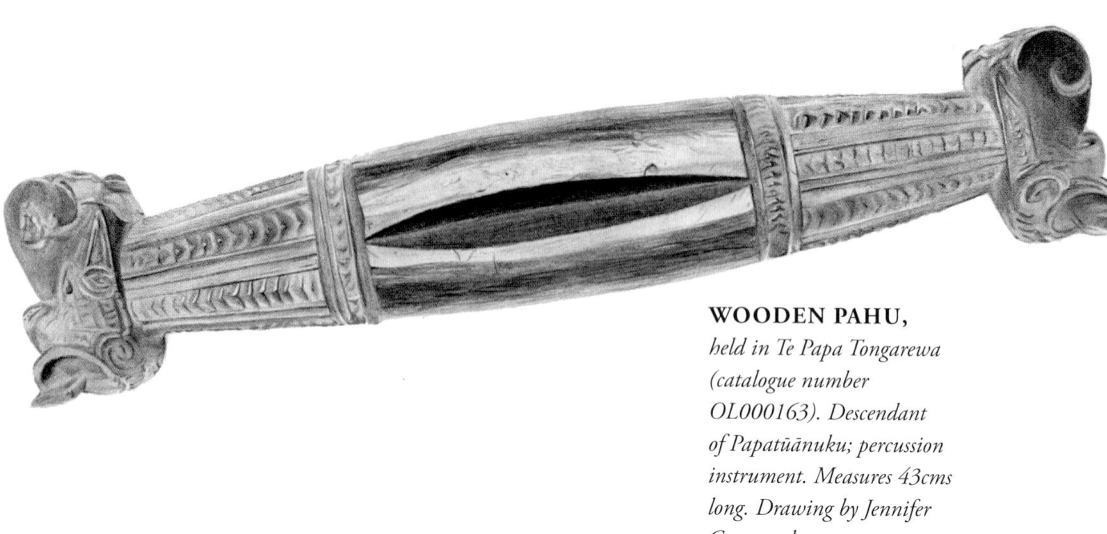

WOODEN PAHU,
held in Te Papa Tongarewa (catalogue number OL000163). Descendant of Papatūānuku; percussion instrument. Measures 43cms long. Drawing by Jennifer Cattermole.

MATAATUA

We have one example of a pahu or patō (gong) from the Mataatua rohe. It is unusual because of its small size: it is only 43 centimetres long. This wooden instrument is believed to whakapapa to Tūhoe.[23] It is a rarity, being the only known example of its kind and not described in any of the existing historical literature. It may have been used to indicate language rhythms when accompanying speech, chanting or singing.[24]

The tarau is another instrument that is possibly unique to Mataatua (specifically to Ngāti Pahipoto and Ngāti Awa). It consists of a leaf from the tarata tree which is slid in between the player's lips and teeth. A flexible tarata twig is then laid by the side of the mouth and flicked with a finger or thumb so that it hits the leaf. The player alters the instrument's pitch by altering their mouth shape. The tarau was played by children as a toy, but may originally have been used by adults for spiritual purposes, as a way to disguise the voice when communicating with ancestors or deities and to prevent other people from overhearing what was being said.[25] Other Māori instruments played near the mouth or utilising the mouth as a resonating chamber had that function, so it is possible tarau did as well.

Finally, the wind instrument pūmotomoto may have once been unique to Tūhoe. This long flute, with its distinctive notched mouthpiece, was played as an aid to conception and to ease labour pains. As noted earlier, it was played over the belly of a hapū woman during pregnancy; information, wishes, hopes and desires for the child were intoned and sung through the instrument into the infant's subconscious.[26]

PŪMOTOMOTO
made from mataī wood. Descendant of Hine Raukatauri; wind instrument. Measures 58.5cms long. Made by Brian Flintoff. ♪

TAIRĀWHITI

Ngāti Porou developed several kinds of taonga pūoro that are not found anywhere else, including a pahu made in two sections, from wood that was hollowed out and then lashed together. Māori long wooden trumpets and flutes were also created this way, so the gong-like percussion instrument may have originated as an application of those techniques to create a different instrument. One, or sometimes two, beaters (sometimes made from whalebone) were used to strike it.[27]

Another uniquely Ngāti Porou percussion instrument is a pākuru made of the bark of the houhi (lacebark) tree around which whītau was wrapped or bound; it was struck with a wooden beater. A pākuru was used to sound the alarm (for example, to warn of enemy attack) and was suspended from the watchman's platform.[28]

A percussion instrument fashioned from a human skull was used in the Tairāwhiti rohe in the highest school of esoteric learning, Te Kauae Runga. (Kauae runga is also the name of the upper jawbone.)[29] This instrument may be unique to Tairāwhiti, though the highly tapu nature of this knowledge means that human skulls could well have been used as musical instruments elsewhere while remaining secret. The head is regarded as especially tapu, and as the part of the body where a person's hamano (their highest, most pure soul) resides.[30]

The tīrango was a type of leaf whizzer (an instrument similar to a bullroarer) known only to Ngāti Porou. A thin piece of kareao stem forms a bow, which is strung with a strip from the base of a raupō leaf. A cord is attached to one end of the bow; the other end is attached to a stick handle. The player holds the handle and swings it around in a circular motion; the taut leaf whistles through the air as it is swung. This instrument was used as a children's toy and in the manukorihi practices surrounding kuku mamau (wrestling) contests.[31] Manukorihi was the ritual for calling down birds to sanctify a games gathering, highlighting the importance of birds as messengers from, or ariā of, ngā atua.[32]

Gourd mouth and nose flutes (kōauau waha and kōauau pongā ihu, respectively) are documented only from the Ngāti Porou rohe. These instruments are made from small hue, dried and with the neck removed, and have one to four fingerholes.[33] Their peaceful, gentle voices were heard during childbirth or when someone was dying.

A possibly unique artefact was found in the Wharerata ranges near Poverty Bay by Leslie Moncrieffe Nutt in 1938. Made of bone, this instrument is thought to be a flute or whistle; it has two wenewene (fingerholes) and a suspension hole. The bore is blocked between the wenewene, meaning two distinct pitches can be blown from either end, one pitch is produced when the wenewene is covered and one when the finger is lifted off.[34] In that respect, this instrument resembles weka callers (karanga weka) and may have served a similar function.

MANAWATŪ

In an account unique to Manawatū, containers full of water were used to imitate the sounds of a waterfall in a game called wīwī. As Vi Hanuera (Ngāti Raukawa) recalled:

> When we were young my mother used to gather us around under our big old oak with a bowl of water each to play wīwī. Some had buckets, some had big metal lids or cans filled with water. We would ripple the water in many ways with our fingers and sing. Then we would be very quiet as my mother would perform our favourite hakura. Her dance would be with slow movements and no sound. If she reached up we gently patted the water, when she lowered herself we lowered our fingers too and bubbled the water in our bowl. When she turned we did the same with our fingers in the water. All the sounds were different … We connected to her every move … with so many of us the music sounded like a babbling brook … we would also mimic the spirit of the sea and our tāheke … At times we would quietly blow on the water and would jump around making tinkling noises … then we would lift it up and it would peal back down.[35]

While this account refers to European-derived metal buckets, the game would have been playable using containers made from customary materials, such as hue.

WHANGANUI

An instrument called whio rōria, made from a cut clump of reeds, was used in Whanganui. The whio rōria was held in the hand and blown on, then discarded after use. It was used as a bird lure when hunting.[36] While the use of leaves as birdcallers was quite widespread, there are no other documented examples of reeds employed in this way.

Taonga puōro that originated in Te Ika a Māui

The available evidence suggests that, in addition to the unique instruments from Te Arawa, Mataatua, Tairāwhiti, Manawatū and Whanganui described above, some other customary instruments were originally found only in Te Ika a Māui. These include conch trumpets with wooden mouthpieces, long wooden trumpets, humming tops, clappers and several varieties of flute (nguru, pererau, ororuarangi, pūmotomoto), as well as instruments termed whio, rehu and pūtōrino that are of a type specific to this island (and that differ from Te Wai Pounamu instruments of the same name).[37]

PŪKAEA-LIKE TRUMPET *made from wood, from Te Mata Hāpuku pā, Waitaha, held in the Canterbury Museum (catalogue number E159.684). Photograph used with permission of the Canterbury Museum.*

It seems likely that the examples of these instruments that have been found in Te Wai Pounamu were imported by people from Te Ika a Māui who migrated south. An instrument found at the site of Te Mata Hāpuku pā on Horomaka Banks Peninsula is the only long wooden trumpet recovered from an archaeological site in Aotearoa to date and the only one predating the taonga pūoro revival that has been provenanced to Te Wai Pounamu.[38] All other examples held in museum collections that have provenance information recorded for them can be traced back to Te Ika a Māui. Te Mata Hāpuku pā dates from the late 18th century, was abandoned in the 1820s–30s, then reoccupied before 1844. The instrument, made from mataī, was found there in a shallow, waterlogged location.[39]

The long wooden trumpet called pūkaea in the north was one of three instrument types – the others being pūtātara and Te Ika a Māui-style pūtōrino – recorded by Georg Forster, a naturalist on Lieutenant James Cook's second voyage. He observed these instruments being traded in Tōtaranui Queen Charlotte Sound on 4 June 1773 by a group from the southwesternmost point of Te Ika a Māui, Cape Terawhiti (originally known as Omere). The group was led by a man whose name was recorded as 'Teiratu'.[40] The trumpet that Dutch explorer Abel Tasman and his crew heard in Mohua (Golden Bay) in 1642, described as being like a 'Moorish trumpet', may have been any of these instruments as all have trumpet voices, though it is most likely to have been pūkaea or pūtātara as they have greater carrying power compared to pūtōrino.[41]

Although the first migrants to Aotearoa had conch trumpets, the addition of a wooden mouthpiece was a Te Ika a Māui innovation. The remains of these pūtātara have, however, also been found at sites in Te Wai Pounamu, including Te Ana o

PŪTĀTARA *made from conch shell with a wooden mouthpiece and wooden insert, held in the Museum of Archaeology and Anthropology, Cambridge (catalogue number D.1912.31), and acquired in 1912. Descendant of Tangaroa; wind instrument. Measures 27.5cms long. Photograph used with permission of the Museum of Archaeology and Anthropology, Cambridge, England.*

Hineraki Moa Bone Point Cave at Redcliffs in Ōtautahi, and at Kaikai Beach and Beaumont in Otago.[42] There is also a place named Putatara in Otago, described as 'formerly a fort' and otherwise known as Rugged Point.[43] A wooden pūtōrino of the type typically found in Te Ika a Māui was lost by Te Rauparaha when he led an attack on Rāpaki pā; one account suggests it was subsequently sold by Rāpaki chief Paora Taki in around 1873.[44]

Taonga pūoro found in multiple rohe

Instruments such as poi, swung slats, spinning discs, short and long straight-bored flutes, birdcallers, dog rattles, shell trumpets (without wooden mouthpieces), percussion rods, lamellaphones and leaf oboes are known to have been widespread throughout the motu. However, it is the presence of comparatively rare instrument types in more than one rohe that reveals the most about inter-iwi relationships and their influence on the development of iwitanga. Similarities typically occur between rohe that are not greatly distant from one another. However, in some cases similar instruments have been found in places that are geographically distant, raising questions around whether these are instances of cultural influence or of convergent evolution. Complicating matters, the name for an instrument in one area can – as we have seen – refer in another rohe to a completely different instrument, or one that varies in form, design or material.

KŌAUAU

The kōauau is perhaps the most ubiquitous Māori musical instrument; it appears to have been used across the entire motu in pre-European-contact Māori society. As noted earlier, this short, straight-bored flute was named for its sound and had associations with both life and death. Kōauau could be made from a variety of materials, including wood, stone, hue, kelp/seaweed, whaletooth, and human, kurī, whale and bird bone. Because the kōauau in its base form was so functional, flexible and broadly used, tracing the variations in design, materials, use and playing technique from rohe to rohe can be revealing.

For example, different methods of determining kōauau fingerhole placement were used around the motu. It is noteworthy that Ngāti Whakaue, in Te Arawa, and Ngāti Whātua, in Tai Tokerau, use exactly the same method. In this method, the lower end of the kōauau is pressed down against a person's extended thumb and laid alongside their forefinger, with their hand forming an 'L' shape. Usually the kōauau is the length of a person's forefinger. The top hole is drilled opposite the top joint of the person's forefinger, the second hole opposite the second joint, and the third opposite the third joint.[45]

Two different fingerhole placement methods have been described by members of Ngāti Porou. In one described by elder Iehu Nukunuku (1828–1928), who lived at Waiomatatini in the Waiapu district, the kōauau's length is measured from the tip of the forefinger of the right hand to the fork at the base of the thumb. The first hole is measured off by placing the forefinger on the instrument nail upward so as to measure off the first two joints, where the first hole is placed. The finger is then doubled over, bringing the first joint nail downward on the bore; the length of the first joint marks the site of the second hole. The second joint is then brought down in the same manner, and its length marks the position of the third hole. The thumb is then placed sideways on the outer edge of the kōauau, and its width gives the measurement for where to cut the end off.[46] Another Ngāti Porou method involved placing the fingerholes in alignment with the stars in Tautoru (Orion's Belt).[47]

There is one notable difference that distinguishes flutes from the north and south islands, and it relates to which end the instruments are blown from. In Te Waipounamu, albatross bone flutes were blown from the end closest to the largest gap between fingerholes, whereas wooden or bone kōauau from Te Ika a Māui were blown from the opposite end (the end nearest to where the fingerholes are closest together).[48]

PŪTŌRINO

As discussed in Chapter 1, the term pūtōrino in Te Ika a Māui typically describes a wooden instrument with a tapering shape and a single fingerhole located near the centre of the bore; while in Te Wai Pounamu, the name was used to refer to very different flutes.

There was also much regional variance rohe to rohe. For example, in the Bay of Islands, the central māngai (mouth) was smaller in comparison to elsewhere in Te Ika a Māui, while some instruments from the neighbouring Tai Tokerau and Tainui regions had three small fingerholes instead of one māngai. A few examples from the Whanganui area have a comparatively large hole at the distal end, which was used as the blowing end for the trumpeting voice.[49]

In Te Tau Ihu o te Waka a Māui, pūtōrino were described as being shorter than kōauau, and as having three koroputa (fingerholes).[50] In this respect, they resemble a small nose-blown pūtōrino with three fingerholes from Tainui that we know of thanks to a single account.[51] In the Banks Peninsula area (Waitaha), pūtōrino are described as being similar to pōrutu, but were not often used. They were made from poroporo with the pith removed. Like those from Te Tau Ihu o te Waka, they had

PŪTŌRINO *made from matai wood. Descendant of Hine Raukatauri; wind instrument. Measures 44.5cms long. Made by Brian Flintoff.* ♪

three fingerholes. They were played with the nose, the player blocking one nostril with a finger and blowing with the other nostril.[52] In Murihiku, pūtōrino were a type of whistle made from kōiwi toroa (albatross bone); the term was defined as 'to make the ears ring', indicating its piercing sound. Bone was also used to make tōrino/pūtōrino in the Mataatua rohe.[53]

HOHO / PŪ HOHO HŌ

Hoho and pū hoho hō are names used by Ngāti Porou in Tairāwhiti and by Tainui in Te Rohe Pōtae, respectively, for the same instrument – the flute known more commonly today as pūtōrino.[54] The instrument is distinguished by a particular playing technique, involving moving (but not lifting) the player's fingers over the central māngai, which features in both rohe.[55]

PERERAU

A one-holed flute made from human bone was found in the Rangitāiki awa in Mataatua. The flute measures 15 to 17.5 centimetres and features a carved human figure, which has a hole in its face. It is uncertain if this was a blowing hole or a fingerhole. While the Mataatua name for this flute is not recorded, in Tai Tokerau it was recognised by a Ngāpuhi informant as a type of flute called pererau.[56] Some artefacts labelled toggles (poro) in museum collections may actually be examples of pererau.

ORORUARANGI

Ororuarangi are long flutes with two fingerholes placed side by side at the midpoint of the tube. Like pererau, ororuarangi have been documented in both the Tai Tokerau and Mataatua rohe.

TOROA BONE ORORUARANGI. *Descendant of Hine Raukatauri; wind instrument. Measures 31cms long. Made by Brian Flintoff.* ♪

Tai Tokerau ororuarangi were made from toroa (albatross) wing bone while, according to a Ruatāhuna elder, Tūhoe used long-necked hue. In the Tūhoe rohe, players rolled their index finger back and forth over the two fingerholes, creating a voice that oscillated between the high and low registers. The high voice may relate to the practice of men singing in falsetto.[57]

Long-necked hue (hue kakau roa) are different from the traditional type of gourd, which has a shorter neck, and they may have been introduced after the arrival of Europeans.[58] Given this, the Tūhoe ororuarangi was likely a comparatively late development.

TŪTEURE AND PŌRUTU

Tūteure is a type of straight-bored Ngāti Porou flute used to accompany song.[59] To form the bore, the pith of dried tutu is burned using coals of mānuka or another hardwood. Fingerholes are then drilled using a cord drill (tūwiri).[60] Pōrutu, as noted earlier, is a similar type of flute that is commonly found throughout Te Wai Pounamu. Tūteure and pōrutu are both longer versions of kōauau but their names are very different, which suggests that those two flutes were likely invented independently of each other.

TARAKIMERE

Tarakimere are reported to have been used by Te Aupōuri in Tai Tokerau, Ngāti Kahungunu in Tākitimu, and Tūhoe in Mataatua. This instrument consists of a small leaf clamped between two slivers of wood bark or bone, which is placed between the player's lips.[61] With a combination of lip pressure and blowing, the leaf vibrates as a reed. It can be used to play the rangi (tune) of mōteatea and waiata koroua (traditional chants).[62]

HUE RARĀ

Rattles made from dried gourds (hue rarā) have been reported only from Tai Tokerau and Tokomaru Bay in Tairāwhiti. Ngāti Porou hue rarā were made from hue approximately the size of tennis balls. While growing, the hue was bent around a hoop to create a shape that could comfortably fit in the hand of a kaiwhakatautau (ceremonial mourner) or kaikanikani (dancer) while being played.[63] These hue rarā used the gourd's seeds to produce the rattle. In Tai Tokerau, the gourds had their seeds removed and replaced with small smooth river pebbles. This key difference means these instruments could have been invented independently.

HUE RARĀ *made from gourd with small quartz pebbles inside. Descendant of Hinepūtehue; percussion instrument. Measures 11cms long. Made by Brian Flintoff.* ♪

BUBU / PŪPŪ

In Te Wai Pounamu, toitoi shells were used as musical instruments. In Waitaha (specifically in the Ngā Kohatu Whakarakaraka o Tamatea Pōkai Whenua Port Hills area), the conical points were removed from the shells, which were then played as trumpets called pū.[64] Both there and in the Murihiku rohe, these shells were also played as flutes called bubu or pūpū to perform rangi.[65] In Murihiku, James Beattie's informants reported that the shells customarily used were blue or white, and longer than those available at the time of Beattie's research in the early 20th century (and since).[66]

PŪHUE / REHU

Gourd trumpets reported from Haranui marae at Te Awaroa in Tai Tokerau and from Taranaki share similar physical attributes, which may indicate a cultural connection between iwi from these two regions. Both had incised decorations in the form of

BUBU *made of toitoi (Cook's turban) shells. Descendants of Tangaroa; wind instruments. The larger shell (measuring 8.5cms in diameter) was shaped by David Cattermole and the smaller one (measuring 4cms in diameter) was found by Jennifer Cattermole at Te Mamaku Ruby Bay, Tasman district.*

GOURD TRUMPET *with kauri wooden mouthpiece. Descendant of Hinepūtehue; wind instrument. Measures 47.5cms long. Made by Jen and David Cattermole.* ♪

double spirals and notches. There were, however, some key differences. The Tai Tokerau version had one fingerhole bored in the neck a few inches from the blowing end and was fairly large (30.5 centimetres long); the Taranaki version was shorter and had two to three fingerholes. The Tai Tokerau example also had a hole at the top of the gourd's neck that functioned as a mouthpiece, and was shaped like a cow's horn, with a double curve.[67] None of the descriptions of these instruments mentions a hole at the end opposite the blowing end, though this would have been necessary for them to have functioned as trumpets. This is the case for one Māori instrument held in the British Museum – a gourd instrument with a small bone mouthpiece 'which was perhaps used as a trumpet, with the gourd's base cut out to form a bell'.[68]

Ngāti Porou gourd trumpets featured a wooden mouthpiece and had no fingerholes or incised decoration. This type may therefore have been invented independently. Ngāti Porou leader Matutaera (Tuta) Nihoniho, born in the Waiapu valley in 1850, described the hue used to make trumpets as elongated with a curve at the stem. A piece was cut off the large end, which served as the mouth of the instrument from which its voice projected. A small piece was cut off the stem, and a wooden mouthpiece was affixed.[69]

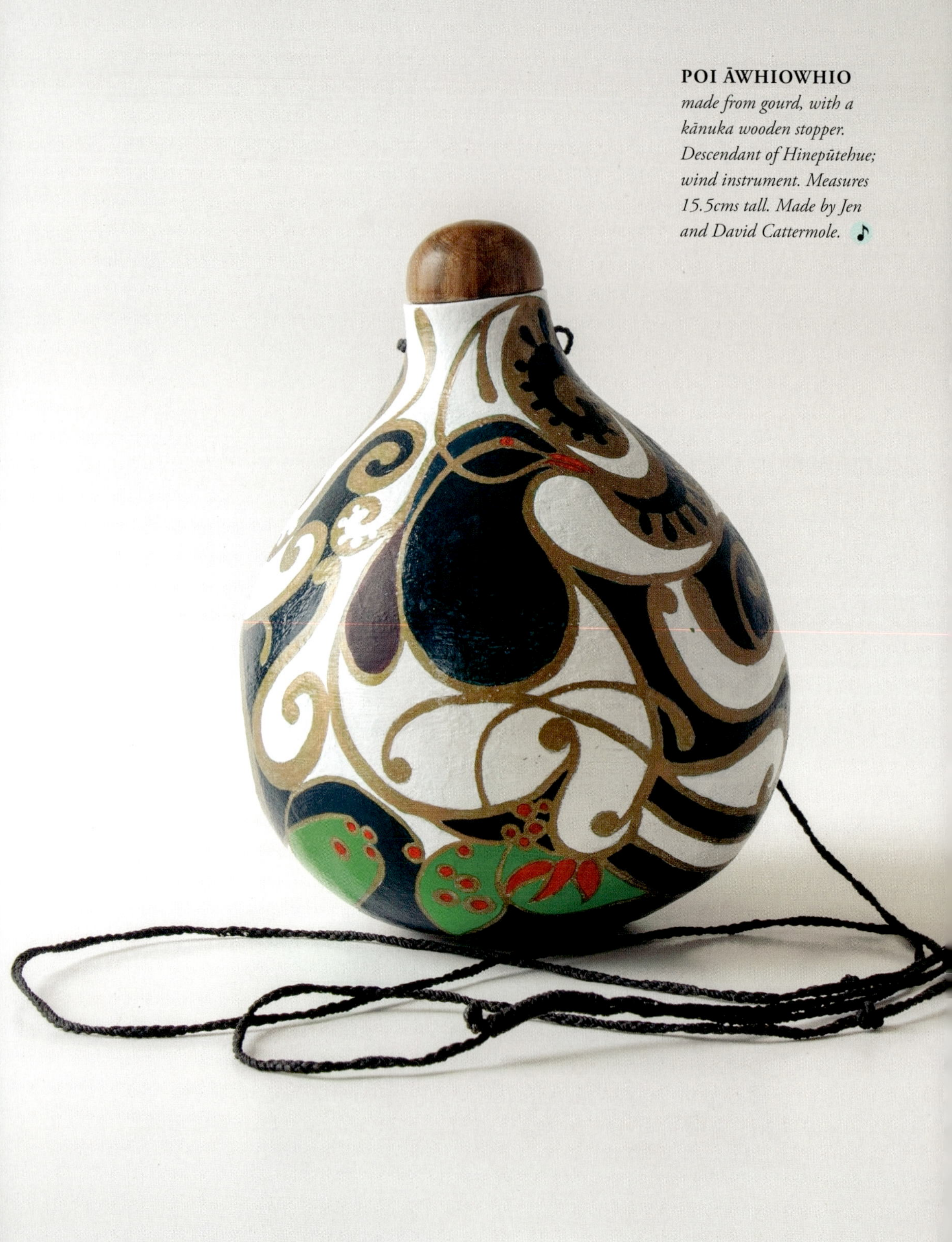

POI ĀWHIOWHIO
made from gourd, with a kānuka wooden stopper. Descendant of Hinepūtehue; wind instrument. Measures 15.5cms tall. Made by Jen and David Cattermole. ♪

POI ĀWHIOWHIO

Poi āwhiowhio are instruments made from small- or medium-sized gourds with one to four holes in the body.[70] Historically, they were used by Tūhoe and Ngāti Kahungunu to summon birds, particularly kererū/kūkupa,[71] though the voice of this instrument also resembles mātātā (fernbird), riroriro (warbler) or a flock of tauhou (waxeyes).[72] Birds were summoned both to be killed and eaten, thereby sustaining human life, and also to communicate messages for tohunga. Poi āwhiowhio were played during rituals that were undertaken to open the season for taking kererū when they were fat. According to a Ruatāhuna elder, Tūhoe played these instruments after reciting appropriate karakia.[73]

Ngāti Kahungunu people also used this instrument to attract lovers.[74] Both poi āwhiowhio and some birds, particularly miromiro, were used to convey ātahu (love charms/spells).[75] Miro means 'spin, twirl, whirling, moving in spirals', which aptly describes the motion of both the miromiro and poi āwhiowhio.

Āwhiowhio (whirlwinds) feature in pūrākau: as noted previously they were the force that drew Rangi and Papa together into their loving embrace and they assisted Tāne's ascent to the highest heaven to obtain the three baskets of knowledge. Poi āwhiowhio reflect these whirlwinds. Their spinning motion creates a vortex, which draws in desired objects (birds; a lover) with its irresistible force. When spiralling upward in flight, the instrument enables enlightenment and communication with the spiritual realm.

OVAL-SHAPED PAHU WITH THIN WALLS

A rarely documented form of percussion is a large, oval-shaped pahu or patō that was hollowed out as thinly as possible, and placed in useful locations. Instruments matching this description were reported twice. The first example, described in 1869, was located on a hill at Te Whaiti in Te Urewera, overlooking the Whirinaki valley. Named Opato, it was made from a block of resonant timber approximately 1.2 metres long and suspended from a sapling resting on two other poles.[76]

The second example, described in 1850, was from Ngā Tukitiki a Hikawera pā on Te Aroha-a-uta mountain in the Tainui rohe. This pahu was suspended from a post on top of a high platform in the centre of the pā and beaten with a heavy piece of wood to give warning of wartime attack.[77] A similar instrument described as a 'war bell' was recorded at Matamata in 1836. It was an oval pahu partly hollowed out in the centre, suspended from cords on a platform 4.5 to 6 metres from the ground, and beaten with a mallet.[78]

PAHU MADE FROM HOLLOW TREES

Ngāti Tūwharetoa used wooden logs or hollow trees as gongs and employed a simple signal language to send messages long distances across Lake Taupō via staging posts.[79] Similar instruments, made from hollow living trees, were used in the neighbouring Tūhoe rohe.

One example, a hollow tōtara located near Te Kakau on the bush track from Ruatāhuna to Maungapōhatu, was called Tōtara-pakopako. Travellers approaching Te Kakau would signal their approach by striking the tree using a wooden beater.[80]

Another example, described in 1869, was formed from a hollow living tōtara tree around 30 metres tall. It was located on a hill near Te Apu, on the track from Whirinaki to Ahikereru in the Te Whaiti area. The 'tongue' of this pahu was elaborately carved and the instrument was struck with a maire club. It was so resonant that it could be heard at Tahataharoa near Ruatāhuna, about 30 kilometres away.

Smaller pahu were located on several hilltops in the area. One was located on a hill above a kāinga near Maungapōhatu and another at a pā in the Waimana valley below Tawhana. These were beaten to sound the alarm in the event of an enemy attack.[81]

The only wooden pahu reported from Te Wai Pounamu was a hollow log used to wake muttonbirders in the Tītī Islands near Rakiura Stewart Island.[82] The geographical distance separating these iwi, and the fact that hollow logs naturally lend themselves to such uses, suggests that this pahu was a case of independent invention as opposed to cultural connection or influence.

STICK GAMES

Stick games were played in many locations. Usually, the players would avoid touching sticks, but there were localised variants of the game in Tai Tokerau and Te Arawa in which the players touched sticks together to produce sound.[83]

In Tai Tokerau, the game was called titi tourea or titi tōrea and was accompanied by chanting. Two people would stand about 1.2 metres apart, each holding a prepared rod of kaiwhiria (pigeonwood) approximately the length and size of a walking stick. The players would throw their sticks, which must touch while passing in the air and give out 'the exact note required' before being gently caught by the other player.[84]

This game had a similar name in Te Arawa (tī rākau or touretua) and was also accompanied by chanting, but here the two sticks were beaten together as well as thrown.[85]

TREE PAHU. *Drawing by Jennifer Cattermole from an image in Best,* Games and Pastimes, *p. 107.*

KURĪ RATTLES

Rattles made from several pieces of wood or bone were reported across Aotearoa. These rattles were tied around the necks of kurī when hunting ground-dwelling species such as kiwi, kākāpō, weka and kiore. The sound of the rattle would alert hunters to the whereabouts of the kurī and hence their prey. Names for this instrument varied. For example, the neighbouring Te Arawa and Tūhoe iwi both used the name kākara, while rattles from Whanganui were named tātara – a related term.[86]

Instrument-making materials specific to particular rohe

Many iwi utilised widely available materials (such as whale, human, dog and bird bones; whale teeth; shells; wood, gum, leaves and plant fibres; and stones) in a locally distinctive way, and some iwi made their musical instruments using materials that were unique to their rohe. Such instruments play an important role in the iwitanga concerning taonga pūoro. As taonga pūoro player and maker Alistair Fraser says: 'If we look at the availability of resources at a regional level we see an interaction and musical conversation with the environment that can be seen as a unique musical voice of the people from that geographic area'.[87]

The discussion below largely excludes flora, except for those plants that are known to have grown within a limited area. It is very difficult to ascertain where unprovenanced taonga pūoro made from plant materials held in museum collections originally came from. Wood gains a dark patina with age, making visual identification of tree species from its grain and colour very difficult. Moreover, the instruments' taonga status rules out the use of destructive testing methods that could be used to identify the plant species. We know from historical accounts the kinds of plant species used to make taonga pūoro (see Appendix 2), but there are currently no studies that map all these species' distributions geographically.

KELP/SEAWEED FLUTES

Kelp was often used to make flutes. In the Banks Peninsula area and in Te Tau Ihu o te Waka a Māui, rimurapa (bull kelp) stipes were used to make kōauau, and the words kōauau and rimurapa were used interchangeably there.[88] Rimurapa is a cool, temperate species found only on the most exposed headlands in northern Te Ika a Māui. It becomes more common towards Te Moana o Raukawa Cook Strait and thrives on Te Wai Pounamu shores.[89] Rimurapa stipes are usually solid and need to be hollowed out to form flutes; this is usually done using a stick while the stipe is fresh.[90]

In Murihiku, rimurimu may have been used in addition to rimurapa. One of Beattie's informants specified that kōauau kelp had '"crackers" hanging in strings', though they also used the term in a more general sense for 'weeds cast up by the sea'.[91] The description matches rimurimu, as the dry kelp pods crackle and pop beneath the feet when one walks along the high-tide line. The pods are hollow inside and, with one or both ends broken off, can be played as birdcallers and flutes. Kelp pods can be played when wet or dried. When fresh, the walls of the pod are thicker, more resilient and more resonant.

Flutes are also made from seaweed in Te Ika a Māui. Around Te Kaha, in the Mataatua region, Te Whānau-ā-Apanui make flutes from seaweed stems and use kōauau as a term for both seaweed and flutes made from seaweed stems. These stems are very small and delicate, about the size of the tip of the little finger.[92]

Taonga pūoro practitioner and scholar Robert Thorne (Ngāti Tumutumu) once used an oceanic microalgae organism (probably *Eklonia radiata*, the stipes of which can be solid or hollow) found on a beach in Napier to make a kōauau. Similar materials have been found in Palliser Bay and on the Coromandel Peninsula. Thorne discovered kelp stipes (identified variously as sea grass, crayfish kelp and bull kelp, though further research is needed to identify the species) at Schooner Bay, Aotea Great Barrier Island, which form naturally hollow woody/leathery tubes when dried. Due to their hollowness, these can reasonably be labelled kōauau kelp.[93]

KŌURA

Crayfish are widely distributed in coastal waters all around Aotearoa. Historically, it was only in the Murihiku area that the larger leg sections of kōura were used to make kōauau.[94] The antennae of large crayfish could also be played as flutes.

KŌAUAU KŌURA *made from crayfish leg (top), measuring 9.3cms long and antennae (bottom), measuring 9.8cms long. Descendants of Hine Raukatauri; wind instruments. Made by Alistair Fraser and James Webster.* ♪

PŪNUI / BŪNUI

Flutes were made from the hollow branches of pūnui/būnui (Stewart Island rhubarb), which is unique to Rakiura (and nearby islands such as Te Wharawhara Ulva Island).[95] Pūnui/būnui flutes were restricted in their geographical distribution, owing to the limited area in which this plant grows.

HUE

Hue can be grown north of Ōtautahi, though the voices of gourd 'instruments would have been more commonly heard in the top of Te Waipounamu and in Te Ika a Māui'.[96] While gourd vines cannot generally grow south of Ōtautahi, as the climate is too cold, harvested gourds were traded all across the motu.

KŌHATU

The origin of stone instruments can often be traced using geochemical analysis. Therefore, when found in a particular location, instruments made from stone help map the movements of trade items and people. This information can then be compared with oral and written historical accounts.

In southern Te Wai Pounamu, steatite has historically been used to make birdcallers. This soft and talcy material is easy to shape. It is more dense than wood, which means that birdcallers made from steatite have quite a loud, piercing voice.

In the north of Murihuku, naturally occurring hollow ironstone from the Maerewhenua awa may have been used historically as rattles and flutes. Both instruments have certainly found their way into the contemporary whānau of taonga pūoro. The rare 'rattling stones' or 'rattle rocks' (also found in Bushy Creek, which flows into the Maerewhenua) are hollow concretions with sand inside, while tubes of ironstone that are either completely hollow or closed at one end can be played as flutes using the cross-blowing technique.

Kōau made from pounamu and pakohe (argillite) are held in private collections by southern people whose tūpuna knew how to cut, drill, hollow and polish the stone to create flutes that 'sang with a clarity and sweetness like no other'.[97] Pounamu is also used to make pahu, with stone of the highest quality creating exquisite ringing tones.[98]

Pounamu may also have been used to make `gārara, swung slats. The stone's density, weight and spiritual significance made it appropriate for `gārara used as weapons as well as in healing.[99]

As pounamu was and remains a highly valuable trade commodity, this Te Wai Pounamu material also found its way to Te Ika a Māui. Two taonga pūoro made

IRONSTONE KŌAUAU *(descendants of Hine Raukatauri; wind instruments) and rattle stones (descendants of Papatūānuku; percussion instruments) from the Maerewhenua awa, near Duntroon, Murihiku. Measuring (top) 18cms long; (bottom, from left to right) 9, 10.5 and 12.5cms long, respectively. The flute in the middle of the bottom row was shaped by David Cattermole.* ♪

NGURU *made from pounamu (left) and kōauau made from pakohe (right). Descendants of Hine Raukatauri; wind instruments. Measuring 10.7 and 14cms long. Made by David Cattermole and Clem Mellish, respectively.*

POUNAMU XYLOPHONE AND TUNING FORKS. *Descendants of Papatūānuku; percussion instruments. Made by Russell Beck. Photographed by Jennifer Cattermole.*

from pounamu were used at Maungakiekie (One Tree Hill) in Tāmaki Makaurau: a pahu pounamu and a pūrerehua pounamu. The pounamu they were made of came from a great distance away. Long-distance trading in materials or goods may have commenced as early as the 16th century but is more likely to have been later. By the 18th century, pounamu was being traded across the motu via trade networks centred on the east coast of Te Wai Pounamu.[100] When the pūrerehua at Maungakiekie was played at dusk its voice could be heard simultaneously in the Waitematā and Manukau harbours, which means it must have been extraordinarily loud and powerful.[101]

The pahu was suspended above a stage or platform located at the top of Maungakiekie, or possibly at Maungawhau (Mount Eden). It was also played at dusk and was used as a war signal or as a signal for people from nearby kāinga to gather; its voice could be heard for several kilometres.[102] Names recorded for this taonga include Whakārewhatāhuna, Whakarewa-tāhuna and Kahotea. Owned by a chief named Kiwi Tāmaki of Waiohua, the taonga carried the mana of the Tāmaki district;

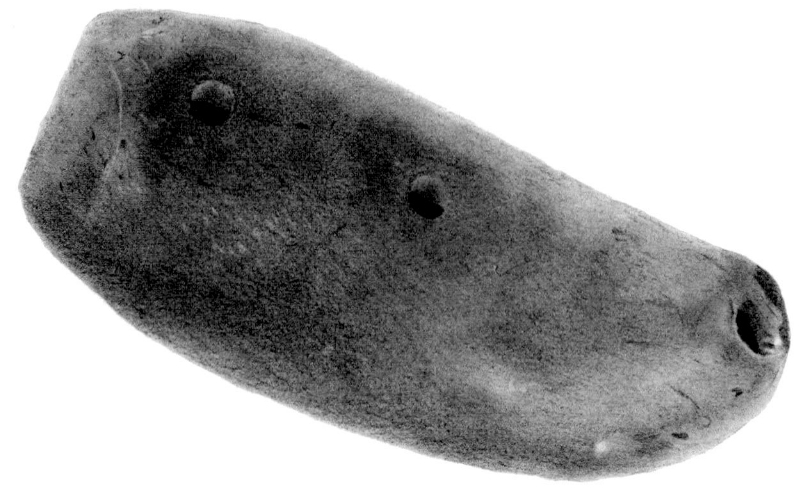

STONE NGURU *from the Oruarangi pā site, Hauraki district, held in Tūhura Otago Museum (catalogue number D33.1595). Descendant of Hine Raukatauri; wind instrument. Measures 7.4cms long. Drawing by Jennifer Cattermole.*

possession of it was evidence of ownership of the land. This instrument is said to have been buried for safekeeping somewhere on Maungakiekie, or near Maungawhau, before the battle where the Waiohua people lost their lands to Ngāti Whātua (specifically, Te Taoū) around 1740.[103] It was never recovered.

In Te Ika a Māui, historically, flutes were made from other types of stone. At Oruarangi pā in the Tainui area, nguru and kōauau were made using fine- and coarse-grained sandstone, rhyolite, tuff, ignimbrite and pumice. Some of that material was not sourced locally. For example, the marine tuff possibly came from the Auckland area, and the sandstones from North Auckland or Waikato.[104] Another sandstone nguru was found at the Oue pā site, also located within Tainui – two kilometres northwest of the Wairoa awa, South Auckland.[105] Stone nguru have been reported from the Tairāwhiti East Cape area, and a kōauau made from sandstone or pumice was found on Te Pane o Mataoho (Māngere mountain) in Tāmaki Makaurau.[106]

CLAY

Clay is important in a spiritual sense as, according to pūrākau, the body of the first woman, Hineahuone, was made from this material. Historically, clay was not commonly used, but there is evidence that Māori did make some instruments from this material.[107] For example, nguru from the Oruarangi pā site were made from wet, unfired clay, as were vessel flutes called ukutangi (or pūtangitangi, ipūtangi, or būdagidagi). These taonga were traditionally associated with mourning and are now also used to mihi to whenua, to connect with land.[108]

LAND SNAILS

Pūpūrangi (kauri snails) are found only in Tai Tokerau. When these snails retreat into their shells and turn into the breeze, they make an eerie whistling sound that is difficult to pinpoint.[109] It is likely that this mysterious sound inspired local Māori to use empty snail shells as flutes – instruments that are said to be favoured by the patupaiarehe, a type of supernatural being.

Pūpū harakeke (also called pūpūwhakarongo taua or pūpū korari) are another type of land snail specific to a particular location whose shells are played as flutes. As we saw in Chapter 1, for the Ngāti Kuri people of the far north, these snails were treasured as kaitiaki. The sound of the snails retreating suddenly into their shells when disturbed alerted people to the presence of an invading war party, giving advance warning of their approach and saving lives.[110]

MARINE BIRD BONE

Flutes made of the bones of marine birds such as albatrosses, mollymawks and giant petrels have been found in all the main islands of Aotearoa.[111] In coastal sites in eastern Te Wai Pounamu, there is evidence of such flutes dating from at least the late 16th century, but they are more common in the archaeological record in the 18th and early 19th centuries.[112]

Albatross wing bones were used in Murihiku to make pōrutu as well as shorter flutes called whio or rehu.[113] These were played at times of grieving, recalling a connection between toroa and Hawaiki. The tears of the albatross – roimata toroa, the extrusion of excess salt through their nostrils – were regarded as tears of homesickness for Hawaiki. Toroa flutes were blown from the end that has the widest space between the top and middle wenewene – the opposite of the practice when playing wooden and human bone flutes from Te Ika a Māui.[114] Although it was not until until 1920 that toroa formed a breeding colony at Taiaroa Head on Muaūpoko Otago Peninsula – the only place in mainland New Zealand that they breed – albatross bones do occasionally wash up on the east coast and in southern areas of Te Wai Pounamu, providing material for flutes.[115] They also wash up on the shores of Rakiura thanks to breeding colonies on islands nearby.[116]

Marine bird bone flutes were also played in some parts of Te Ika a Māui. On the Hauraki plains, in the Tainui rohe, they have been found in the upper layers of sites Māori ceased occupying in the early 1800s (such as Oruarangi pā). In Tai Tokerau,

KŌAUAU KŌIWI TOROA *held in Tūhura Otago Museum (catalogue number D39.1399). Descendant of Hine Raukatauri; wind instrument. Drawing by Jennifer Cattermole.*

both kōauau and ororuarangi were made from kōiwi toroa. A surviving example of the former is unusual in having four pairs of holes placed in pairs side by side.[117] These Te Ika a Māui flutes likely developed independently from those in Te Wai Pounamu, utilising bone sourced from nearby (for example, the west coast beaches of Tāmaki Makaurau), though the possibility that they were inspired by or were trade items from Te Wai Pounamu shouldn't be discounted.[118]

The proliferation of kōiwi toroa flutes was spurred on by demographic changes and by the extinction of moa in around 1450–1500.[119] Kāti Māmoe, Rangitāne and other groups came to Te Wai Pounamu in the 16th century, and Kāi Tahu arrived in the 17th and 18th centuries.[120] These peoples came from the east and south coasts of Te Ika a Māui, where no kōiwi toroa flutes have been found despite these bones being available along those shores. It is unlikely then that these flutes were introduced to the south via the introduction of 'Classic' Māori culture from Te Ika a Māui, even though their proliferation is concurrent with these population changes, particularly the most recent ones.[121] Waitaha people were using bird bone flutes before northern peoples migrated to Te Wai Pounamu; these flutes subsequently became a shared aspect of iwitanga as the populations became integrated. 'Despite this "blending," the new occupants may have been the catalysts for new behaviours in Murihiku such as [with the decline of moa] … intensification of muttonbirding.'[122] An increased reliance on muttonbirding – and hence spending more time on offshore islands – would have meant more toroa bone was available to be made into flutes.

Taonga pūoro uses

In examining the names of taonga pūoro (in Chapter 1), and their distribution, iwitanga and specific materiality (in this chapter), we have covered a number of the ways they were customarily used in Māori society, from sacred and spiritual practices; communication, alerts and warfare; birth, death and mourning rituals; in wānanga and education practices; healing; hunting; and play and recreation. However, it is worth considering here several further key roles played by these taonga and some revealing differences in their use from rohe to rohe, iwi to iwi.

USE THAT VARIES BY ROHE

Some widespread instrument types were used in quite idiosyncratic ways in certain iwi. Without repeating information presented elsewhere in this book, some notable instrument uses are discussed below.

One example concerns kōauau from the Tai Tokerau rohe. In the Tauhara and Waikaretu kāinga (in the northern Kaipara) in 1887, small bone flutes were sung through by Manihera and Keena Tangaroa in pao (two-lined epigrammatic songs) contests. Each player attempted to outdo the other in order to gain mana.[123]

A specific use of another type of instrument, pōtaka hue, was restricted to Tūhoe and neighbouring iwi. These iwi used pōtaka hue to accompany the singing of whakaoriori pōtaka or oriori pōtaka (songs of lamentation and grief). The tops were spun at the end of each whiti (verse), and the humming sound of the pōtaka hue was a dirge representing the wailing of mourning widows. As noted in Chapter 1, tears and wailing avenged the afflictions of Aituā (the personification of misfortune), as acknowledged in the following expression: ko roimata, ko hupe, anake ngā kai utu i nga patu a aituā (by tears and grief only may the strokes of misfortune be avenged). The spinning of wailing tops (hai ranaki i te mate) thus avenged defeat. Laments were sung out of respect for those killed in battle; it is known there was one such performance after the battle of Ōrākau – the last major battle of the Waikato War – in 1864. An oriori pōtaka was performed after the battles at Maketu that same year and Pukemaire the year after in which Ngāti Porou and Te Whakatohea were defeated. Often, after the defeat of a group of warriors, friendly visitors would call at their pā to pay their respects to the memory of the fallen and grieve with their loved ones. People would gather at the marae and chant a lament for the dead, accompanied by pōtaka hue. Afterwards, the tops – along with presents such as clothing – would be given to the visitors.[124] The use of this specific instrument in lament bears out the practice of using taonga pūoro to express grief in all rohe of Aotearoa.

While shell trumpets were used for a variety of signalling purposes across the motu, one specific to Tai Tokerau was to warn of shark sightings: 'groups from the northern tribes, collecting shellfish from reefs, were alerted to the presence of sharks by short, loud blasts on a small pūtātara played by an observer who was stationed on a suitable vantage point'.[125]

Similarly, among the documented uses of bullroarers as lures (e.g. to call lizards or rainclouds), one account from Waitaha stands out as being unusual. In this account, famous Kāi Tahu and Kāti Mamoe writer Keri Hulme (1947–2021) recalls bullroarers being used to call dolphins when she was a child.[126]

LOVE AND SEDUCTION

In Te Ika a Māui, flute playing was associated with sexual attraction and procreation. Kōauau, pūtōrino or whio were all used for this purpose.[127] For example, in Tai Tokerau, skilled pūtōrino players could attract women, although the whio was generally considered a more effective instrument. If a man could not play the whio, he pretended to play while sitting near an adept player in a dark or dimly lit house. If he won his desired woman's affection, he rewarded the player with a gift of a garment, weapon or food.[128]

In most stories, the player of the kōauau is successful in wooing his woman.[129] However, sometimes a clever rival could thwart the seductive powers of a kōauau player. In Kaitāia, for example, two men – Huarahi and Putere – both admired a woman named Moewai.

> Putere was an 'accomplished player on the kōauau' and Moewai was a 'passionate lover of music'. Huarahi, however, was of higher rank than Putere but 'could not play a note' on the kōauau. Huarahi lit a fire on the rock where Putere played his kōauau to Moewai causing him to jump off the rock because of the heat, and land on top of Moewai who was awaiting a loving tune. In the end, this event causes Moewai to get angry and eventually [she] falls in love and marries Huarahi.[130]

The shapes, carvings and playing techniques of pūtōrino and kōauau all relate to procreation and recognise that both male and female attributes are necessary to create new life. For example, the tapering shape of pūtōrino, and of some kōauau, is reminiscent of the female vulva. In Tai Tokerau a Te Aupōuri women's haka refers to the three openings of the female pelvic floor and the sounds they make, mapping these onto the three fingerholes of kōauau. The first hole makes the sound of water; the second, the sound of a baby's movement through the birth canal ('Kei roto koe i taku puta … Shaaa'); and the third the sound of wind.[131] Male genitalia are also represented on some kōauau, with shapes and carvings that represent a phallus.[132]

Among Te Arawa, in order to aid conception, players scalloped their finger over the third hole of the flute to replicate the action of rolling back the foreskin of a penis (te mea whakatehe).[133]

CROP FERTILITY

The use of flutes to aid human reproduction also likely extended to crop fertility across Te Ika a Māui. Although no historical accounts refer to kōauau being used in connection with kūmara fertility rituals, they appear in many pūrākau and karakia connected with kūmara planting and may have been used for this purpose.[134]

Raukatauri, goddess of flute music, appears in the following karakia associated with kūmara fertility: 'Te hiki Raukata-uri, Raukatamea [me] Itiiti-ma-Rekareka' (The lifting karakia of Raukatauri, Raukatamea, Itiiti and Rekareka).[135] As noted earlier, one of the ariā of Raukatauri is the kihikihi (cicada), which is associated with spring and harvesting.[136] Cicadas employ sound as a key element of their mating practices, as do casemoths, which are another manifestation of this goddess.

Other instruments fulfilled similar functions. As mentioned earlier, Ngāti Porou used swung slats (huhū, tūrorohū, tarari) to facilitate crop growth. Similarly, among the neighbouring Ngāti Awa and Tūhoe iwi, the pūkaea was used to open kūmara-planting rituals.[137]

DIVINATION AND SPIRIT COMMUNICATION

As we saw in Chapter 1, several taonga pūoro were likely used to communicate with and receive communications from the spirit world – especially when seeking omens to confirm a decision or intention. This practice seems to be common across Te Ika a Māui. For example, tohunga could interpret the harmonics generated by pūtōrino as omens used in matakite (foretelling). Similarly, in the Tainui rohe, humming tops were used historically in divination, with tohunga making a judgement based on the instrument's voice.

Humming tops were famously used in the Waikato district to determine the identity of the first Māori king. Each iwi made their own humming top. Matai was the favoured material; however, Pōtatau Te Wherowhero's humming top, called Te Ketirera, was made from a large gourd. His pōtaka hue defeated all its competitors by humming the loudest, and thus Pōtatau Te Wherowhero was elected.

Generally, humming tops can be used to receive messages from the atua and ancestors. When a top hums loudly, the answer to a question is yes; and when it hums quietly the answer is no. The wind sometimes influences the sound, and tohunga can hear words being communicated. When the tone alternates from higher to lower, this is seen as a good sign.[138] Porotiti and pūrerehua are, similarly, associated with matakite: 'The howling and eerie sounds of the winds are often acknowledged as messages from the spirit world. Sometimes porotiti [and pūrerehua] produce unexpected sounds which are considered special as they are perceived as spirit voices joining in with the song'.[139]

HUMAN COMMUNICATION

As well as channelling messages from the spirit world, taonga pūoro, through the agency of ngā atua, give words spiritual power, potency and efficacy within the human realm.[140] We have a range of examples of this from across Te Ika a Māui. For Māori generally, the chief role of musical instruments is speaking or singing the relevant words.[141] Māori instrumental music mirrors and incorporates language, and esteemed players can enunciate the words of waiata, karakia and messages into various types of flute (pōrutu, kōauau, pūtōrino and pūmotomoto).[142] Tohunga sometimes communicated cryptic coded verbal information through instruments like pūtōrino,[143] but other ideas could be conveyed too. For example, in the Te Kūiti district, Tangiwharau sang a love message through a pūtōrino to a woman named Parekarau, who lived five to eight kilometres distant.[144] The instrument was not amplifying his words in a literal way, but because of its divine nature was able to convey his meaning from afar. Flutes are not only vehicles for transmitting kupu across vast distances, but also a means of ensuring those kupu have their desired effect (in this case, seducing the desired person).

There are some wonderful kōrero concerning the use of flutes to communicate secret messages. The best-known Māori love story is that of Tūtānekai and Hinemoa. Tūtānekai (and/or his friend or slave Tiki) from Mokoia Island played flutes to seduce Hinemoa.[145] They would perform in the evening or at night from an elevated platform on a hilltop.[146]

> Hinemoa was the daughter of a great chief named Umukaria and his wife Hinemaru. Their home was at Ōwhata on the shores of Lake Rotorua. Because of Hinemoa's high rank she was made a puhi, or betrothed daughter, Umukaria intending her for someone also of noble birth. Hinemoa secretly desired Tūtānekai, a stepson of Whakaue whom the Mokoia chief had accepted into his household. Because of his humble birth, Tūtānekai had not even considered asking permission to marry her, though he felt love for her. At the great communal gatherings of the people held at Ōwhata to discuss communal matters, they had often glanced at one another. Tūtānekai had even contrived to give the secret sign of love by pressing the palm of Hinemoa – and the squeeze had been reciprocated, evidence of the fondness they mutually felt. Each evening, as the sun went down, Tūtānekai and his friend Tiki would go up to the rise called Kaiwaka and play their flutes, Tūtānekai on the pūtōrino, Tiki on the

kōauau. Both were skilled players. The plaintive sounds wafted across the lake from Mokoia and were heard by Hinemoa as she sat on a rock by the shore. The music filled her with longing for her beloved. At the end of one great sporting contest, in which Tūtānekai had shown his unsurpassed skills at wielding the taiaha and mere, Hinemoa told him that the next time she heard the notes of his flute, she would take a canoe and paddle to Mokoia. But her people had begun to suspect a romance was blossoming and took the precaution of hauling all the canoes well up the beach. At last Hinemoa decided the only way she could join her lover was to swim across to the island. She obtained six large empty gourds to use as floats, tying them together with flax. Then, casting off her clothes, she entered the water in the dead of night, guided only by the sound of Tūtānekai's flute. At last Hinemoa reached the rocks of Mokoia, cold and weary. In the morning it was known to the people of the pā that Hinemoa had become the wife of Tūtānekai.[147]

The kupu or the words Tūtānekai sang through his flute for Hinemoa, and their English translation, are as follows:

Na-a te waka ra-a
Kai te Kopua-a
Hai-i wa-aka mai mo-ou
Ki-i Mokoia-a.
Kai rangi na koe-e
Kai rangikura-a te tau e-e!
Ko'ai ra-a i runga i-a-a Iri-iri-Kapua?
Ko Hinemoa pea-a,
Ko te-e tamahine o-o Umuka-ria-a;
Hai tau naaku ki te whare ra-a.

There is the canoe
On the shore at Te Kopua
For you to paddle
To Mokoia Island.
You are indeed heaven-sent
With lover's crimson blush
O darling of my heart!
Who is that beguiling shape
On Iriirikapua rock?
It can only be Hinemoa,
Maiden daughter of Umukaria;
Who I will take as my loving wife.[148]

Tūtānekai 'convey[ed] his messages of love through his koauau', and one evening Hinemoa could 'almost hear the message asking her to go across [Lake Rotorua]'.[149] As Ngāti Whakaue kaumātua Te Kiwi Amohau (c. 1859–1927) said, all the tunes played on kōauau had words; players would sing the words into their instruments.[150]

A similar love story to that of Hinemoa and Tūtānekai concerns a young chief named Te Ngaru (Ngāti Te Takinga), who played waiata aroha on his pūtōrino for his love, a young chieftainess named Rahera Te Kahuhiapo (Ngāti Pikiao). The kupu of this waiata (and an English translation) are as follows:

Tenei au kei te tiwa i Motutawa,
Kei Pukurahi i nga tami e ia maku ti e-i.
Ka ritorito te ahi ki Pukurahi; he ahi
Pai, e hine, nga tami e i maku ti e-i.
E titi ra e atarau ki Pukurahi,
Kopuretia ki nga tami e i maku ti e-i.
Tangi te rino, kihai to rino he karanga mo
Nga tami e ia maku ti e-i.

Lonely I sit
On Motutawa's cliff,
Ever gazing towards Pukurahi,
Where dwells my love.
The fires burn low
On Pukurahi hill;
The moonlight beams
On Pukurahi hill;
By that pale light
We would love again!
My sad flute song
Floats out across the lake,
But thy lament
Ne'er falls upon mine ear.[151]

Rahera's family disapproved of Te Ngaru and removed her to Pukurahi pā on the opposite side of Lake Rotoiti. That particular tale, unlike that of Hinemoa and Tūtānekai, has an unhappy ending (from the couple's perspective), as the lovers were never united.

Flutes were also used to communicate secret messages between lovers in Tainui. What follows are two versions of the same tale. The first was recounted by Hare Hongi (Ngāpuhi; 1859–1944), who had heard the story from an old man at Whatiwhatihoe, near Pirongia mountain.

> [A] young chief Kōmako … was captured with his wife by a Waikato party in a raid upon Taranaki. The chief's wife was expert in raranga (weaving), and so spared, while her husband was to be put to death in satisfaction of utu. He asked for one last request, to play a farewell on his kōauau. This was granted, and he entranced his captors with his beautiful playing. With the kōauau, he also coded a message to his wife on where she could meet him when he had made his escape. At the conclusion of his performance, the audience sat in 'breathless admiration', and Kōmako plunged into the nearby Waipā river, and escaped, later meeting with his wife who had quietly made her way to the agreed rendezvous.

The second version, which was retold by writer and ethnologist Johannes Andersen, is based on Hare Hongi's account, but is slightly different.

> A handsome toa (warrior) fell in love with a puhi (woman reserved for a high-ranking marriage) on a visit to a kāinga in the Mokau area (located between Maniapoto and Taranaki). Being low-born, he was not acceptable to her family. His meetings with her were seen as a hara or transgression. After being warned off, he was seized and was about to be thrown from a cliff when he begged to play his kōauau one last time. Because he was a tohunga whakatangi kōauau (expert kōauau player), his final request was allowed. 'He put the koauau to his lips, the mellow sounds floated out, he played his farewell.' He then lulled his captors into a trance-like state by playing his kōauau, enabling his escape. While playing, he also communicated a coded message to his lover regarding where they could be reunited: his kāinga (home) of Piopio, in the Waitomo district, south of Te Kūiti. He then leapt from the cliff [on] which he stood into the sea. His brothers were waiting for him in a canoe, and sped him away. After a few months, the family relaxed their guard on the young woman, and she took off to join her lover. The last words her iwi heard her speak, as she paddled away, were: 'Ki a Piopio'.[152]

A similar tale from Taranaki that also involves subterfuge and a daring escape – that of Toheriri – shows that expert Ngāti Maru pū (flute) players could make their instrument 'me he reo tangata' (speak mouth words).

> When [Toheriri] and his lover were captured by a war party, he communicated a covert message to her via his playing, telling her where to go to await him. He played to divert his captors' attention and cover his lover's escape, performing

> a *whakataratara* (inciter to action) when he first noticed her absence, to which his captors performed a war dance. Finally, he played a *whakaoriori*, lulling his captors to sleep and then effecting his own escape.[153]

Kōauau can also be played to convey other kinds of love, such as the love felt by a mother for her children and iwi. This is conveyed clearly in the Ngāpuhi version of a narrative titled 'Ko Kame-tara rāua ko Te Wahine-Tupua' (Kametara and his Ogre Wife).[154]

> Kame-tara took a second wife, who one day went fishing with the first or senior wife. The second wife tricked the senior wife into diving under the canoe to see why the anchor could not be raised. While the senior wife was under the water, the second wife, who was in fact an ogre, cut the anchor rope, and returned home. The senior wife had to call upon a taniwha (water spirit) to rescue her, and she settled in another place, bringing up twin sons. Missing her other children who had been left behind, the senior wife composed a waiata aroha (love song), and told them to make a flute: 'Ka oti, ka hanga nga puta e toru, katahi ka whakatangihia e te wahine ra tana waiata aroha mo tana tane me tona iwi, ki roto i tana whio.' Eventually they also fashioned a canoe, returned to their mother's original home, and played the kōauau song over and over to identify themselves. When they had told the people their story, everyone travelled to settle where the woman now lived, although Kame-tara himself had gone away to live at the place of his ogre-wife.[155]

In this narrative, a waiata aroha sung through the kōauau was composed by Kametara's first wife for her children, husband and the people from whom she'd been separated. It was played by her children not only to convey their mother's love to their estranged older siblings, but also as a means of confirming their identity upon returning to their mother's home.

As we will see in Chapter 4, this type of communication via taonga pūoro was based on practices in tropical Polynesia, but other instruments and instrument uses were innovations developed in response to opportunities and challenges in the new lands of Aotearoa and Rēkohu.

CHAPTER 3: Discovering new voices

OVER SEVERAL HUNDRED YEARS OF ISOLATION, the indigenous peoples of Aotearoa and Rēkohu explored the wide range of flora and fauna offered by their lands, used already familiar materials (gourds, human and dog bone, whalebone and teeth) in new ways, and created their own distinctive instrument traditions.

The instruments described in this chapter are almost certainly Māori and Moriori inventions, as there is no evidence that the same instrument types existed in tropical Polynesia. If they did, then no trace of them or any variations on them remains in oral or written histories, or in the material record (though instruments made from perishable materials would not have survived in any case). Some Māori instrument names have linguistic ties back to tropical Polynesia, but the instrument types that the names relate to are different, supporting the idea that Māori invented them independently – that is, they are examples of convergent evolution.

Similarities between Māori instruments and those from Melanesia, Micronesia and the Polynesian outliers are noted below. However, these regions lie beyond the area that the immediate ancestors of Māori are believed to have come from – with the possible exception of parts of East Melanesia (Fiji, Vanuatu and New Caledonia). These similarities may point towards shared ancestral traditions predating the voyages of the immediate ancestors of Māori and Moriori, but are more likely examples of convergent evolution and therefore unhelpful in terms of shedding light on where those voyaging ancestors came from.

Māori innovations

HUMMING TOPS

Whip tops – spinning tops that are set in motion using a whip – are found in Polynesia, but Māori added a spindle to them to create an innovative form of humming top or pōtaka. String is wound carefully around the spindle, then pulled to set the top spinning. This invention has some advantages over whip tops: the addition of a spindle requires less of the player's energy to activate the top and typically makes the top spin longer.

HUMMING TOP
made from wood, held in Tairāwhiti Museum (catalogue number 54/234). Descendant of Tāwhirimātea; wind instrument. Measures 15cms long. Photograph taken by Jennifer Cattermole and used by permission of Tairāwhiti Museum.

SPINNING DISCS

One form of the spinning disc porotiti also appears to be a Māori invention, unless it was an old form of the instrument that subsequently became obsolete everywhere else in Polynesia except Aotearoa. These were 'made of a piece of the rind of a gourd cut into a disc ... [with a] ... wooden centre on which to spin when set twirling'; or 'made from a piece of rind of a gourd with a peg inserted'.[1] The inspiration for this type of porotiti may have come from a Cook Islands object type called pōtaka miro. This was 'made from a miro berry through which a piece of coconut leaflet midrib was thrust until the point protruded a short distance to form the spinning point. The long end was rolled between the palms to cause the toy to spin'.[2]

KURĪ RATTLES

Rattles worn by dancers are found in Melanesia and West Polynesia (Fiji and Tonga), but are reported in East Polynesia only from Hawai`i, where they are called kūpe`e niho `īlio (leg ornament).[3] There is no evidence that Māori tied rattles to their bodies while dancing, but they did tie rattles around the necks of their kurī while on hunting expeditions. Woven from muka, these featured albatross bone, māpara (heartwood kahikatea or rimu), heartwood mataī, small slivers of whalebone, or shell.[4] As noted earlier, the sound of the rattle enabled hunters to track the dog, particularly when hunting nocturnal species such as kiwi and kākāpō, and it also acted as a lure or goad for their prey.

Although rattles tied around the necks of domesticated dogs was a Māori innovation, this instrument has linguistic links back to the Southern Cooks and the Society Islands. For instance, two Māori names for dog rattle, kākara and tātara, are similar to the term for 'rattle' in Rarotonga (pārarā), which reconstructs to the Polynesian kalalā, meaning 'sizzle'.[5] Kākara is used by Te Whānau-a-Apanui as a term for conch shell trumpets, but refers to dog rattles among Te Arawa and Tūhoe.[6] This term may derive from kā`ara, the name for large log gongs in the Southern Cook Islands (Aitutaki, Mangaia and Rarotonga), which were often used in conjunction with conch trumpets (pū).[7] The name for the Cook Islands signalling instrument was transferred to different signalling instruments in Aotearoa.

Another Māori term for dog rattle, patete, relates to the Tahitian atete or `atete, meaning 'to rattle or tinkle'. A Māori equivalent term is ngatete, meaning 'crackle' or 'move'. In te reo Māori, as we saw in Chapter 1, patete has related meanings connected with the rattle's use in hunting.[8]

SHELL RATTLES

Māori used pāua to make a musical instrument called kī pāua. Small pieces of broken shell were placed inside two pāua shells, which were then bound together. Often, a flax cover was woven around this instrument. The kī pāua – or a similar shell- or stone-filled gourd – was used in a game called kītē (also known as tīoreoreo), which involved two or more players.[9] Kī pāua could also be attached to kites or hung in bunches from tree branches in order to communicate messages,[10] or be swung like pūrerehua.[11] There are no accounts of shells being used to create similar instruments elsewhere in Polynesia.

PAHU

Although the instrument name pahu is shared across Aotearoa and central East Polynesia, the name applies to a variety of different percussion instruments. Sharkskin-headed drums have been used throughout East Polynesia (in the Societies, Cooks, Australs, Tuamotus, Marquesas, Mangareva and Hawai`i), but are absent in Rapa Nui and Aotearoa. Pahu (and its cognates) is the name applied to these instruments, whereas Māori use this word to refer to gongs made from hardwood or pounamu.[12] This poses quite a conundrum; as Richard Nunns and Allan Thomas observed: 'One of the great unanswered questions in our work with taonga pūoro is why drums, so prominent in the musical traditions of the rest of Polynesia, do not feature in Māori music.'[13]

The Proto Central Pacific term *(v,b)asu and Central Eastern Polynesian (or Proto Nuclear Polynesian or Proto Polynesian) *pasu refer to 'a drum' or 'to thump, pound'.[14] In Tahiti, for example, the term means 'thumping blow' and 'drum'.[15] If these linguistic reconstructions are correct, then the implication is that the ancestors of Māori would have had sharkskin-headed drums.

If they are incorrect, then this may explain the absence of sharkskin-headed drums in Aotearoa. Could sharkskin drums be an innovation that postdated the departure of the ancestors of Māori and Moriori from the tropics? Around the time they left, did pahu actually refer to that kind of instrument or a different kind of percussion instrument, or only to thumping or pounding? If the latter, it would be understandable that a term relating to the action of striking percussion instruments ended up being applied to very different kinds of percussion in Aotearoa compared to tropical East Polynesia.

However, assuming the linguistic reconstructions are correct, this leads us back to the question: why are skin-headed drums absent from Aotearoa? Te Rangi Hīroa suggested that the ancestors of Māori may have known of skin-headed drums called pahu but deliberately discontinued their manufacture and use in Aotearoa, with the name of the obsolete instrument being applied instead to completely different, newly created types of percussion.[16] He noted that their abandonment may have been due to Māori replacing drums with body percussion to accompany dance, and due to changes in the practice of religious ritual observances.[17] A woman elder from Moorea, Tahiti, provides another possible reason. Speaking with Jerome Kavanagh (Mōkai Pātea, Ngāti Maniapoto, Ngāti Kahungunu), she said that pahu were intentionally left behind by the ancestors of Māori when they departed for Aotearoa because of their association with war.[18] According to these kōrero, the ancestors of Māori had the knowledge, skills and materials to make skin-headed drums, but deliberately chose not to. The change does not appear to be related to a lack of sharkskin relative to other materials, or the respective labour involved in making these instruments.

Pahu were used in similar ways in both central East Polynesia (particularly the Societies, Southern Cooks and Tuamotus) and Aotearoa. The most prevalent use of Māori pahu was to sound the alarm during wartime.[19] Pahu also served a wartime purpose in Tahiti, where they were used to summon warriors and to incite them prior to battle.[20] As in Aotearoa, Tahitian pahu were also used to summon people to a gathering. Log idiophones were used for this purpose in the Southern Cooks and Tuamotus.[21] While these similarities are noteworthy, they are not proof of cultural transmission, given that any loud percussion instrument lends itself well to these kinds of uses. There are significant differences as well. For example, pahu were used in Tahiti to accompany dance (just as log idiophones were used to accompany dance in the Southern Cooks), though there are no written records that indicate pahu were used in this way in Aotearoa.[22]

Māori created a variety of different types of pahu, some of which were similar to instruments from tropical Polynesia. One such pahu on Te Aroha-a-uta mountain, discussed in Chapter 2, resembled a percussion instrument reported from Hawai`i: a sounding board consisting of 'a hollow vessel of wood, like a platter'.[23] The Te Aroha pahu was oval-shaped, had very thin walls, was beaten with a heavy piece of wood, and was suspended from a post.[24] Unlike Māori pahu, which were typically beaten with wooden mallets, the Hawaiian instrument was stamped on with a foot, like the stamping boards of Papua New Guinea and Torres Strait, and the Rapa Nui keho (pit drum).[25] Although physically similar, the playing method differed completely, and so they are unlikely to be related.

A different type of pahu, formed from hollow tree trunks by Ngāti Tūwharetoa and Tūhoe, resembles instruments from New Caledonia, Vanuatu and Papua New Guinea.[26] Another similarity between log idiophones in Papua New Guinea (specifically Buka and Tami islands) and Aotearoa comes in the form of narratives that mention someone striking an instrument, hiding, and eventually being discovered.[27]

Hollow logs readily lend themselves to percussive uses, while hiding after striking such instruments says something more universal about human mischievousness and fear of reprisal.

The slab form of Māori pahu was the most common form of gong in Aotearoa. Some were plain slabs, while others had a shallow groove in the centre. Most had an elliptical or oval hole pierced through the centre. The slabs typically had rounded ends, though some were rectangular in shape. This type of gong varied from around 2.4 to 9.1 metres long, 61 to 122 centimetres wide and around 15 centimetres thick. They were typically suspended from both ends and struck using wooden beaters or mallets, though one account mentions an example suspended from one end only and struck with a stone.[28]

Ethnomusicologist Mervyn McLean believes that this instrument, along with the pūkaea (long wooden trumpet), was invented by Māori to meet a need for louder signalling instruments as they began building pā (fortified villages), a process that began c. 1500 in most districts.[29] Te Rangi Hīroa also believed this type of pahu to be a Māori invention but, unlike McLean, argued that it resulted from a natural sequence in experimentation as an extension of bowl or canoe making.[30] Both explanations are plausible.

Could slab-form pahu have been an adaptation of sounding boards or struck wooden plaques that originated in West Polynesia before finding their way to East Polynesia? Sounding boards in various forms have been reported from Fiji, Sāmoa, Tonga, Tokelau, `Uvea and Futuna. One type from West Polynesia features a crescent-shaped board, though sometimes objects with hollowed-out cavities are used instead.[31] These are played resting on the ground with the concave surface facing downwards. Sounding boards are also used in the Polynesian outliers (Mungiki and Munggava, Tikopia, Luangiua and Nukumanu), as well as in central East Polynesia.[32] For example, a crescent-shaped board-type instrument is used in Mungiki, long, thin weaving boards are used for this purpose in Tokelau, and large wooden bowls are used in Munggava.[33]

However, none of the names for sounding boards in tropical Polynesia, where they have been recorded, resemble pahu. If sounding boards were, in fact, the inspiration for the slab form of Māori pahu, their name would likely have been papa rather than pahu. Papa, in te reo Māori, refers to 'anything broad, flat and hard', which is in keeping with other definitions of papa: 'board, plank' in Malayo-Polynesian, and 'flat hard surface' in Polynesian.[34] Moreover, the playing methods are different. The instruments described above are played using two small sticks, one in each hand, or a coral stone in the case of Tikopia.[35] Māori pahu are typically beaten using wooden mallets, which are more robust than the beaters used for tropical Polynesian sounding

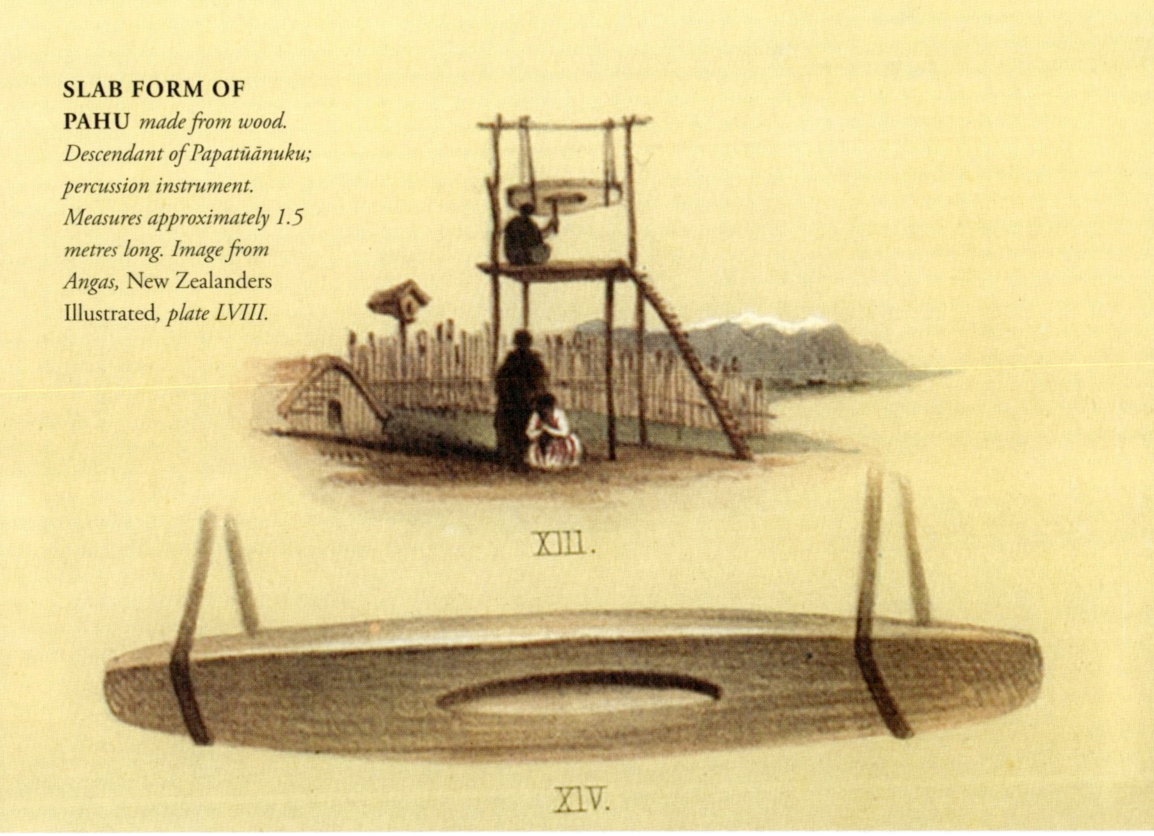

SLAB FORM OF PAHU *made from wood. Descendant of Papatūānuku; percussion instrument. Measures approximately 1.5 metres long. Image from Angas,* New Zealanders Illustrated, *plate LVIII.*

boards (a necessity given the larger size of the instruments being struck), though the essential playing technique is the same. While it is possible that sounding boards were a precursor instrument to the slab form of Māori pahu, this seems unlikely.

UPTURNED CANOES

Upturned canoes have been used as percussion instruments on Pukapuka, as well as in Futuna, Pohnpei and Papua New Guinea. Similarly, they were used as pahu substitutes in Aotearoa, specifically in the Te Arawa rohe.[36] As with hollow logs, canoes readily lend themselves to being used as percussion instruments, so these similarities are almost certainly due to convergent evolution.

CLAPPERS

Clappers made from a variety of materials are used throughout Polynesia, though none of the terms used for those instruments correlates with any of the names used for clappers in Aotearoa: pākēkē, pākōkō, tōkere, tokerangi and māpara.[37] Any of the Polynesian instruments may have provided inspiration for the development of tōkere by Māori, though the etymology of the term suggests it was a Māori innovation.

TŌKERE *made from scallop shells. Descendant of Papatūānuku; concussion instrument. Measures 9.5cms wide. Made by Brian Flintoff.* ♪

The Central Eastern Polynesian term for a generic 'wooden percussion instrument' was *tookere, though it could have been used more generally as the verb 'to tap'; the Hawaiian cognate term ko`ele was used in the latter sense to denote a 'tapping sound (wood on wood)'.[38] If these definitions existed at the time Māori ancestors departed for Aotearoa (i.e. the term did not then necessarily relate to a specific musical instrument), it would make sense that the term tōkere was subsequently applied to castanets/clappers in Aotearoa, and to log idiophones throughout much of East Polynesia. Log idiophones (tōkere, tō`ere or tōkele) were used in the Cook Islands (Aitutaki, Atiu, Mangaia, Mauke, Mitiaro and Pukapuka), and subsequently spread to the Tuamotus; the term tō`ere is also found in Tahiti and the Marquesas.[39] That Māori gave this name to clappers rather than to log idiophones supports Te Rangi Hīroa's hypothesis that the introduction of log idiophones to central East Polynesia postdates the departure of the ancestors of Māori from tropical Polynesia.[40]

IPU KŌRERO OR POI PIU

An instrument similar to poi is called ipu kōrero or poi piu.[41] This may have been struck against the body as a mnemonic device, to act as a memory aid or to punctuate the recitation of whakapapa or stories.[42] If so, this instrument played a similar role to Sāmoan fue (ceremonial fly whisks used by tulāfale, talking chiefs), though fue are constructed very differently from ipu kōrero and the names are linguistically dissimilar. Ipu kōrero are, therefore, almost certainly a Māori invention.

CONCH TRUMPETS WITH WOODEN MOUTHPIECES

Shell trumpets are found historically throughout Oceania.[43] Although some Māori shell trumpets did not have wooden mouthpieces, the use of such mouthpieces is a distinctive characteristic of these instruments, differentiating them from similar instruments elsewhere.[44] Māori may have added mouthpieces to conch shell trumpets 'to make the smaller shells of the cold-water [native] species more similar in sound to the large shells of the tropics'.[45] Māori could have been inspired by end-blown conches from the Southern Cooks, and/or conch trumpets with bamboo mouthpieces found in Tahiti, Tubua`i (Australs), the Marquesas, Vao (Vanuatu) and Fiji.[46] For the latter, a round hole was made in the side of the conical end of a triton shell, typically on the third whorl from the tip of the shell, in which a bamboo mouthpiece was inserted.[47] In contrast, Māori attached a wooden mouthpiece to the apex of the shell.

WOODEN TRUMPETS

Both Mervyn McLean and Te Rangi Hīroa considered the pūkaea an independent Māori invention. As mentioned earlier, McLean believed their invention coincided with the development of pā. Te Rangi Hīroa instead proposed that the invention of this instrument was driven by a shortage of shells suitable for making trumpets in Aotearoa, with the pūpakapaka (a conch shell trumpet with a long wooden mouthpiece) a likely precursor instrument.[48]

Another possibility is that this instrument was based on flax oboes, invented in order to create louder and more durable instruments. If flax oboes were the precursor to the wooden pūkaea, then there is an instrument that could be regarded as transitional: the Murihiku pūkaea iwi. Instruments closely resembling pūkaea iwi were also used in the Caroline Islands in Micronesia, which lies outside the 'Hawaiki zone'. Marquesan wooden trumpets also bear some similarity, though pūkaea iwi feature bone instead of bamboo for the mouthpiece and harakeke instead of wood for the main body. These significant differences point towards the pūkaea iwi being a Māori invention.[49]

Although long wooden trumpets were almost certainly invented independently by Māori, it is possible that the ancestors of Māori brought the idea of wooden trumpets with them from the tropics. A wooden trumpet similar to a Māori pūkaea, attributed to the Gambier Islands, is held in the Linden Museum, Stuttgart.[50] This is likely a misattribution, given the lack of corroborating evidence for the existence of wooden trumpets in that part of French Polynesia.[51] With the exception of Aotearoa and the Marquesas, wooden trumpets are not known to have existed anywhere else in Polynesia.

In the Marquesas, wooden trumpets (called pū`akau, or pū rohoti in the northern Marquesas) may have been a late 19th-century innovation.[52] Structurally, they are very different to Māori wooden trumpets.[53] They were 'made from a hollowed piece of wood about two feet [60 centimetres] long and eight inches [20 centimetres] in diameter narrowing to a small hole at one end, to which was attached a large bamboo a foot [30 centimetres] or more long that served as a mouth piece'.[54] In contrast to Marquesan trumpets, Māori wooden pūkaea do not have an inserted mouthpiece and do feature the use of tohe (inserted wooden pegs). Some pūkaea had a fingerhole in the middle of the instrument, a feature not noted in wooden trumpets elsewhere in Oceania.[55] These physical differences, and the possible late development in the Marquesas, support the idea that in Aotearoa long wooden trumpets were invented independently.

Physically, the instruments most similar to Māori pūkaea are the end- and side-blown wooden trumpets used in Papua New Guinea. The side-blown type is remarkably similar to a side-blown example from Aotearoa currently held in the Dresden Museum. Side-blown trumpets most likely evolved independently in both Papua New Guinea and Aotearoa, modelled on side-blown conch trumpets.[56]

Some of the uses of the Māori pūkaea are similar to those of wooden trumpets elsewhere in Oceania. For example, Māori sometimes delivered words of challenge or insult via pūkaea. Similarly, the speaking of words into trumpets has been reported

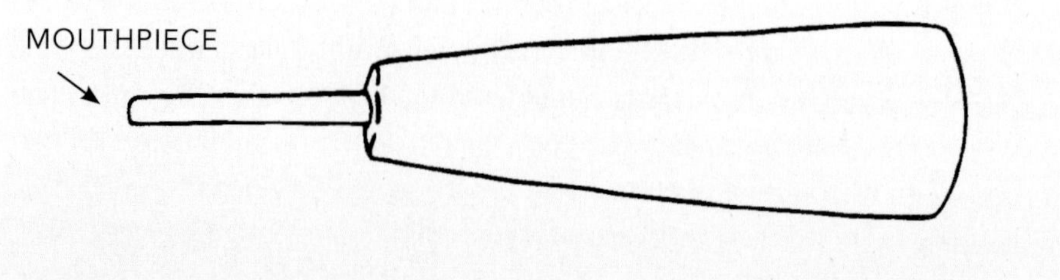

MARQUESAN TRUMPET. *Drawing by Jennifer Cattermole from an image in Fischer,* Sound-producing Instruments, *Plate XXVII, ill. 439.*

from Vanuatu (Malekula, Ambryn) as well as the Marquesas.[57] In the Solomons, an instrument known as suke has been labelled a 'war bassoon', and various warfare usages are similarly associated with pūkaea.[58] The loudness of these instruments makes them ideally suited for use in such contexts.

GOURD TRUMPETS

Gourd trumpets were made in Aotearoa but are otherwise not reported from tropical Oceania except for Papua New Guinea. A Wantoat instrument consisting of a section of bamboo tube with a gourd resonator is remarkably similar to a Ngāti Porou gourd trumpet, although the Māori instrument features a wooden mouthpiece instead of one made from bamboo.[59]

A SLIDING TRUMPET

As noted in Chapter 2, one type of Māori trumpet is said to have consisted of two sliding tubes, the larger one overlapping the smaller one.[60] There are no direct analogues for such an instrument in tropical Oceania, meaning it was likely invented by Māori. However, its description does somewhat resemble those of flutes from elsewhere in Oceania. Botanist Joseph Banks, for example, noted the Tahitian practice of tuning flutes by rolling up a leaf and sliding it over the bore at the distal (non-blowing) end, rather than inside the bore, as per the Māori instrument.[61] This Māori trumpet also resembles descriptions of piston flutes from northeast Papua New Guinea.[62]

LEAF WHISTLES / RIBBON REEDS

In the Torres Strait and among the Elema people of the eastern Gulf of Papua, a leaf is placed – sometimes doubled – between the thumbs and blown on to produce a sharp, shrill tone. This instrument is used as a children's toy. Children also blow over blades of grass held between their thumbs in New Caledonia, and on the Polynesian outlier Anuta, children blow onto a blade of grass or a leaf held between the thumbs of their cupped hands to make a buzzing sound rather than a sharp whistle.[63]

Similar instruments were used in Aotearoa, though as birdcallers rather than toys. Using instruments to mimic and lure birds was a necessary hunting skill. These birdcallers consisted of a single leaf folded around its spine, pinched at either end to create a reed, or placed between the player's lips and either blown on or sounded via a quick inhalation of breath.[64] A variety of leaves are used; certain varieties are used to lure certain bird species. Their songs send invocations to Tāne to seek his blessing on the season for catching manu, which are his children.[65]

Elsewhere in Oceania, including Rēkohu, 'imitations of bird cries were produced mainly with the mouth, purely vocally or by whistling. Enticing instruments are mentioned extremely seldom and seem to have occurred only on New Guinea and in New Zealand' – though only in Aotearoa were leaves documented as being used for this purpose.[66] Leaf birdcallers were thus a Māori innovation.

STRAIGHT-BORED FLUTES WITH A HOLE (OR TWO ADJACENT HOLES) IN THE CENTRE

Māori ororuarangi, whether made of bone or hue, are distinguished by having two wenewene side by side at the midpoint of the tube, though in some examples the holes are joined together to form a mouth-like shape.[67] The Moriori bone flute named pauawau shares the latter characteristic, raising the possibility that flutes of this type were developed during the time when the ancestors of Māori and Moriori were in contact.[68] It is also possible that some Moriori artefacts labelled toggles or cloak pins in museum collections are, in fact, flutes – particularly those that are longer than is typical. As there are no similar examples of these flutes elsewhere in Oceania, they could be an early innovation shared by Aotearoa's first migrants.

NOTCHED FLUTES

Flutes with notched mouthpieces similar to the Tūhoe pūmotomoto are found in Melanesia – for example, in Vanuatu, New Georgia (Solomon Islands) and Papua New Guinea.[69] These Melanesian flutes are associated with courtship, while the Tūhoe pūmotomoto was associated specifically with childbirth. All these flutes are, broadly speaking, associated with procreation.[70]

PŪTŌRINO / HOHO

The Te Ika a Māui instrument commonly known as pūtōrino (and in some rohe as hoho) is unique.[71] There is no other instrument like it anywhere in the world. It is said to have arrived with the ancestors of Māori from tropical Polynesia, and it is mentioned – like kōauau – in a narrative concerning the arrival of the Pukeātea-wainui and Arawa waka. However, its name may have been interpolated later into that narrative, or the original form of the instrument may have been quite different to the form that developed in Te Ika a Māui.[72] Its invention predates the late 18th century, as it is mentioned in European accounts dating from as early as 1769.[73]

According to Māori pūrākau, the casemoth is the personification of Raukatauri, who loved her flute so much that she chose to live inside it, becoming the goddess of flute music.[74] This is reflected in names used to describe the cocoon (tūngoungou) of

PŪTŌRINO *made from wood. Descendant of Hine Raukatauri; wind instrument. Measures 48cms long. Made by Warren Warbrick.*

the female casemoth: pū a Raukatauri (Raukatauri's flute) and whare atua (a deity's house).[75] The āhua (shape) of the pūtōrino and some kōauau echoes the shape of this cocoon.

Raukataura (a variant spelling of Raukatauri) is a goddess also known in tropical Polynesia, though in the Society Islands she and her sister (Rau`ata-ura and Rau`ata-mea, respectively) were goddesses of the forest rather than of the pleasurable arts like music and entertainment.[76] A vestige of this idea is preserved in the idea that Raukataura is a daughter of Tāne, god of the forests, and in the naming of the aruhe (bracken fern), which is known as ngā makawe a Raukatauri rāua ko Raukatamea (the hair of Raukatauri and Raukatamea).[77]

Across tropical Polynesia there is a strong connection between nose flutes and love/fertility. In Mangaia, in the Southern Cook Islands, for example, a flute could be played near the are karioi (house of entertainment) to send love signals from the player to a woman inside.[78] This idea is also found in Melanesia and West Polynesia. Fijian flutes had the power to attract women, even on behalf of another person, and young people of both sexes played love songs on the flute in Sāmoa.[79] The ancestors of Māori brought these ideas with them to Aotearoa.

The pūtōrino may have originated in response to the ancestors of Māori observing a new species, the casemoth, explaining its mating habits in the context of their ideology, and designing an instrument that encapsulated those ideologies. The Māori use of these instruments in seduction relates to stories about the female casemoth singing to attract a mate.[80] In the absence of any visable clues as to how the insect attracted a mate, Māori found a sonic explanation: that her singing was inaudible to (most) humans, but able to be heard by male casemoths.[81] In this idea, the spiritual power and efficacy of words spoken, chanted or sung into the instruments of Raukatauri – particularly in connection with love – is explained. The female casemoth is a powerful symbol of one of humankind's ultimate mysteries: the creation of new life.

The powerful spiritual symbolism of the casemoth could have been a further reason for the instrument's invention. The pūtōrino could 'encode esoteric associations because a cocoon is a liminal state between caterpillar and moth, which may be accepted as a representation of the interface between spirit and human worlds'.[82] The pūtōrino is a highly esoteric instrument used by tohunga.[83] The harmonics generated when singing into pūtōrino while playing the instrument, like those that sometimes occur during vocal performance, may have been considered spirit voices – tohu used in matakite.[84]

The pūtōrino is also notable for its multifunctionality and the variety of its voices. Its male trumpet voice (te kōkiri a te tāne) typically sounds when the player blows from the large end of the bore, pursing their lips together so they vibrate. The player alters the tension of their lips to alter the pitch. The female voice, that of Hine Raukatauri (te waiata a te wāhine), is activated by using the cross-blowing – or oblique embouchure – technique. When the player holds their instrument so it angles downwards by approximately 45 degrees and to the right, their blowing edge will be on the left (or vice versa if the instrument points leftward). Shaping their lips as though they are going to whistle, the player places their lips just behind but not touching the blowing edge, lightly pressing the rest of the bore against their face. The splitting of the airstream across the blowing edge, so part blows across the edge and part down the bore, activates the instrument's voice. Changing the force of the player's breath, tongue position, angle of the instrument relative to airstream, and lip shape and proximity to the blowing edge, can all alter the pitch – especially when combined with fully or partially (un)covering the māngai using a finger. A range of other mysterious and often unexpected voices attributed to Wheke – a daughter of Hine Raukatauri – can also be activated. These include a softer, more mellow feminine flute voice when the player blows directly over the central māngai; quiet whistling overtones when the player blows very gently using the oblique embouchure technique; and multiphonic sounds when the player vocalises a drone while cross-blowing.

The invention of the pūtōrino may have been driven by the need for varied functionality. As Richard Nunns asks, 'Why was a multi-purpose instrument needed by Māori? Was it envisaged that the player would want to switch from one voice to another [trumpet/flute]? What circumstances would require this?'[85] Mauri Tirikatene provided an example of one such circumstance: te kōkiri a te tāne could call people together, for instance, to mourn tragic news; then te waiata a te wāhine could lead weeping and other expressions of grief. Different voices of the instrument may have been used by tohunga during the opening of a newly constructed house and the lifting of a tapu on it.[86] Another example of multifunctionality is found in a different version of the tale of Tūtānekai and Hinemoa to that related earlier, with the feminine flute-like voice playing a role in seducing Hinemoa, and the masculine trumpet voice of the instrument being used to communicate signals to her.[87]

Some experts believe the name pūtōrino refers to its multifunctionality. The name suggests 'the plaiting of several sounds': its male and female voices, as well as the unexpected and unexplained voices of Raukatauri and her daughter Wheke. It could also relate to 'the binding of two voices', the voice of the taonga and the voice of the player, to produce a third spirit voice.[88]

The pūtōrino shares some remarkable similarities with Melanesian water flutes, and this is most obvious when we consider the instrument under its alternative Te Ika a Māui name, hoho (plus cognate terms pūhoho or pū hoho hō). Players sang into the hoho, and while doing so they moved their fingers up and down over the central māngai. By doing this, the instrument's voice sounded as though it were coming from a distance, as though through a spring of bubbling water.[89] A Māori flute called tō, described as a 'water-blowing instrument', perhaps a 'flute blown into water or a specially made vessel in which water was placed and then played', may or may not be the same instrument.[90] These descriptions closely resemble Papua New Guinea water flutes, as well as a description of a Loyalty Islands (Drehu, Nengone and Iaaï) flute called hoho: 'smaller pieces of cane, made up at one end, and filled, or partly filled, with water, according to the pitch of the tone desired, were blown'.[91]

A similar term to hoho, hohoni, is used in Tonga to refer to a water-carrying vessel made from a large coconut shell, but not to a musical instrument. It reconstructs to the West Polynesian sosoni, meaning 'water container'.[92] Although Ngāti Porou flutes were not filled with water, as in the Melanesian examples, they were ascribed a water-like sound when played in a particular way. The use of the same instrument name, hoho, in both New Caledonia and Aotearoa is noteworthy, and it is possible the terms share the same derivation though instrument transmission is unlikely.

The idea of gendered voices (the female flute voice and male trumpet voice) for the hoho resembles the way flutes are gendered in Papua New Guinea.[93] Another similarity comes in the form of a Simbo Island (Solomons) instrument which, like the hoho, is both a flute and trumpet, though in that case, the flute and trumpet voices sound simultaneously rather than separately.[94]

DOUBLE FLUTES

An unusual, possibly unique Māori instrument was found in the Wharerata ranges near Tūranganui a Kiwa Poverty Bay. Made of bone, this instrument has a blockage between its two fingerholes. The instrument most closely resembles end-blown bamboo pipes from New Britain in the Bismarck Archipelago, Papua New Guinea, which have a node in the bore, meaning that different notes are produced when the player blows from each end. It also somewhat resembles side-blown 'double flutes' from Vanuatu.[95]

NGURU

Nguru is another unique type of Māori flute. The name nguru has tropical Polynesian connections. In te reo Māori, it means to 'utter a suppressed groan, sigh or grunt', 'murmur' and 'rumble'. This term and its cognates have similar meanings in Rēkohu and in Rarotonga and Penrhyn in the Cook Islands.[96] The Māori term reconstructs to the Malayo-Polynesian gulu (grunt, rumble), and Polynesian terms *sa(a)gulu (grunt, rumble) and *ta(a)gulu (deep-toned sound).[97]

McLean suggests that the shape of this flute type was modelled on sperm whale teeth (niho parāoa) or curved hue necks.[98] Both of these materials were present in tropical Polynesia. However, if flutes were made in this form from those materials in the tropics, no record of them has been found to date. If this flute type was invented by Māori in Aotearoa, it is likely that the first nguru were made from hue necks. This material, being naturally hollow and relatively soft, lends itself easily to flute manufacture. In support of this theory, the oldest known example of a nguru was made from hue. Dating to around 1500, this nguru was recovered from the Kauri Point swamp near Tauranga.[99]

KŌAUAU HUE *made from gourd. Descendant of Hinepūtehue; wind instrument. Measures 14.5cms long. Made by Jen and David Cattermole.*

♪

NGURU *made from sperm whale tooth. Descendant of Hine Raukatauri; wind instrument. Measures 8.5cms long. Made by David Cattermole.* ♪

Nguru may have been created in order to reproduce the lower pitches of tropical Oceanian bamboo flutes in a shorter flute form. Such an innovation might have been suggested by pūtōrino, some of which have closed off bores at the distal end.[100] The natural shape of curved hue necks and whale's teeth ideally lent itself to being used to create flutes with closed bores. Instruments that are modelled on their shapes made from wood, stone or clay were likely developed later.

PLAYING METHODS: THE NOSE- VERSUS MOUTH-BLOWING CONTROVERSY

In Aotearoa, many flutes are mouth-blown. A key reason for developing a primarily mouth- rather than nose-blown flute-playing practice in Aotearoa may have been that, '[i]n blowing sideways, the lips are free to move … [to blow] words into the koauau'.[101] Nose-blown flutes are predominant elsewhere in Polynesia, though mouth-blown bamboo flutes may also have existed in central East Polynesia at the time the ancestors of Māori and Moriori departed the region. For example, it is not known when the `akatangi ko`e (a type of bamboo mouth flute used in Aitutaki) was developed.[102]

While there is substantial historical, physical and linguistic evidence that nose-blowing continued alongside mouth-blowing as a practice in multiple rohe of Aotearoa, McLean argued that playing flutes with the nose was not practised here, with the exception of a single blowing technique. His understanding of this method was derived from an account by the distinguished scholar of te reo Māori Herbert Williams, who witnessed a kōauau being played as a nose flute. The player – thought to be Te Whānau a Apanui rangatira Tūteranginoti, who died in 1836 – blocked one end with their upper lip and blew into the nearest hole with their left nostril, blocking the right nostril with their right thumb. This technique mirrors early European accounts of bamboo nose flute playing from tropical Oceania.[103]

Using Tūteranginoti's technique, McLean experimented with, and succeeded in, nose-playing a kōauau that appeared purposely designed to be played as a nose flute in a similar way to bamboo examples in the tropics, with the blowing hole drilled through the bore near the proximal end.[104] His reluctance to accept nose-blowing more broadly was based on his own physical assessment of surviving flutes and scepticism that they could be played by Tūteranginoti's method.

There are, however, historical accounts of the nose being used to play nguru and kōauau, particularly among people from Te Tai Tokerau, and some of these instruments can be played with the nose using a technique different to that trialled by McLean. This technique involves players blocking one nostril with their thumb, and blowing across the end of the bore rather than across one of the holes drilled through the walls of the bore. A variation of this method was used in Murihiku, whereby an old man 'had a hole through his nostrils and stuck the kōauau through it and played away'.[105] Nguru with a larger than usual hole at the top of their piko (upturned end) can be played by blowing over that hole with the nose using the same technique, with a hand held over the other end of the bore (i.e. the end that would typically be blown using the mouth). These instruments can, therefore, be played with the nose or the mouth.[106]

Kōauau intended to be played with the nose are purposely designed differently to those designed to be played with the mouth. They have an extra-large hole for the nostril just below the proximal edge, and the three wenewene are smaller than those of the mouth-blown kōauau.[107] Moreover, for Ngāti Porou, flutes played with the nose (kōauau pongā ihu, kōauau whakatangi ihu) and those played with the mouth (kōauau waha) have different fingerhole placements. For kōauau pongā ihu, the first fingerhole is placed the width of a forefinger from the end of the tube. The distance to the next fingerhole is a thumb's width, and the one after that is the combined width of the forefinger plus middle finger. (The fingerhole placement for kōauau waha, based on finger measurements, was outlined in Chapter 2.)[108]

Nose playing is highly valued, both aesthetically and spiritually, because the breath of the nose is pure – a manifestation of mauri. Flute performances that employ nose-blowing have been very well received by contemporary Māori audiences for these reasons.[109]

KŌAUAU PONGĀ IHU (LEFT) AND KŌAUAU WAHA (RIGHT).

Descendants of Hinepūtehue; wind instruments. Measuring 9.5 and 12cms tall. Made by Brian Flintoff, and Jen and David Cattermole, respectively.

Moriori innovations

Moriori developed a variety of unique instruments on Rēkohu during the period in which they had no contact with other peoples, from c. 1500, around the time of the Little Ice Age, until the arrival of Europeans in 1791.

FLUTES

One kōauau-like flute found on Rēkohu, and believed to be Moriori, is made of hopo (royal albatross) bone.[110] Given the rarity of albatross bone flutes in Aotearoa's archaeological record from the period when Rēkohu was initially settled, the existence of this flute raises the possibility that Moriori may have developed albatross bone flutes independently.[111]

The flute, held in the Canterbury Museum, measures around 16 centimetres long and 1.3 by 2 centimetres in diameter. From the collection of Rēkohu resident Edward Chudleigh, it entered the museum's collection in 1921. It has four fingerholes plus a partially drilled suspension hole (and in this regard differs from the one named Moriori flute we know about, the single-holed albatross-bone pauawau).[112] Charcoal was originally rubbed into the incised decorations, making them stand out against the bone.

Albatross have profound spiritual significance for Moriori, and their bone 'appears to have been a valued material used in a variety of artefacts'.[113] Juvenile albatross taken from Rakitchu The Sisters, Motchuhara Forty-Fours and Tarakoikoia The

MORIORI FLUTE *made from albatross bone, held in the Canterbury Museum (catalogue number E181.217) and acquired in 1921. Wind instrument. Measures 16cms long. Photograph used with permission of the Canterbury Museum.*

Pyramid were a valuable food resource as well as a supply of bone, though Moriori middens contain the bones of both juveniles and adults.[114]

However, the strong resemblance of this flute to Māori kōauau could also mean that this kind of instrument was in use when the ancestors of Māori and Moriori were in contact; it may even have been a late introduction from Aotearoa.

PERCUSSION INSTRUMENTS

Moriori used a variety of percussion instruments for different purposes. One account, for example, speaks of the use of stones pounded together to attract fish: 'To employ his leisure, a headman owning sheltered deep-water gulches, there trained pet moki to come at the call of pounding on the rocks, to be fed and fattened on paua'.[115]

Percussion instruments were also used to influence the weather. For instance, a particular mushroom-shaped limestone rock near the shore of the Te Whanga lagoon, known as Rua's Bell (nowadays known as Bell Rock), was struck by Māori rangatira Rua as he travelled across the lagoon in his canoe; 'if it rang out like a bell, rain would follow'.[116] Although Rua was Māori (who were not present on Rēkohu until after 1835), the origin of such a practice may be Moriori as certain trees, when struck, would similarly produce rain.

Rectangular cutouts in the bark of particular kopi trees could be struck with wands (presumably thin lengths of wood) to change the wind direction to one that was more favourable. These cutouts were karakii (invocations) addressed to the etchu (deity, patron spirit) inhabiting the tree. They measured around 13 to 20 centimetres in area, though some were more than a metre high, and they were typically located around a metre from the ground. The performer struck the cutout facing the wind direction they wanted to change. Cutouts could be found 'at most of the arbours', but there were concentrations at Kairae and a site that dendroglyph (tree carvings) scholar Christina Jefferson named Matarakau Coast 3. In two examples near Tennant Lake, the cutouts faced northwest and east-northeast, the directions of the onshore and offshore breezes respectively. Other examples were located near the harbour of Te Raki (near Operau), in Taia Bush Reserve, at Te Whakaru and Mairangi.[117] It's not known how many of these dendroglyphs still survive.

Moriori may have also used kelp to make percussion instruments. When Europeans first arrived at Rēkohu in 1791, they fired their guns to try and scare a group of Moriori, at which the Moriori remarked: 'Hear the crack of the kelp of their god Hauoro!' possibly alluding to the report made by thrashing long arms of bull-kelp on a sea-beach.[118] Strands of kelp, when struck on the ground whip-fashion, produce a sound like a gunshot; as do two strands of kelp held together at each end (or a single strand doubled over), with the player's hands pushed together then suddenly pulled apart. There are no accounts of Moriori having used kelp in any of these ways, however.

Another possibility is that kelp was placed in a fire, causing crackling sounds. Ethnographer William Baucke recalled going fishing for mararii and koiro at night as a small boy with Kirapu, one of the Moriori chiefs from Kaingaroa: 'We arrive. He lights a fire of dry wood above the high water mark and performs certain rites by drawing green flax blades through the blaze, and listening to the light explosions scorching flax blades make, intermittently repeating certain charms ... The whole was an offering of placation to Maru and Tangaroa (fish and sea deities) not to be angered that his food necessities compelled him to destroy their children.'[119]

This practice is similar to the ways in which Māori tohunga interpreted the harmonics generated by pūtōrino or humming tops in divination, with tohunga making a judgement based on the tohu or signs indicated by the instrument's voice. The term tohu has the same or similar meanings in Tahiti, Rarotonga, Penrhyn and Rapa Nui; it reconstructs to the East Polynesian tofu, meaning 'point out, indicate'.[120] The use of sound in divination is not documented elsewhere in Polynesia. This might be because it did not take in Polynesia other than in Aotearoa and Rēkohu, but it seems more likely that such knowledge is so sacred that it has remained secret. It is certainly a practice that links Māori and Moriori, despite differences in the instruments used. It may have developed in the time when these peoples were in contact, or later independently.

Chapter 4: Echoes of the ancestors

Examining similarities between instrument traditions can provide clues about where in the tropics Aotearoa and Rēkohu's first settlers originated. However, trying to untangle which instruments may have been borrowed or adapted from Polynesia, and when, is a hugely complex task. The comparative approach taken in this chapter is purposely selective and may be subject to confirmation bias.[1] It is also, by necessity, speculative. There is no way to know for sure whether any similarities offer proof of musical instrument adoption or adaptation, or whether they are mere coincidences. People move and cultures and languages change over time, so trying to understand cultural transmission that occurred several hundred years ago (c. 1200–1400) from information dating from a few hundred years later is fraught with difficulty.[2]

There are many challenges with the existing evidence. Instruments held in museum collections are sometimes incorrectly provenanced, few examples of instruments made from perishable materials have survived in the archaeological record, and the early written historical record is incomplete and biased. Early European writers documenting Polynesian musical traditions for the first time were not music experts and their own Eurocentric biases colour their writing. Some instruments garnered much attention, while others were poorly documented or not documented at all. Several of the instruments mentioned in this book are the single known physical examples of their kind or are described in a single historical account. It is impossible to know if such examples are simply anomalies or the sole extant examples of a more widely used type. It is certainly not possible to generalise or extrapolate about nationwide instrument types and practices based on such singular examples. Considering all of these limitations, what follows is an exploration of different theories; there are no definitive answers.

Midway I.
HAWAIIAN IS
Tropic of Cancer
MARIANA
ISLANDS
Wake I.
Johnson I.
Guam
MICRONESIA
Bikini
MARSHALL IS.
Palau
Truk
CAROLINE
ISLANDS
GILBERT IS.
(KIRIBATI)
Palmy
Washi
Baker I.
Nauru
Banaba
WEST
PAPUA
PAPUA
NEW
GUINEA
New Ireland
PHOENIX
ISLANDS
ELLICE IS.
(TUVALU)
SOLOMON IS.
New
Britain
TOKELAU IS.
Timor
Port
Moresby
SANTA
CRUZ IS.
WALLIS &
FUTUNA
Louisiade Arc.
SAMOA
Rotuma
MELANESIA
AMERICAN
SAMOA
VANUATU
CORAL
SEA
FIJI
TONGA
NIUE
LOYALTY IS.
NEW
CALEDONIA
Tongatapu
AUSTRALIA
Sunday (Raoul)
Norfolk I.
KERMADEC IS
POLYNESIA
Sydney
TASMAN SEA
Tāmaki Makaurau
AOTEAROA
TE IKA A MĀUI
Pōneke
TASMANIA
Rēkohu
TE WAI POUNAMU
Auckland Is.
Macquarie I.

Oceania | Te Moananui a Kiwa

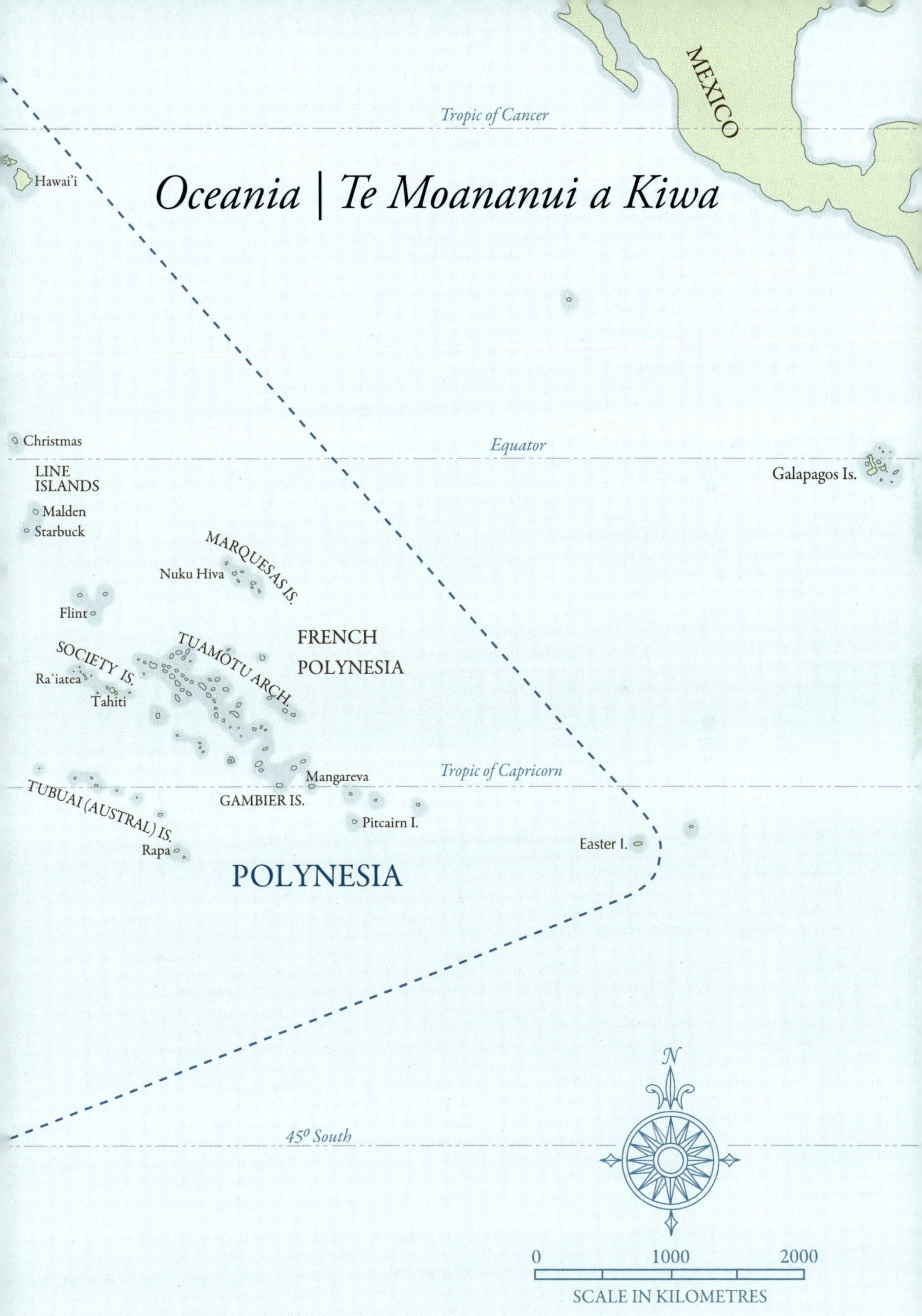

MEXICO
Tropic of Cancer
Hawai'i
Christmas
Equator
Galapagos Is.
LINE ISLANDS
Malden
Starbuck
MARQUESAS IS.
Nuku Hiva
Flint
FRENCH POLYNESIA
TUAMOTU ARCH.
SOCIETY IS.
Ra'iatea
Tahiti
Tropic of Capricorn
Mangareva
GAMBIER IS.
Pitcairn I.
TUBUAI (AUSTRAL) IS.
Rapa
Easter I.
POLYNESIA
45⁰ South
N
0 1000 2000
SCALE IN KILOMETRES

Current origin theories

Māori and Moriori ancestors came from a broad regional interaction sphere, or series of interrelated spheres, underpinned by centuries of long-distance voyaging involving trade and migration.[3] This extensive interconnectedness makes it unlikely that the ancestors of New Zealand Māori came from a single island or even a single region.[4]

EAST POLYNESIA

The weight of current research favours the theory that ancestors of Māori and Moriori originated from central East Polynesia: the Societies, Cooks, Australs, Tuamotus, Marquesas and Mangareva. This view is supported by material, cultural, linguistic and genetic studies.[5] Several Māori instruments almost certainly whakapapa to this region.[6]

There is a question mark over the possible settlement of Aotearoa from the Tuamotus, which may have been settled fairly late (c. 1300–1400) due to sea levels prior to that time having been too high.[7] Off-wind sailing routes were open from the Southern Cook Islands and the southern Austral Islands to Aotearoa between 1140 and 1260. After around 1300, however, voyaging to Aotearoa from central East Polynesia would have been difficult because the onset of the Little Ice Age created poor climatic conditions, making long-distance voyaging risky.[8] Long-distance voyaging to and from Aotearoa and Rēkohu resumed following these islands' European 'discovery', with Polynesians joining European ships' crews. So while knowledge of musical instruments from the Tuamotus could have reached Aotearoa, there may have been only a narrow time window in which that took place during the first phase of Aotearoa's human settlement.

Evidence concerning the ancestors of Māori and Moriori having voyaged from the Marquesas is inconclusive – it is supported by placename, skeletal, linguistic and archaeological evidence but refuted by genetic studies of an important commensal species, the Pacific rat or kiore (*Rattus exulans*).[9] There is evidence of trade from the Marquesas to the Cook and Society islands, however, which would have enabled indirect cultural transmission from those islands to Aotearoa.[10] There are notable similarities between some Marquesan and Māori musical instruments, but it is important to note that those instruments are also found elsewhere in central East Polynesia.

Similarities between percussion rods from Manihiki and Aotearoa show that the Northern Cook Islands may also have been a place Māori ancestors voyaged from or had contact with. There are also similarities between other Māori percussion instruments and those from Pukapuka in the Northern Cooks. However, it should be remembered that while most Cook Islands languages relate closely to te reo Māori, Pukapukan is an exception.[11]

Some Māori instruments resemble those from Hawai`i and Rapa Nui. Hawaiian oral histories support voyaging from Hawai`i to Tahiti, returning via the Tuamotus. These histories are supported by archaeological data: the material of a stone adze recovered from the Tuamotus is similar to hawaiite (an olivine basalt) from Kaho`olawe Island.[12] Return voyaging from Rapa Nui to central East Polynesia was also possible during the periods 1090–1120 and 1200–1250.[13] It is, therefore, possible that the ancestors of Māori knew of instrument types from these islands before voyaging to Aotearoa.

Comparative studies of musical instruments from far-flung islands across East Polynesia reveal some similarities. This means that they were either invented independently, or they were the result of cultural transmission, or these instruments (or a common progenitor) existed in central East Polynesia before outlying Polynesia was settled, later becoming obsolete across most of the region except for the marginal areas.[14] All of these possible explanations are plausible but there is no way of knowing for certain which is correct. Mervyn McLean favours the third theory, the 'stone in the pond' model of cultural diffusion, whereby ripples spread from the central point of origin to the margins while retaining traits once characteristic of the centre.[15]

WEST POLYNESIA AND EAST MELANESIA

A small amount of genetic evidence supports the ancestors of Māori having had contact with West Polynesians and East Melanesians. For example, a population of Pacific rats found in southern Te Ika a Māui has a possible West Polynesian origin.[16] Rats from the same genetic population are also found in Vanuatu, New Caledonia, Fiji, Sāmoa, Tokelau and Kapingamarangi.[17]

West Polynesian and East Melanesian linguistic traces remain in the names of some instruments present in Aotearoa.[18] In terms of the instruments themselves, leaf whizzers and a variety of percussion instruments are similar to those from West Polynesia. The following survey of instruments by type will tell us more about the ancestry of taonga pūoro in various parts of Polynesia and other islands of Te Moananui a Kiwa Oceania.

Swung, thrown or spun instruments

JUGGLED OR SWUNG BALLS

The artefact type currently known as poi is a light ball on a string that is juggled, twirled and tapped in time to an accompanying song. It is a Māori adaptation of pan-Polynesian juggling traditions, particularly those of central East Polynesia.

In Aotearoa, the earliest poi were stringless balls called kī, which is Tahitic in origin and means 'full'.[19] We have evidence of these from Murihiku. A player would toss kī in the air and catch them with alternate hands.[20] Poi could also be played in groups, with players standing facing each other in two rows, throwing the balls in time with an accompanying song.[21] The missionary William Colenso observed that poi was 'a pleasing and dexterous game' performed by young women using a stuffed and ornamented hand ball.[22]

These descriptions of Māori poi resemble East Polynesian juggling games called pei. In the Tuamotus, four to six popo (balls) were used. Each toss of a ball from the left to right hand coincided with the word of a chant. Similarly, in the Marquesas balls were tossed in time with an accompanying chant. Juggling accompanied by a chant was a child's game in Hawai`i. In Mangareva, pei was played exclusively by women, performed in a seated position, often at festivals and competitions. The winner was the player who could go the longest without dropping a ball, or who could juggle the most balls in time with a chant. In the Southern Cooks between four and eight balls were tossed vertically and from one hand to the other in an anti-clockwise direction in time with chanted verses. The aim was to juggle for as long as possible. Pei was also played in Tahiti and Fiji.[23]

In Aotearoa, over time, a long string was added to create toa or poi toa. The long string meant players were spaced further apart and the poi was swung more slowly.[24] In the 1840s, long-stringed poi were superseded by poi with shorter strings. These are the poi used in the performances familiar to contemporary audiences.[25] The transition from long- to short-stringed poi may have happened at different times in different places around Aotearoa, and is a topic that deserves further study.

One of ethnographer James Beattie's Murihiku informants recalled that poi were unknown in Hawaiki. Rather, they were invented in Ōpunake, near Parihaka in western Taranaki.[26] According to that kōrero, a girl named Pari lived at the Tahi-marae pā. As she was gathering raupō in a swamp, she worked some of it into balls, which she would juggle in time to songs sung by other girls. When Pari's father heard of this, he got her to perform in front of him and then in front of a large social gathering. In this narrative, the word 'poi' once meant singing. Despite this story's claims, it is unlikely that poi originated in Taranaki.

Descriptions closely resembling poi can be found elsewhere in Oceania. For example, British anthropologists working in New Guinea in the early 20th century described a dance that was very similar to Māori poi. The dance was performed by young women and involved manipulating balls or small netted bags attached to strings. It is not known if this is an example of convergent evolution or if it possibly reflects Māori cultural influence in Papua New Guinea.[27]

The next closest matches to Māori poi are from the Tuamotus, Hawai`i and the Marquesas. In the Tuamotus, popo were made from pandanus leaf or strips of plaited coconut leaf, and in Hawai`i, juggled balls were called lau hala, referring to the leaves (lau) of the hala tree used in their making. In the Marquesas, balls made from fau leaves bound with pandanus were called pei.[28]

The Marquesan game called pohutu featured the use of pei balls around five centimetres in diameter. A strip of pandanus leaf, a few centimetres long, formed a handle. When played solo, the ball was batted by the player's free hand; when played in pairs, one player would hold the handle while the other player hand-batted the ball.[29] This description resembles an 1859 account of Māori poi, where poi is described as a game in which 'the string is held in one hand and the ball is struck with the other'.[30] Given the first poi in Aotearoa were stringless balls, the addition of a handle in the Marquesas and of a string in Aotearoa is likely to be an example of independent localised innovation.[31]

Further parallels between Māori poi and Tuamotuan pei can be seen in the legend of Tinirau and Kae. Three women are mentioned in both the Tuamotuan version of this narrative and a version from one of Beattie's informants from the Otago Heads.[32] In the Tuamotuan version, two of the three sisters of the whale brothers Tutunui and Togamaututu are named Ruatohu and Ruatogaegae (also known as Katouri and Katomea, respectively). The latter names are cognates of Raukatauri and Raukatamea, whose names (and their variants) are found in different Māori versions of this narrative. The Tuamotuan version also mentions juggling as being among the games and amusements performed by these three women, and the Murihiku version is the only documented Aotearoa record of this tale that mentions poi.

The closest linguistic matches to poi in the tropics are found in central East Polynesia.[33] For example, the Tuamotuan term poi means 'to toss up and down, as in waves in a storm', and Māori definitions for poi include 'ball, lump' and 'toss up and down'.[34]

Pei – and cognates pe`i or pe`ipe`i in the Southern Cooks – was also used to describe juggling with ball-like objects of various kinds.[35] Stones or limes were juggled in Tahiti, whereas tamanu tree fruit or candlenut tree seeds were used in the Southern Cooks.[36] In the absence of tropical fruits and nuts in Aotearoa, Māori created poi using materials such as raupō and houhi.[37] Ngāti Porou occasionally made poi from light wood such as houama or mako.[38] In Tuahiwi in the Waitaha rohe, poi was a game that involved throwing up and catching pebbles in various orders, which is reminiscent of the juggling of stones practised in Tahiti.[39]

There is also a linguistic connection between Māori poi and West Polynesian juggling traditions. Hiko is the name for a juggling game in Tuvalu, East `Uvea and Tonga that may have been a precursor to Māori poi.[40] In te reo Māori, hiko means 'move at random or irregularly' and 'snatch'; hihiko means 'brisk, quick'; and hikohiko means to 'move from one thing to another'. These terms all aptly describe the Tongan game observed by William Mariner, an early European visitor to Tonga. This game was usually played by women and involved juggling five stones or small fruits, keeping four in the air at once, while chanting in time with the movements.[41] Each successfully completed chant marked one ulu (game). Players that reached the pre-agreed number of ulu won.[42]

Some of the chants used to accompany Tongan hiko included the recitation of names.[43] This fits with another meaning of the Māori term hikohiko: to 'recite genealogy'. Similarly, in the Marquesas, mothers teaching children their genealogies used both pei and pohutu to accompany a chant naming important patrilineal ancestors.[44] A related usage was found in Mangareva, where pei was associated with prenatal ceremonies.[45] In this instance, it was performed by women as a form of rest between two parts of the `uki`uki (pains of childbirth) ceremony: the `akatotou (concealment) and tu`i (showing), and the pahunu (a navel ceremony).

Māori used poi to accompany oriori, songs performed to the children of high-ranking individuals to educate them in matters appropriate to their descent, including knowledge concerning their whakapapa.[46] In Taranaki, poi used to keep time in the chanting of whakapapa were termed poipoi whakapapa.[47] Pātere (chants) could also be performed with poi accompaniment. A well-known example is the mid-19th century 'Poia atu taku poi' composed by Erenora Taratoa (Ngāti Raukawa), in which the composer's poi figuratively touches on places where her illustrious ancestors dwelt.[48]

SPINNING DISCS

Hawaiian spinning discs were known as pokakā. These were typically made from hau bark, perforated with two holes through which a cord was passed, though music scholar Ernest Dodge mentions an example made from a gourd.[49] There is no apparent linguistic connection between the Hawaiian pokakā and the various names for spinning discs in Aotearoa (see Appendix 1), but most Māori spinning discs match the pokakā's physical description.

Spinning discs might have been widespread across Polynesia around the time the ancestors of Māori departed the tropics, subsequently becoming obsolete everywhere except Hawai`i and Aotearoa. Another possibility, based on the late date of ethnographer Stewart Culin's accounts – 1899 – is that Hawaiians may have learnt of this instrument from Aotearoa or elsewhere in post-European contact times.

SWUNG SLATS (BULLROARERS)

Swung slats were predominantly found in Micronesia (Sonsorol, Pulo Anna) and Melanesia (Vanuatu, Papua New Guinea). They were comparatively rare in tropical Polynesia, though they were used on the Polynesian outliers Mungiki and Munggava, where they were known as hakatangikugu.[50] There is an account of wooden swung slats being used as children's toys in Hawai`i, where they were known by the onomatopoeic names oeoe, kowaliwali and koheoheo. In Aotearoa and Rēkohu, wood and whalebone were used to make swung slats.[51]

None of the Polynesian terms for swung slats resemble the terms used by Māori (see Appendix 1), which reduces the likelihood of recent cultural transmission having taken place. Linguistically, a commonly used Māori name for these instruments, pūrerehua, is related to the Malayo-Polynesian terms pulele-fua and Samoic–Outlier Polynesian lelefua – both of which refer to 'moth or butterfly'.[52]

The distribution of swung slats across Oceania supports McLean's views concerning cultural diffusion,[53] and the presence of this instrument type in both Aotearoa and Rēkohu lends further weight to this possibility.[54]

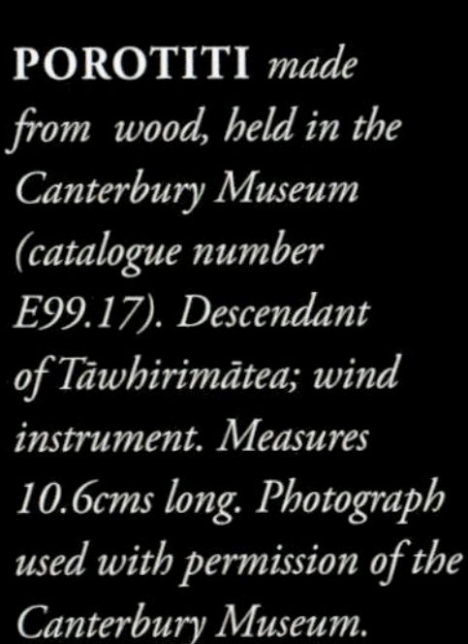

POROTITI *made from wood, held in the Canterbury Museum (catalogue number E99.17). Descendant of Tāwhirimātea; wind instrument. Measures 10.6cms long. Photograph used with permission of the Canterbury Museum.*

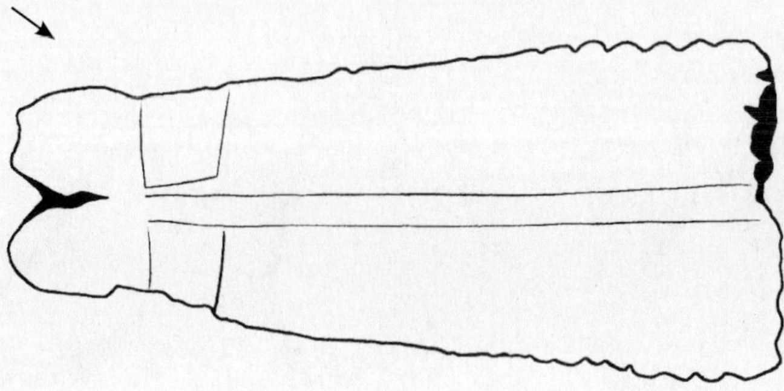

MORIORI SWUNG SLAT *made from whalebone. Wind instrument. Drawing by Jennifer Cattermole from an image in Dendy, 'On some relics', plate VI, figure 12.*

Swung slats were used in very similar ways in Aotearoa and Papua New Guinea. In both countries, they were played during rituals associated with crop fertility: as noted earlier, Ngāti Porou used them to summon a gentle rain at the time of kūmara planting, and the Kiwai and Kwoma peoples of Papua New Guinea played them when planting yams.[55] Swung slats were also associated with warfare in these two countries. In the Murihiku region, some `garara were used as weapons.[56] For the Anga people of Papua New Guinea, swung slats were played to intimidate the enemy during attacks rather than as weapons.[57] Swung slats also played a spiritual role in farewelling the dead. In Taranaki, pūmamae or mamae were played to summon tears during tangihangi and to ward off or disperse evil spirits.[58] Similarly, at Latangai Island in Papua New Guinea, the sound of the whirling swung slat indicated that the ancestors had appeared to receive the soul of the deceased.[59]

LEAF WHIZZERS

Leaf whizzers were widespread across tropical Oceania, so it is likely that the ancestors of Māori knew of this instrument type.

There are no direct linguistic connections between the Māori name for leaf whizzers (tīrango) and East Polynesian names for this instrument.[60] However, in both Aotearoa and West Polynesia leaf whizzers were named after the sound made by insects: 'rango' in tīrango refers to a hovering blowfly and in Tokelau the name ligoligo was shared with a chirping insect.[61]

Physically, the tīrango also closely resembles West Polynesian leaf whizzers. In Tonga, as in Aotearoa, a bow is used as part of the instrument.[62]

PŪREREHUA *made from wood, held in the Canterbury Museum (catalogue number E99.17) and acquired in 1899. Descendant of Tāwhirimātea; wind instrument. Measures 52.6cms long. Photograph used with permission of the Canterbury Museum.*

GOURD HUMMING TOPS

Instruments similar to the hue humming tops found in Aotearoa – specifically, in the Mataatua region and Waikato – were found in Hawai`i and Vanuatu. In the Cook Islands, Marquesas and Mangareva, humming tops were made from coconut shell and in Melanesia (Papua New Guinea, the Solomons, Vanuatu), as well as Polynesian outlier Luangiua, fruit shells or nuts were used.[63] Gourd humming tops may once have been widespread throughout East Polynesia, subsequently becoming obsolete everywhere in that region except Aotearoa and Hawai`i, but it is more likely that Māori began using hue as a substitute material for coconuts, which were unavailable to them.

The Southern Cook Islands is a strong contender for the place where this type of Māori instrument originated, as pōtaka is a term used in both Aitutaki and Aotearoa for spinning tops.[64] The term reconstructs to the East Polynesian poo-taka, meaning 'to revolve, go around; revolving or spinning object; round' – meanings that are apt for this instrument.[65]

Instruments featuring mouth resonators

Throughout tropical Oceania, the term utete and its cognate ukeke are used to describe various forms of percussion instrument that utilise the mouth as a resonating chamber: ū meaning 'to bite' and tete meaning 'to vibrate'. The latter derives from the Proto Polynesian term *tete, meaning 'shiver' or 'tremble'. Utete 'was applied independently to the Jew's harp in Western Polynesia and to the musical bow, which operates on a similar principle, in Hawai`i and the Marquesas Islands'.[66]

PERCUSSION RODS

Percussion rods or sticks are found in Melanesia (Fiji) as well as across Polynesia: in the West (`Uvea), the Polynesian outliers (Luangiua, Tikopia, Mungiki, Nuguria, Nukumanu, Nukuoro) and the East (Rapa Nui, Hawai`i, the Marquesas, Manihiki and Tahiti).[67] In Manihiki in the Northern Cooks, Hawai`i and Aotearoa, the rods are described as being unevenly sized, with the smaller rod being struck against the larger.[68]

In Manihiki and Aotearoa, the key thing that sets these instruments apart from their counterparts elsewhere in Polynesia is that they involve the use of the human oral cavity as a resonator. In Manihiki there are two types of percussion rod (titāpū). One type consists of a coconut leaflet held across the mouth, struck with the midrib of another leaflet. The second type consists of two unevenly sized cyclindrical wooden sticks.[69] The latter type most closely resembles wooden examples from Aotearoa.

The names for these instruments in Manihiki (titāpū) and the Marquesas (koufou, pahu koufau, papaki `akau) are dissimilar to names used for percussion rods in Aotearoa (see Appendix 1).[70] However, some Hawaiian terms for this instrument are related. Kāla`au or kālā`au (meaning 'to strike wood') or la`au (wood) are equivalent to the Māori term rākau, and relate to one of the Māori terms for percussion rods (pakakau) as kakau/kau refers to plant stalks.[71] This similarity is the result of a widespread Polynesian practice of naming instruments after the materials used in their construction.

LAMELLAPHONES

Although none of the names used for lamellaphones across Polynesia resemble those used by Māori (rōria, tararī, tarau and kūkau), this instrument is likely to have been brought to Aotearoa by the ancestors of Māori as its use is so widespread across Oceania.[72] It is possible, however, that Māori, who were captivated by metal Jew's harps introduced by Europeans, created their own functional substitutes using kareao and a variety of woods (mataī, maire, mānuka, tītoki and mamaku).

Some of the ways Māori used these instruments are the same as those described elsewhere in Oceania. For example, in West Polynesia they are often used as children's toys; the same usage is reported for Māori rōria from the Waitaha rohe.[73] In Papua New Guinea, Sāmoa and the Marquesas, these instruments are associated with generating love and with communication between lovers.[74] Likewise, at Waiomatatini in the Tairāwhiti rohe in Aotearoa, lovers would sit side by side with their heads close together speaking very softly while playing their kūkau, with one hand covering both the instrument and their mouth.[75] In the Marquesas, lamellaphones are used to converse in secrecy and code; and in Hawai`i, players project their voice against the instrument.[76] In Aotearoa, word-based melodies are played using lamellaphones; players often sing or hum with the instrument's sound. The instruments are used to rehearse and accompany mōteatea and karakia. The changing shape of the player's oral cavity creates different resonances, which are perceived as different words and messages. These instruments function as voice modifiers and disguisers, conveying sounds imbued with lexical meaning for the purpose of secret, intimate communication, something that relates to 'the Polynesian delight in indirect speech and cleverly veiled meanings'.[77]

RŌRIA *made from supplejack vine. Descendant of Tāne; percussion instrument. Made by Brian Flintoff.* ♪

MOUTH BOWS

The Māori mouth bow, kū (sometimes also called kūkau), was almost certainly transmitted from Tahiti, the Tuamotus, the Australs and/or possibly the Cook Islands, where similar instruments can be found. However, the instrument name titapu (or cognate tita`apu), used in the Marquesas and Australs (Ra`ivavae and Rapa), is dissimilar to the Māori name for this instrument, and there are no records of its original name elsewhere in central East Polynesia to compare to its Māori names.[78] On Mangaia, in the Southern Cooks, the term ko`e (named for the bamboo the instrument is made from) is used for mouth bows, though it is unclear whether this was a traditional instrument and, if so, whether that was its original name.[79]

The use of dog intestine for the string in a Māori kū may offer one possible explanation for its name (another was explored in Chapter 1): kū is an abbreviation of Polynesian terms for 'dog' (kurī and its cognates).[80] Te Rangi Hīroa, however, provides a third explanation for this instrument name's etymology. Hawaiian terms for mouth bow include ukēkē and `ūkēkē.[81] He notes that the first syllable of the latter term would be the same as the name of the Māori mouth bow, with the initial glottal stop substituting for 'k'. The Māori term could therefore be an abbreviation of one of the Hawaiian terms for this instrument.[82]

The Māori kū is most similar in terms of its size and manufacture to mouth bows from Papua New Guinea.[83] Hawaiian and Marquesan mouth bows resemble the Māori kū, but differ from it in several important respects. Māori kū are described as being around 25 centimetres long, whereas Hawaiian instruments tend to be around 40 to 60 centimetres long, and Marquesan utete even longer, around 1 to 1.5 metres.[84] Both Hawaiian and Marquesan mouth bow strings can be plucked with a plectrum; and in Hawai`i and Aotearoa the player can use their fingers. Māori kū players can also tap the strings with a rod or use their knuckles to strum or stroke the string. Hawaiian instruments have a peg around which one end of the string is wound, and both the Hawaiian and Marquesan instruments have a bridge – features that are absent from the kū. Kū are described as being single-stringed, though if a lyre-like instrument described by French explorer Jules Dumont d'Urville that had three or four strings was a form of mouth bow, then it was multi-stringed like Hawaiian mouth bows, which had two to three strings. However, there is no guarantee that the instrument observed by d'Urville was, in fact, a kū. Given the description comes from his 1840 visit to Aotearoa, it seems more likely that the instrument was a transitional one modelled on a European lyre.[85]

Percussion instruments

CANOE-SHAPED PAHU

As noted earlier, in central East Polynesia the name pahu is used for sharkskin drums, while Māori use it for hardwood or stone gongs. Late 19th and early 20th century accounts report Māori using a canoe-shaped wooden gong like the slit gongs found elsewhere in Polynesia (and known there by very different names – lali, logo, nafa, kā`ara, tōkere and their cognates): 'a block of sound heartwood hewn into the form of a canoe and hollowed out carefully … so as to leave a long narrow aperture that widened out to a large hollow space in the interior'. It is, however, described as being rare.[86] John White used the name 'pahu kahatu' to describe the instrument, but that may have been incorrect as the term kahatū (or its cognate tahatū) refers to the upper edge of a canoe sail, whereas the instrument's shape and manufacture more closely resemble a canoe's hull.[87]

Some pahu in Aotearoa were fashioned like a kumete (trough), suspended with the opening downward and struck on the bottom.[88] British writer John G. Wood (1827–1889) describes an instrument matching this description: 'a block of hard wood about six feet (1.8 metres) long and two (61 centimetres) thick, with a deep groove in the centre … suspended horizontally by cords, and struck by a man who squats on a scaffold under it. With a stick made of heavy wood he delivers slow and regular strokes in the groove.'[89] Regrettably, no examples of this type of pahu survived, with the exception of a small version (possibly a model) that was made in Ruatāhuna in 1899.[90] This trough-shaped Māori instrument, while resembling East Polynesian slit gongs, is physically dissimilar to Melanesian and West Polynesian log idiophones.[91] It has the most in common with canoe-shaped examples from Papua New Guinea (tongtong), the Solomon Islands, Espiritu Santo in Vanuatu and Fiji,

RUATAHUNA PAHU *made from wood, held in Te Papa Tongarewa (catalogue number ME000466). Descendant of Papatūānuku; percussion instrument. Measures 73cms long. Drawing by Jennifer Cattermole from an image in Best,* Games and Pastimes, *p. 165.*

particularly in terms of the instruments being suspended off the ground and being only partially hollowed out.[92]

Music scholar Hans Fischer asserted that the similarities between Māori canoe-shaped (or trough-like) pahu and similar instruments from Melanesia are 'too great to ascribe independent development to New Zealand'.[93] Te Rangi Hīroa, however, disagreed: as noted earlier, he believed that log idiophones were not known to the ancestors of Māori at the time they departed for Aotearoa, as this type of instrument was absent from other parts of marginal Polynesia (i.e. Hawai`i and Rapa Nui), in which case their presence in Aotearoa represents an independent invention.[94]

Canoe-shaped wooden gongs could have been transmitted from tropical Polynesia to Aotearoa. They may have been adopted by Aotearoa's founding human population on the basis of cultural contact with West Polynesia. Another possibility is that Māori first encountered these instruments either while voyaging in tropical Oceania with early European explorers and whalers, or that knowledge of them was brought to Aotearoa by visiting Polynesian members of such crews. Māori crew members were being taken on by whaling ships as early as 1805 and, although none of the informants Beattie talked to in 1920 had heard of wooden pahu being used in Te Wai Pounamu, one had heard Pacific Islanders who arrived in the 1860s aboard whaling vessels talk about theirs.[95] As all accounts of Māori instruments resembling slit gongs date from the late 19th and early 20th centuries, they are most likely a 19th-century development.[96]

STRUCK MATS

One type of Māori percussion instrument, the Ngāti Porou pākuru, consists of whītau wrapped around houhi bark.[97] It may have been an adaptation of a rolled mat percussion instrument from Pukapuka, though this seems unlikely given there is only one account of rolled mats being used as an improvised percussion instrument from there.[98] Instruments that most closely match the Ngāti Porou pākuru include a Sāmoan percussion instrument called tu`itu`i, which was made from a mat wound tight around a framework of reeds or lengths of bamboo. Similarly, in Tonga rolled mats (tafua) were wrapped around lengths of bamboo.[99] These West Polynesian instruments were beaten with two sticks, whereas the pākuru described above was struck with a single wooden beater. As with the pahu discussed above, the Ngāti Porou pākuru may have been a late introduction to Aotearoa from West Polynesia, given Best first published information about this instrument in 1923. The perishability of these instruments means none have survived in the archaeological record, so we may never know whether this type of pākuru was invented independently by Māori, or whether it was a borrowing or adaptation of instruments encountered through later contact with tropical Polynesian peoples.

Kuru is used as a term in the Northern Cooks (Manihiki, Rakahanga) as well as in the Southern Cooks (Rarotonga), meaning 'to strike, pound or knock against', which is consistent with definitions of kuru in Māori and Moriori languages. The term kuru reconstructs to the Nuclear Polynesian word kulu, which means 'apply force to, strike'.[100] Kuru was, therefore, a very suitable term for Māori to use in percussion instrument names (in the same way the term pahu was).

PERCUSSION BEAMS

Percussion beams, found across West Polynesia, are made from bamboo, though wooden logs or large sticks have been used in West Futuna, Tokelau and Sāmoa.[101] These instruments differ from Māori pahu, but there is one Māori instrument these percussion beams resemble: a type of pākuru from Waitaha.[102] This instrument, as noted earlier, was made from a thick hollowed stem of tutu rākau around a metre long, plugged at each end. It was played by only one person (rather than several men, as in West Polynesia), owing to its smaller size in relation to similar Polynesian instruments. However, the hollow tube plugged at both ends strongly recalls bamboo. As with other percussion instruments described above, this type of pākuru may have been introduced to Aotearoa in the 19th century from West Polynesia; equally, it may simply be an independent invention.

Concussion instruments

CLAPPERS, CASTANETS

Māori tōkere are castanets typically made from wood or bone, which can be separate or hinged. These instruments may be adaptations of similar instruments from tropical Polynesia, though there is no linguistic correlation between them. Tahitian castanets are made from two mother-of-pearl shells held together by a piece of cord acting as a hinge, and are termed paraow or tete.[103] Coconut shells are also used as clappers in Fiji, as well as in Sāmoa (ipu), Malekula and Fiji (qānibilo).[104] Hawaiians have a pebble castanet called `ili`ili, in which separate pebbles are held between the dancer's fingers.[105] Pebble castanets have also been reported from Rapa Nui, as well as clappers made from bone (etimoika).[106]

STICK GAMES

Stick games like those played in Tai Tokerau and Te Arawa are found elsewhere in Oceania. For example, sturdy wooden poles are cracked together during stick dances and games in Micronesia (for instance, in Chuuk and the Marshall Islands) and

Melanesia (Tanna).[107] They are also found in West Polynesia. An `Uvean stick dance called eke spread to Tonga in the 1830s, and later to Fiji's Lau archipelago, Sāmoa and Tokelau.[108] They could perhaps have been a late introduction to Aotearoa, or an independent invention.

CONCUSSION STONES

Tumutumu, used in the Murihiku rohe, are hand-held percussion instruments made from bone, stone or wood. Similar instruments made from stone (lithophones) are found elsewhere in Polynesia. For example, in the Southern Cooks, two stones are struck together.[109] The Mangarevan pore`o is described as 'a flat stone that was beaten'.[110] Another instrument, consisting of two stones struck together (maea or ma`ea poro), has been reported from Rapa Nui, and is used to accompany song.[111] Māori may have adapted such instruments for their own purposes, or invented tumutumu independently. Certainly, the Māori use of tumutumu as learning aids appears to be unique within Oceania.

Etymologically, the Māori term whakatumutumu is similar to a Niuean definition of tumutumu: 'collection, gathering together, to heap up'. Across West Polynesia (Tonga, East Futuna, Sāmoa, East `Uvea, Tokelau and Tuvalu) and the Polynesian outlier Tikopia, tumutumu refers to 'summit, top, peak, highest point'.[112] Any of these meanings could relate metaphorically to the attainment and accumulation of knowledge. These meanings relate to the Māori definitions of tumutumu noted in Chapter 1: tumu referring to 'foundation or bed' and whakatumutumu meaning 'heaped up'.

Gourd instruments

Several Māori gourd instruments share physical characteristics and uses with instruments from Hawai`i, West Polynesia and Melanesia. The strong similarities between several Māori and Hawaiian gourd instruments in particular raise the possibility of shared ancestry.

GOURD VESSEL FLUTES

Māori kōauau pongā ihu, as we saw in earlier chapters, are made from a small hue, dried with the neck removed, and feature one to four fingerholes. They are played with the nose.[113] A similar instrument is the Hawaiian ipu hōkiokio (also known as ipu hoehoe or pu`a). In 1934, ethnologist Johannes Andersen referred to a Māori 'gourd whistle' named pua – which is very similar to pu`a, one of the names for the

Hawaiian instrument – though he did not specify that it was played with the nose.[114] Hawaiian ipu hōkiokio generally have three fingerholes plus a nose-blowing hole, though they can have between two and five holes.[115] Like kōauau pongā ihu, ipu hōkiokio are primarily made from gourds; kamani nut shells can also be used.[116] This instrument type, blown with the mouth, may have been present in Tahiti (though similar instruments depicted by British anthropologist James Edge-Partington and attributed to Tahiti are believed to be Hawaiian rather than Tahitian).[117] Sāmoans have a similar instrument, made from the hollowed fruit of the togo (mangrove). Vessel flutes made from gourds, nuts and clay can also be found across Melanesia: in Torres Strait, Papua New Guinea, Vanuatu, Fiji and possibly New Caledonia.[118] Unfired clay is also used to make vessel flutes (ukutangi) in Aotearoa, though nuts were not used, owing to the lack of nuts of a suitable size.

SWUNG GOURDS

In terms of usage, poi āwhiowhio have the most in common with Hawaiian instruments. For example, the Hawaiian ipu hōkiokio is described as a lover's whistle.[119] They were 'used to exchange signals at night by lovers who [swung] them on the end of a cord'.[120] Similarly, as as we saw earlier, poi āwhiowhio were swung by members of the Ngāti Kahungunu iwi to attract a lover.[121] A different Hawaiian instrument also has similar uses to poi āwhiowhio. The matangi, carved from a kamani seedpod, was used by inland people to call birds in the forest,[122] just as Ngāti Kahungunu and Tūhoe used poi āwhiowhio to lure birds, particularly kererū.[123]

Ipu hōkiokio also sometimes replace the tapa balls used in a game called pala'ie, which closely resembles a Tongan game called hapo.[124] In these games, the gourds are tied by string to a long stick. The aim is to toss the balls up in the air and get them to land through a hoop or loop at the end of the stick. There are no records of similar games being played in Aotearoa. The physical similarity of poi āwhiowhio to hapo, however, raises another intriguing possibility: that of West Polynesian ancestry for this instrument. After all, the term āwhiowhio, which in te reo Māori means 'whirlwind, whirlpool', reconstructs to the Fijic *(qaa-)sio-sio, meaning 'whirlwind, tornado, waterspout' – and Fiji neighbours Tonga.[125]

GOURD RATTLES

Apart from Aotearoa (specifically Tokomaru Bay and northern Te Ika a Māui), Hawai'i is the only place within Polynesia where gourd rattles are reported.[126] There are significant differences between the Hawaiian and Māori instruments, but also similarities. In Hawai`i, they are known as 'ulī'ulī, whereas in Aotearoa they are called hue rarā and hue puruwai, so there are no linguistic similarities between these terms.

HUE PURUWAI
made from gourd. Descendant of Hine Raukatauri; percussion instrument. Measures 22.5cms tall. Made by Jennifer Cattermole. ♪

Typically, Hawaiian gourd rattles are decorated using feathers, whereas Māori gourd rattles are not. The Hawaiian rattles have handles consisting of sticks bound and attached with fibre; in the Tokomaru Bay examples, the gourd neck was bent while growing to form a natural handle.

Both instruments are made from dried gourds (or coconut in Hawai`i), either with the dried seeds left inside (hue puruwai) or with the seeds removed and replaced with small pebbles (hue rarā). (`Ulī`ulī also sometimes contain ali`i poe, canna seeds). In Tokomaru Bay as well as in Hawai`i, these instruments are used to accompany dance.[127]

Trumpets

CONCH TRUMPETS

Māori oral histories indicate that their ancestors brought conch trumpets to Aotearoa. For example, pūrākau relate how two pūtātara were made by Tāne's younger brother Tupai to announce Māui's successful return from Rangiātea, the highest of the heavenly dimensions, with the three kete of knowledge.[128] A famous shell trumpet with a wooden mouthpiece named 'Te awa a te Atua' is said to have belonged to Tūwharetoa (founding ancestor of Ngāti Tūwharetoa), who arrived on the Arawa waka.[129] A Tairāwhiti kōrero similarly refers to a prized pūmoana brought from Hawaiki.[130] These narratives all support the idea that conch shell trumpets were a tradition brought from Hawaiki. This idea is further supported by the term pū having been reconstructed linguistically to the Proto Nuclear Polynesian *puu, meaning that it likely existed at the Ancestral Polynesian stage.[131]

The term pū and its cognates are used to describe conch trumpets throughout Polynesia, including in the Societies, Southern Cooks (Aitutaki, Mangaia, Rarotonga) and the Australs.[132] In many Polynesian languages, including te reo Māori, this onomatopoeic term is also associated with concepts of blowing.[133] Another Māori name for these instruments, potipoti, further indicates tropical Polynesian origins. In Aotearoa, this term is used for a small wooden box with a lid hinged with cords in which tohunga house an atua. Some examples of this type of instrument feature stoppers for the shell (and sometimes also the mouthpiece), which perform the same function as the lid on the wooden box, in this case helping 'to keep certain symbolic attributes of sound safe within the trumpet, especially when not in use'. These attributes pertain to Tāne's younger brother Tupai, who made the first two shell trumpets and whom Tūhoe (and other iwi in Mataatua) associate with lightning and thunder. Different names are given to these instruments in various accounts: one is named Puororangi, Hāururangi or Taururangi; and the other is named Te Wharara o te rangi, or Te Rangi Whakārāra.[134]

Given how widespread the name pū is for conch trumpets across Polynesia, it might have been expected that Moriori would have retained this name. However, as noted in Chapter 1, Moriori elders used a different name, tere, in a series of letters to George Grey that included the lyrics of a rongo (song).[135] Beginning with the words 'Kariro ra tere i ho mai', this rongo describes a trumpet announcing the arrival of a group of visitors attending a gathering of two groups for the purpose of establishing friendly and peaceful relations.[136] Although the type of trumpet is not specified, it is likely to have been a conch trumpet given the use of these instruments to announce the arrival of visitors and to indicate that people should gather is well documented in many Polynesian contexts.[137] Conch shells of a suitable size wash up rarely on Rēkohu's beaches. As we saw earlier, in Aotearoa, the cognate word pūtētere is a term that was used for conch trumpets, while another cognate term – tētere – was used to describe conch trumpets, long wooden trumpets and flax leaf oboes. Unfortunately, neither pūtētere or tētere appear in POLLEX, the Polynesian Lexicon Project Online database, and none of the entries for tere relate to trumpets, meaning that the etymology of the term remains a mystery.

Like thunder, the voice of conch trumpets is loud and resonant. This idea relates to the Ngāti Porou definition of oro, which is likened to rolling or sustained thunder. Several accounts from across Polynesia, likewise, note that particular shell trumpets are the embodiment or abode of gods, especially gods of war.[138] For example, the voice of a shell trumpet used only by the king or high priest of Mangaia represents Rongo, the war god and principal god of that island.[139] There is a deep connection between the sacredness and spiritual power of such instruments and that of the leaders who used them. Indeed, in the Southern Cook Islands, pū is both a term for conch trumpets and for 'ruler' or 'chief'.[140]

Conch shells can also be the abodes of female spirits. This is illustrated by the ability of these instruments to be played as flutes using the oblique embouchure (or cross-blowing) playing method. One pūrākau concerns a shell sourced from Matakaoa, near Wharekaika (Hicks Bay), located within the Ngāti Porou rohe:

> When fishing off Matakaoa Point, fishermen would often hear strange songs coming from the deep water beneath their canoes. One day, the men in one canoe raised their stone anchor and a pūpū-tara (*Septa tritonis* shell) was found clinging to it. This shell had been responsible for the singing the fishermen had been hearing. A mouthpiece was fitted to the shell, and the name given to the completed instrument was Hinemokemoke, The Lonely Woman, describing the mystery of her song. The trumpet was used for many years, and was viewed as a tipua [supernatural being].[141]

In tropical Polynesia, shell trumpets are used for a variety of signalling purposes, some of which are shared by Māori. Tūhoe used them to signal the approach of enemies, warning their warriors to gather and mobilise to confront the threat; the commanding chief used this instrument to direct or rally his fighters during battle.[142] The same uses have been reported from Tahiti and Mangaia, as well as elsewhere in East Polynesia (the Marquesas, Hawai`i and Rapa Nui), West Polynesia (Tonga, Sāmoa, Tokelau) and Melanesia (Fiji, Papua New Guinea).[143] In Te Urewera, conch trumpets are used to summon people to a village gathering.[144] When played by tohunga, they call people together and usually signify the beginning of a time of tapu, a time to be quiet before a public ceremony is about to begin.[145] This usage has also been reported in Tahiti and the Cook Islands.[146] Māori sometimes use conch trumpets to signal the arrival of a group or a high-ranking man at their destination; this use is also noted in Tahiti and the Cook Islands.[147] These similarities may be examples of cultural transmission, or they may simply be apt uses of such a loud signalling instrument.

Leaf instruments

LEAF OBOES

Leaf oboes are found across Oceania in Melanesia, Polynesia, and central and western Micronesia.[148] In Polynesia, they are invariably described as noise-making toys played by children, mirroring accounts from Aotearoa (specifically from Te Tau Ihu o te Waka, Kaiapoi, the Murihiku region and among Tūhoe), where their playing is described as being a common amusement for children – particularly boys.[149] Children sometimes chant songs into these instruments too.[150]

Pū is the onomatopoeic name of these instruments in the Southern Cooks, as well as in Tokelau, Niue and the Marquesas.[151] Leaf oboes are always found where shell trumpets are used, and the name pū was likely transferred from shell trumpets to leaf oboes due to their similar sound. Pū is a Polynesian term for 'hole; perforated, punctured, holed'.[152] This meaning of the term is evident in Aotearoa, where pū is a prefix for the names of a variety of musical instruments that feature hollow tubes, including leaf oboes (see Appendix 1).[153]

The leaves of various plants – most commonly pandanus or coconut, but also banana and tī – are used to make leaf oboes across tropical Polynesia, and the instrument names reflect the types of leaves used. For example, instruments made from coconut leaves include the pu`i kikau in the Southern Cooks.[154] This naming practice was common across Polynesia, and was continued in Aotearoa, where the names kōrari and pūharakeke refer to the flax flower stalk and leaves used in making the instruments.[155]

Flutes

WHIO

Te Rangi Hīroa noted that Māori developed a number of flute types not found elsewhere in Polynesia (as discussed in Chapter 3).[156] The names of these flutes are dissimilar to any found in tropical Oceania, with one exception: whio.[157] This term may derive from the Central Eastern Polynesian term *wiwo (flute), though linguist Andrew Pawley argues it instead originates from the Proto Eastern Polynesian *fio. A cognate term, vivo, is used to describe flutes in the Societies, Cooks, Tuamotus and Marquesas.[158] Another cognate term, hio, is used in Tahiti.[159]

In Aotearoa, the name whio was given to a variety of flutes, including ones made from albatross bone, and a type of long flute made from mataī (as discussed in Chapter 1).[160] Of these types, the long mataī flute resembles the central East Polynesian vivo, in terms of length and the number and placement of fingerholes – particularly vivo from Tahiti (some of which could have a hole on the underside) as well as those from the Southern Cooks.[161] The crucial difference is that in Aotearoa, unlike in the tropics, whio were not closed at one end. This particular type of whio may be an adaptation of the central East Polynesian vivo, whereas the other whio described above have a linguistic but not a physical connection to central East Polynesia.

PŌRUTU

The origins of the Māori term pōrutu, used for different types of flute in the north and south, are debated (as we saw in Chapter 1). Pōrutu is often believed to be a transliteration of 'flute', though Māori linguist and lexicographer Herbert Williams argued against this.[162] Porutu is possibly a Tahitian term meaning 'loud, clamorous', which is apt for musical instruments. Given it reconstructs to the Central Eastern Polynesian poo-rutu (strike hard), however, its etymology shows the term is actually better suited for percussion instruments than flutes.[163]

The Te Ika a Māui transverse flute called pōrutu (or rehu) may be a transitional instrument, given its physical similarity to Western flutes.[164] Te Rangi Hīroa, however, believed this flute type was 'more likely to have been derived from the old Polynesian form than from a European source'.[165] East Polynesian bamboo nose flutes do resemble this type of pōrutu in being closed at one end and having a blowing hole

PŌRUTU *made from matāī wood. Descendant of Hine Raukatauri; wind instrument. Measures 34cms long. Made by Brian Flintoff.*

REHU *made from rimu wood, with pounamu stopper and pāua shell inlay. Descendant of Hine Raukatauri; wind instrument. Measures 41.3cms long. Made by David Cattermole.*

♪

near the proximal end and fingerholes near the distal end.[166] However, the Māori flutes were purposely designed to be played with the mouth rather than the nose, which is a key difference. In that respect, they more closely resemble Melanesian side-blown flutes from Papua New Guinea, Aoba (Vanuatu), New Caledonia and Nissan Atoll (Solomons); and also the Sāmoan fa`aili fa`asipa.[167]

KŌAUAU

The kōauau is reportedly an instrument brought by the ancestors of Māori to Aotearoa: 'Ehara i te mea poka hou mai, nō Hawaiki mai anō' ('It is not something of recent origin, but a tradition from Hawaiki').[168] Evidence supporting a tropical Polynesian origin for kōauau was given by Ngāti Kahungunu tohunga and historian Te Matorohanga in 1876:

> No te wa i a Uenuku-rangi raua ko Tāne-herepi, ko Tāne-here-maro ka kitea e Roere e hoki ana ngā wairua i te moana, e tangi ana, e waiata ana etahi, e whakatangi koauau ana, e poroporoaki ana ki Maui-iti, Maui-nui.

A translation of this quote by ethnologist S. Percy Smith, edited by Jo'el Komene, reads:

> and in the times of Uenuku-rangi, Tane-herepi, and Tane-here-maro, Roere discovered that the spirits returned from there across the ocean, crying and singing, playing flutes [kōauau], and all the while bidding farewell to Maui-iti, Maui-nui.[169]

The kōauau is also mentioned in a story concerning the arrival of the Pukeātea-wainui and Arawa waka to Aotearoa. The story may be summarised as follows:

> Ruaeo's wife Whakaotirangi was abducted by Tamatekapua, who was kaihautū (captain) of the Arawa waka. In Te Rangikāheke's version of this tale, Ruaeo voyaged on the Pukeātea-wai-nui waka, which arrived in Aotearoa before the Te Arawa waka. When the Te Arawa waka arrived, he sat under its side and played his flute. This wakened Whakaotirangi, who recognised the sound as her husband's flute and went to him. He instructed her to tell Tamatekapua about a dream in which Ruaeo played flute and pūtōrino. Angered, Tamatekapua struck her, giving her cause to return to her husband. After a fight between the two men, won by Ruaeo, Ruaeo tells Whakaotirangi to go back to Tamatekapua, and that he will play the kōauau and pūtōrino for them to hear. In this instance, the sound of those instruments communicates heartbreak; a lament for a lost lover.[170]

There is no reason to doubt the veracity of these narratives, though it is possible that kōauau may have been invented after the arrival of the ancestors of Māori to

Aotearoa and interpolated retrospectively into these narratives; or that the term may originally have applied to instruments different to those we now recognise by that name.

Although there are no equivalent terms to kōauau (or pauawau) in tropical Polynesia, these flute names have linguistic ties to this region. As we saw in Chapter 1, the name kōauau may relate to te reo Māori onomatopoeic terms for the howling of dogs: auau, au and ao. Similar terms for the barking or howling of dogs are used in Rarotonga and the Tuamotus (aoa) and Ra`ivavae (`aoa). These terms reconstruct to Central Eastern Polynesian, with the protoform being *ao(a).[171]

There are possible physical connections as well as linguistic ones. Although kōauau are markedly shorter than the bamboo nose flutes observed in tropical Polynesia by the first Europeans to visit there, it is possible that short flutes were used in East Polynesia at the time the ancestors of Māori migrated to Aotearoa. Across Polynesia, materials other than bamboo are used to make flutes or whistles. These instruments are often played by children. Hollow bamboo substitutes include papaya leaf stalks, which are used to create flutes or whistles in the Cook Islands (pu`i nita or pū nīnītā).[172] Cook Islands nose flutes (vivo) can be made from hibiscus bark, or from hardwoods such as tamanu, tīra, pua or pūrau.[173] Making flutes from hollow or pithy materials, as well as hardwoods, is therefore not unique to Māori in the Oceanic context.

Knowledge that such materials could be used to make musical instruments likely informed flute-making experiments by the ancestors of Māori when they reached Aotearoa's shores. As we saw earlier, in addition to experimenting with newly available woods, Māori also experimented with materials not utilised for flute-making in tropical Oceania, including stone, bone, kelp and new wood varieties, which were not available in the tropics. The substitution of such materials for bamboo could have necessitated a shortening of flute length. As scholars Ernest Dodge and Edwin Brewster suggest, 'Possibly the absence of bamboo and the general shortness of the hollow portions of humori and tibiae, along with the difficulty of boring out wooden blocks without metal tools, accounts for the prevalence in New Zealand of so uncommonly short a pipe as the koauau.'[174] Dodge and Brewster assume that the ancestors of Māori would have brought knowledge of long bamboo flutes from the tropics to Aotearoa, despite the possibility that short flutes were also in use there at that time.

KŌAUAU *made from cow bone. Descendant of Hine Raukatauri; wind instrument. Measures 16.5cms long. Made by Brian Flintoff.* ♪

Instrument usages with tropical Polynesian origins

There are two other key usages of taonga pūoro that can be traced back to tropical Polynesia: altering weather conditions and communicating messages.

The Māori use of incantations in conjunction with instrumental performance to appeal to the gods, in order to bring about a change in the weather, certainly derives from tropical Polynesia. Māori oral histories note that tohunga took hue puruhau – large gourds that can produce sound by a person blowing across the top – on the great voyaging canoes and used them to call and calm winds. When the canoe was stalled through lack of wind or when food stores were running low, the gourd's stopper would be released to call a suitable wind.[175] One such puru (container), called Te Ipu Oraka Maumau, voyaged on the canoe of Taranaki. Taranaki historian Te Kāhui Kararehe referred to 'Ko te Ipu a Rakamaomao' when writing about this phenomenon.[176] Rakamaomao was the brother deity to Tāwhirimatea; they are gods of the winds.[177] Tūhoe knew of a hue puruhau called Ata ra te unuhia te puruhou a Rakamaomao (releasing winds for a specific purpose).[178]

A similar practice occurred in the Cook Islands. The lower section of a gourd was perforated with small holes blocked by wads of cloth; each hole represented a wind direction.

> Should the wind be unfavourable for a grand expedition, the chief priest began his incantation by withdrawing the plug from the aperture through which the unpropitious wind was supposed to blow. Rebuking this wind, he stopped up the hole, and advanced through all the intermediate apertures, moving plug by plug, until the desired wind-hole was reached. This was left open, as a gentle hint to the children of Raka that the priest wished the wind to blow steadily from that quarter.[179]

Similarly, when at sea, the leading tohunga would blow a pūtātara to pacify Tangaroa, calling on him to ease the storm and protect the voyagers in a ritual called whakamairetia. A basis for these instrument uses is found in a pūrākau about Māui catching the winds. His power to control the north, south and east winds (the province of the goddesses Hinerōriki, Hinearoaropari and Hinehauone, respectively) was stored in a large seashell. It had holes all around it. When he wanted to invoke any of the winds under his control, 'he only had to blow its horn and cover up the holes of the winds he did not want to blow'.[180]

As we have seen, Ngāti Porou used swung slats in conjunction with karakia to cause rain, and Moriori used a variety of sound-producing instruments for similar purposes. For example, the act of striking a particular tree or stone released the karakii (invocation) in much the same way as removing the stopper from hue puruhau.

Finally, the Māori practice of communicating verbally via musical instruments, particularly in connection with seduction (as discussed in Chapter 2), also has tropical Polynesian antecedents. Accounts from the Marquesas and Hawai`i, for example, refer to bamboo nose-flute players 'talking' to women they desired through their instruments.[181] Similarly, in the Cook Islands, 'young men were able to express love messages by means of its [bamboo flute] plaintive notes'.[182] Marquesans also used reed whistles to communicate speech.[183]

Echoes from Hawaiki

In charting the ancestral links many taonga pūoro Māori have with the islands of East Polynesia and even further across Te Moananui a Kiwa and back through time, we are hearing echoes from Hawaiki itself – echoes that reverberate through both he ira atua and he ira tangata, the spiritual and the human realms. Seeking out, testing and arranging these strands of knowledge about customary taonga pūoro re-weaves the whāriki that Hirini Melbourne spoke of, providing a platform from which today's taonga pūoro players and makers can breathe life into these cultural treasures.

In the Preface, I expressed the hope that collecting this information in a book might help Māori and Moriori reconnect with their specific instrument-playing traditions and assist them on their revival journey. As the hue puruhau may be unstoppered to release knowledge or encourage the winds to blow, I hope the kōrero in this book will support the further flow of breath and mauri from the taonga pūoro players of the past to those of the future.

HUE PURUHAU
made from gourd. Descendant of Hinepūtehue; wind instrument. Measures 16cms tall. Made by Jennifer Cattermole and David Cattermole. ♪

Appendix i: Names of instruments

The two Moriori and many Māori instrument names given here are drawn from historical accounts. I have included only the names of instruments that existed prior to European contact.[1] The whakapapa of these taonga is acknowledged, but I have (by and large) not organised the information below into their respective whānau, which I acknowledge goes against Māori taxonomies that emphasise the importance of whānaungatanga. Instead, the instruments are primarily grouped by instrument type, with different instruments that share the same names being grouped in close proximity. The reason for this is simply to make some of the naming similarities easier to see.

Spun or swung instruments: descendants of Tāwhirimātea

Swung slat
`gārara
hamumu ira ngā ngārara
mamae
pororohū
pūmamae
pūrēhua
te reo o te whaea
whēorooro

Spinning disc
hūkeke
kōrerohua
kōrorohū
pīrori
pīrorohū
porotiti
porotītiti
takawairore
takawairori
taraere
te reo o ngā atua
tōtara wera
wairore
wairori

Terms used for both swung slats and spinning discs
huhū
pūrerehua
pūrorohū
rangorango
tararī
tīrango
tūrorohū

Leaf whizzer
tīrango

Humming top
pōtaka
pōtaka hue
pōtaka huhū
pōtaka kukume
pōtaka tākiri
whitireia

Wailing top
hai ranaki i te mate

Swung (or thrown) ball
poi
poi awe
poi āwhiowhio
poi kōkau
poi waeroa

Flax poi
ipu kōrero
poi piu

Mouth percussion

Mouth bow
kū

Lamellaphone
rōria
tararī
tarau

Term used for both mouth bow and lamellaphone
kūkau

Tapping rods
kīkīporo
pakakau
pakure
pākuru
panguru whakatangi
panguru

Other percussion instruments

Bark wrapped in harakeke
pākuru

Clappers
ngutu rakiraki
māpara
pākēkē
pākōkō
tokerangi
tōkere

Gong
pahu
pahu kahatū
pahu pounamu
pakū
patō
rarī

Hand-held percussion
tumutumu
pako
kōhatu

Trumpets, leaf oboes and dog rattles

Shell trumpet
kāeaea
kākara
potipoti
pū
pūhāureroa
pūhoho
pūmoana
pūpakapaka
pūpūtara
pūtētere
pūtoto
pūwhāureroa
tūteure
tere (rē Moriori)

Long wooden trumpet
kāea
koea
pūtahoro
pūtara pūtara
putare
tātara
titi mataī
wharawhara

Flax oboe
kōrari
pūharakeke
pūkaea iwi
pūkihi
pūpatea

Term used for long wooden trumpet and flax oboe
pūkaea/pūkāea

Terms used for long wooden trumpet, flax oboe and conch trumpet
pūtara
pūtaratara
pūtātara
tētere

Dog rattle
kākara
patete
rore
tātara

Flutes: The descendants of Raukatauri

Short straight-bored flutes
kōau
kōauau
kōauau hoariri
korowhiti
pererau
pororua
pūtōrino
rehu
whio

Long straight-bored flutes
ororuarangi
pauawau (rē Moriori)
pōrutu
pū
pūmotomoto
pūtōrino
tūteure
whio

Short semi-closed bore flute with upturned end (piko)
ngunguru
nguru

Clay vessel flute
būdagidagi
ipūtangi
pūtangitangi
ukutangi

Marine shell played as flute
bubu
hoputea
whakai i tama/whakai o tama

Land snail shell played as flute
pūpū harakeke
pūpū korari
pūpūrangi
pūpū whakarongo tauā

see also names of gourd vessel flutes, below

Birdcallers / leaf whistles

harakeke papaki
karanga manu
karanga weka
kōauau pūtangitangi
korowhiti
pehe manu
pepe
pīpipi
pipi-karetu
poi āwhiowhio – *see section titled 'Swung (or thrown) ball' above*
rau
tarakimere
tuarōria
tuarōria hoki
whakahihī
whakapipi
whakataki
whio rōria

An instrument that can be blown as both a flute and a trumpet

hoho

pōrutu

pūhoho

pū hoho hō

pūtōrino

pūtōrino kakau rua

tōrino

Gourd instruments

Gourd trumpets

pūhue

rehu

Gourd rattles

hue puruwai

hue rarā

Nose-blown gourd vessel flutes

kōauau pongā ihu

kōauau whakatangi ihu

pongā ihu

pua

Mouth-blown gourd vessel flute

hue puruhau

Appendix 2: Names of plants, animals and other materials

This appendix lists the names of plants, animals and other materials customarily used to make taonga pūoro and other Polynesian instruments. Makers of contemporary taonga pūoro sometimes experiment with new materials; these have not been included.

PLANTS USED TO MAKE TAONGA PŪORO

Reo Māori name	Scientific (Latin) name	English name
aka		supple stems of climbing plants, aerial rootlets and small subterranean roots
aute	*Broussonetia papyrifera*	paper mulberry
harakeke	*Phormium tenax*	New Zealand flax
houama (hauama, houhou, puahou, whau, whauama, whauwhau)	*Entelea arborescens*	corkwood, cork tree
houhi (houhere, hoihere)	*Hoheria populnea*	lacebark
hue[1]	*Lagenaria siceraria*	bottle gourd
kahaka	*Astelia nervosa*	
kaiwhiria (kaiwhiri, porokaiwhiria, pōporokaiwhiri)	*Hedycarya arborea* or *Hedycaria dentata*	pigeonwood
karamū	*Coprosma robusta*	
kareao (pirita)	*Rhipogonum scandens*	supplejack
kiekie (kiakia, giegie)	*Freycinetia banksii*	
kōrari, koari	*Phormium tenax*	harakeke flower stem
kōtukutuku	*Fuchsia excorticata*	New Zealand tree fuchsia
māhoe (hinahina)	*Mellicytus ramiflorus*	whiteywood
maire rau ririki	*Nestegis lanceolata*	white maire
maire raunui	*Nestegis cunninghamii*	black maire

PLANTS USED TO MAKE TAONGA PŪORO *Cont'd*

Reo Māori name	Scientific (Latin) name	English name
mako (makomako)	*Aristotelia serrata* and *Aristotelia racemosa*	wineberry
mamaku	*Cyathea medullaris*	black treefern
mangemange	*Lygodium articulatum*	bushman's mattress
manono (kanono)	*Coprosma grandifolia* or *Coprosma lucida*	
mānuka	*Leptospermum ericoides* and *scoparium*	New Zealand teatree
mapara (kapara, kahika, kahikatea)	*Dacrycarpus dacrydioides*	heartwood white pine
mātā	*Austroderia* spp., *Carex diandra* and *Gahnia lacera*	young toetoe, sedge and cutty grass
mataī	*Prumnopitys taxifolia*	black pine
mikoikoi	*Libertia ixioides* and *grandiflora*	New Zealand iris
neinei	*Dracophyllum latifolium*	spiderwood
ngaio	*Myoporum laetum*	mousehole tree
pāpā (whangewhange, hangehange)	*Geniostoma rupestre* var. *ligustrifolium*	privet leaf
pāpāuma (kāpuka)	*Griselinia littoralis*	broadleaf
patete (patē, patatē)	*Schefflera digitata*	seven-finger, umbrella tree
pēpepe (tūrutu)	*Dianella nigra* and *intermedia*	inkberry
pīngao (pīkao)	*Ficinia spiralis*	sand sedge
pōhuehue generic term for climbing or trailing plants e.g. *Calystegia sepium*, *Clematis* spp., *Muehlenbeckia complexa*, *Passiflora tetrandra*		
poroporo (pōporo)	*Solanum aviculare*	nightshade
pūnui (būnui)	*Stilbocarpa lyallii* spp.	Stewart Island rhubarb
ramarama	*Lophomyrtus bullata*	
raupō	*Typha orientalis*	bulrush
rimurapa	*D'Urvillaea* spp.	bull kelp

PLANTS USED TO MAKE TAONGA PŪORO *Cont'd*

Reo Māori name	Scientific (Latin) name	English name
rimurimu	*Macrocystis pyrifera* or *Laminariales lessoniaceae*	bladder kelp
taraire	*Beilschmiedia taraire*	
tarata	*Pittosporum eugenioides*	lemonwood
tataki (tatangi)	*Gahnia lacera*	cutty grass
taupata	*Coprosma repens*	mirror bush, New Zealand laurel
tī kōuka	*Cordyline australis*	cabbage tree
tītoki	*Alectryon excelsum*	
tōtara	*Podocarpus totara*	
tunguru (tanguru)	*Olearia furfuracea* and *Olearia albida*	
tutu (tūpākihi)[2]	*Coriaria arborea*	
upokotangata	*Mariscus ustulatus*	

TROPICAL OCEANIC SPECIES USED TO MAKE INSTRUMENTS

Scientific (Latin) name	English or indigenous name	Place of origin
Aleurites moluccana	candlenut tree	
Calophyllum inophyllum	kamani	Hawai`i
Fagraea berteroana	pua	Cook Islands
Hibiscus tiliaceus	fau	Marquesas
Hibiscus tiliaceus	hau	Hawai`i
Hibiscus tiliaceus	purau	Cook Islands
Melia azedarach	tīra	Cook Islands
Pandanus odorus/latifolius	pandanus	
Pandanus tectorius	lau	Hawai`i
Scaevola sericea	ngahu	Manihiki

HARDWOODS USED TO MAKE TAONGA PŪORO

	matai	tōtara	maire	mānuka	tara	tītoki	tunguru/ tanguru	kareao/ pirita	mamaku	māpara/ kahikatea	ramarama
kōauau	•	•	•								
kū	•										
māpara										•	
pahu	•	•	•								
pākuru	•		•		•		•			•	
porotiti	•									•	
pōrutu	•									•	
pōtaka	•									•	•
pūkaea	•	•									
pūrerehua[3]	•									•	
pūtōrino	•	•									
rōria	•		•	•		•		•	•		
whio	•										

SOFT/PITHY WOODS USED TO MAKE TAONGA PŪORO

	porokaiwhiria/ kaiwhiria	neinei	tutu/tupakihi	poroporo	whau/houama	māhoe	kōtukutuku/ kahikātoa	mako	ngaio	kōrari
kōauau	•	•	•	•	•	•	•	•	•	•
pahu	•									
pākuru	•									
porotiti	•									
pōrutu	•	•	•	•	•		•			
pūkaea			•							
pūrerehua	•									
pūtātara	•									
whio			•							

SHELLS USED TO MAKE INSTRUMENTS

Reo Māori name	Scientific (Latin) name	English name
bubu (pūpū)	*Lunella smaragda* and *Zediloma aethiops*	
hoputea		whelk
kākahi	*Hyridella menziesi*	freshwater mussel
kākara nui	*Penion sulcacatus*	northern siphon whelk
pāua	*Haliotis iris*	rainbow abalone
pūpū (pūtātara)	*Charonia lampas rubicunda*, *Charonia lampas capax*, *Charonia capax euclioides*, *Septa rubicunda*, *Septa tritonis* and *Murex tritonis*	
pūpū harakeke (pūpū korari, whakaronga taua)	*Placostylus hongii*, *Placostylus ambagiosus*	flax snail
pūpūrangi	*Paryphanta busbyi* and *watti*	kauri snail
pupu rore (puhauriroa, takapu, tikoaka, uere)	*Alcithoe arabica*	Arabic volute
takai[4]	*Struthiolaria papulosa*, *Struthiolaria vermis*	ostrich-foot shell
toitoi (karikawa)	*Cookia sulcata* (also *Petroica toitoi* and *Finschia novaeseelandiae*)	Cook's turban shell
tuangi	*Austrovenus stutchburyi*	Cockle
	Cabestana spengleri	Spengler's trumpet
	Triton australis, *Charonia tritonis*[5]	giant triton
	Turritella communis	common tower shell
	Xenophalium pyrum	helmet shell

OTHER SPECIES USED TO MAKE INSTRUMENTS

Reo Māori name	Scientific (Latin) name	English name
kekeno	*Arctocephalus forsteri*	fur seal
kōura	*Sagmariasus verreauxi*	packhorse crayfish
ngā tangata	*Homo sapiens*	people
moa	*Dinoris* spp.	
pāngurunguru	*Macronectes* spp.	giant petrel
parāoa[6]	*Physeter macrocephalus*	sperm whale
toroa	*Diomedea* spp.	albatross, mollymawk
upokohue	*Globicephala melaena*	pilot whale

SPECIES THAT PROVIDED MATERIALS USED TO DECORATE INSTRUMENTS

Reo Māori name	Scientific (Latin) name	English name
huia	*Heteralocha acutirostris*	
kākāpō	*Strigops habroptilus*	owl parrot
kūri[7]	*Canis familiaris*	dog
ngā tangata	*Homo sapiens*	people
pūkeko	*Porphyrio melanotus*	Australasian swamphen

STONE AND EARTH USED TO MAKE INSTRUMENTS

Reo Māori name	English name
	ignimbrite
	ironstone
pakohe	argillite
pounamu	nephrite
	pumice
	rhyolite
	sandstone
	steatite/soapstone
	tuff
uku	clay

Glossary

The words defined in this glossary are kupu reo Māori unless specified otherwise. For the names of taonga puōro and the materials used to make and decorate them, see Appendices 1 and 2.

āhua shape
Aituā the god of misfortune and death
`akatangi ko`e (Aitutaki) bamboo mouth flute
ake, akeake the shrub or small tree *Dodonaea viscosa*
akepiro, akepiri the tree-daisy *Olearia furfuracea*
amokura red-tailed tropicbird, *Phaeton rubricauda*
apa the messengers and attendants of the whatukura
are karioi (Mangaia) house of entertainment
ariā visible manifestations of gods or deities
aruhe, rarauhe bracken fern, *Pteridium aquilinum* var. *Esculentum*; hanging spleenwort, *Asplenium flaccidum*
ātahu love charm, spell
atua deities and other beings responsible for originating and regulating aspects of the natural world
atua kahu the spirits of stillborn children
awa river
etchu (rē Moriori) atua, patron spirit
hamano a person's highest, most pure soul
hapū subtribe; pregnant
harakeke New Zealand flax, *Phormium tenax*
harakeke papaki flax clapper
hau breath
he ira atua the spiritual realm, the world of the gods
he ira tangata the everyday realm, the world of the people
Hineiterepo the swamp maiden
Hinemoana the goddess/mother of shellfish
Hinenuitepō the goddess of night and death
Hinerauāmoa the goddess of anything pertaining to women
Hineteiwaiwa the goddess of women's arts
hinu fat
hoe paddle
huatapu a fruiting or flowering plant
`ili`ili (Hawai`i) pebble castanet
ihi power
Io supreme deity
ipu vessel
ipu kōrari person who is a holder of stories; also a name for poi
irirangi, rangirua spirit voices
iwi tribe, tribal; bone
iwitanga tribal culture
kahikātoa red mānuka, teatree, *Leptospermum scoparium*
kaikanikani dancer
kaitiaki guardian
kaiwhakatautau ceremonial mourner
kākā the forest parrot *Nestor meridionalis*

kakariki, kākāriki parakeet, *Cyanoramphus* spp.
kāla`au, kālā`au (Hawai`i) to strike wood
karaka New Zealand laurel, *Corynocarpus laevigatus*
karakia invocation
karakii (rē Moriori) invocation
karoro cockle or ribbed Venus shell, *Protothaca crassicosta*; black-backed gull, *Larus dominicanus*
kaumātua elder
kauwae jawbone
kauae runga upper jawbone; *see also* Te Kauae Runga
kauri the large coniferous forest tree *Agathis australis*
kete basket
kihikihi, tarakihi cicada
kiore Polynesian or Pacific rat, *Rattus exulans*
kiwi the flightless bird of the *Apteryx* spp.
kōhatu stone
koiro conger eel, *Gnathophis umbrellabia*
kōiwi bone
kōrari flax-flower stems; also the name of a flax oboe made from that material
kōrero talk, discussion, speech, story
kōrero kākāriki recitation of learning
kōwhai the yellow-flowered tree *Sophora tetraptera*, *Sophora microphylla*
kuku mamau wrestling
kūmara sweet potato, *Ipomoea batatas*
kūpe`e niho `īlio (Hawai`i) leg ornament
kupu word
kurī dog
lau (Hawai`i) leaves
lau hala (Hawai`i) juggled balls
mahi rongoā kōhatu healing with stones
mako wineberry (tree)
mākutu witchcraft
māngai mouth
manu birds
manukorihi ritual for calling down birds to sanctify a games gathering
māpara resinous heartwood of kahikatea or rimu; clappers
mararī, marari butterfish, *Coridodax pullus*
matakite foretelling
mātātā fernbird
mātauranga knowledge
maunga mountain
mauri lifeforce spark or energy
mauri tau balanced lifeforce
māwhai ambush vine, *Sicyos mawhai*
miheke oro (rē Moriori) traditional musical instruments
miromiro white-breasted North Island tit, *Petroica toitoi*
moana sea
moki the fish *Latris ciliaris*
mokimoki fragrant fern, *Microsorum scandens*
mōteatea chant, song; grief
motu island, country; used to mean the land of Aotearoa
muka processed fibre of harakeke
ngā kete o te wānanga the three baskets of knowledge
ngā rangi tuhaha the heavens
ngā tākaro sports games
ngārara, `gārara lizard, reptile; insect
noa non-sacred
niho parāoa sperm whale teeth
oriori lullaby
oriori pōtaka songs of lamentation and grief
oro rumble; sound
pā village, fortified settlement; strike, be struck; act in concert
Pakoti the mother of harakeke
**pala`ie** (Hawai`i) loop and ball game
pao two-lined epigrammatic songs
Papatūānuku Earth Mother
pārarā (Rarotonga) rattle
pātere chant
patupaiarehe type of supernatural being

pia flax gum
pirihau climbing plant or creeper
pōhutukawa New Zealand Christmas tree, *Metrosideros excelsa*
pokakā (Hawai`i) spinning disc
poi swung ball; lump; to bewitch; to toss up and down
poi (Tuamotus) to toss up and down, as in waves in a storm
pū a Raukatauri Raukatauri's flute
poroporoaki farewell
pua (Rarotonga) large tree with fine-grained timber
pua (Mangaia) a variety of tree
pu`i kikau (Cook Islands) coconut leaf oboe
puke pubic mound
pūmotomoto gateway
pūrākau/pakiwaitara legend, story
pūrau (Penrhyn) hibiscus, *Hibiscus tiliaceus*
pūriri the tree *Vitex lucens*
pūtangitangi paradise shelduck, *Tadorna variegata*
rangatira chief, leader
rangi tune; sky; heavens
rangi poi poi tune
rangi tuhaha heavens
Ranginui, Rangi Sky Father
rangirua, irirangi spirit voices
Rarohenga the underworld
Raukatauri goddess of flutes
rohe tribal area
rongo song
rongoā healing
Rongomātāne god of cultivated plants and peace
rua hole, cavities; two
ruru owls
tā moko tattoo
tafua (Tonga) rolled mat instrument
Tāne the god of the forests
Tangaroa the god of the ocean
tangi cry
taonga treasure, prized object
taonga pūoro Māori musical instruments; 'sounding treasures'/'treasured sounds'
tapu sacred
tarakihi, kihikihi cicada
taumata platform
Tāwhitimātea the god of winds and breath
tētere flax oboe
Te Aka the vine of the heavens
Te Ao Mārama the world of light
Te Ika a Māui the fish of Māui; the North Island of Aotearoa
Te Kauae Runga the highest school of learning; *see also* kauae runga
te kōkiri a te tāne male trumpet voice
Te Kore the realm of unlimited potentiality
te mea whakatehe rolling back the foreskin of a penis
te reo o te whaea the voice of the mother
Te Tau Ihu o te Waka a Māui the prow of the waka of Māui; the northern South Island
te Wai o Rongo, te Wai o Rongomai the waters of Rongo
Te Wai Pounamu the waters of greenstone; the South Island of Aotearoa
te waiata a te wāhine female flute voice
te whare o aituā vagina; house of misfortune
tīenga ornately patterned mat
tīra (Cook Islands) a variety of tree
togo (Sāmoa) mangrove
tohe, tohetohe tonsil, inserted wooden peg
tohu sign
tohunga expert in spiritual or material knowledge; priest; healer
tohunga rongoā expert healers
tohutō macron
tōrino, rua tōrino hole dug at the tūāhu
tūāhu a sacred place used for divination and other rites
tulāfale (Sāmoa) talking chief, orator
tūngoungou cocoon
tūpuna ancestors
tūpāpaku deceased person, dead body

tūtangatakino spiritual reptile that causes illness and harm
tutu rākau tutu wood
tūwiri cord drill
upokohue long-finned pilot whale
utu revenge, reparation, repayment, the restoration of balance; reciprocity
waha mouth
wahine hapū pregnant woman
waiata koroua traditional chants
wairua soul or spirit
wānanga knowledge, learning
wehi awe, fear, respect
weka woodhen, *Gallirallus australis*
wenewene fingerholes
whakanoa freer of tapu
whakapapa ancestry
whakataukī proverb
whānau pani bereaved family
whare kura house of learning; the first of three schools of sacred knowledge
whare pūrākau house of stories
whāriki woven mat
whatukura male messenger of Io, the supreme deity
whio blue duck, *Hymenolaimus malacorhynchos*
whītau dressed harakeke fibre
whiti verse

Notes

ABBREVIATIONS

JPS *Journal of the Polynesian Society*
JRSNZ *Journal of the Royal Society of New Zealand*
PNAS *Proceedings of the National Academy of the Sciences*
POLLEX POLLEX-Online: The Polynesian Lexicon Project Online
TPNZI *Transactions and Proceedings of the New Zealand Institute*

PREFACE

1. Hirini Melbourne, *Toiapiapi: He huinga o ngā kura puoro a te Māori* (Wellington: Shearwater, 2016); Richard Nunns & Allan Thomas, *Te Ara Puoro: A journey into the world of Māori music* (Nelson: Craig Potton Publishing, 2014), p. 12.
2. Melbourne, *Toiapiapi*, p. 24; Rachael Ka`ai-Mahuta, Tania Ka`ai & John Moorfield (eds), *Kia Rōnaki: The Māori performing arts* (Auckland: Pearson, 2013), pp. xiv–xv.
3. Mark Evans, 'The Silent Echoes of Chatham Island', in *Refereed Papers from the 2nd International Small Island Cultures Conference, held at the Museum Theatre, Norfolk Island Museum, Kingston, Norfolk Island, 9–13 February 2006*, ed. Henry Johnson (Sydney: SICRI, 2006), pp. 46–53.
4. Ka`ai-Mahuta, Ka`ai & Moorfield (eds), *Kia Rōnaki*, p. 206.

INTRODUCTION: WEAVING NEW STRANDS IN THE WHĀRIKI OF KNOWLEDGE

1. 'Traditional' is a problematic term to use due to its different definitions. Here it refers specifically to Māori and Moriori musical instruments that existed in pre-European colonisation times. This is not to deny that contemporary instruments (such as guitars) cannot also be considered 'traditional' according to various meanings of that term.
2. Te Rangi Hīroa [Sir Peter Buck], *The Coming of the Maori* (Wellington: Whitcombe & Tombs; Maori Purposes Fund Board, 1966); Mervyn McLean, 'A chronological and geographical sequence of Maori flute scales', *Man*, vol. 17, 1982, pp. 123–57; Mervyn McLean, *Maori Music* (Auckland: Auckland University Press, 1996).
3. Nigel Prickett, *Maori Origins: From Asia to Aotearoa* (Auckland: David Bateman & Auckland Museum, 2001), p. 3; Te Rangi Hīroa [Sir Peter Buck], *Vikings of the Sunrise* (Wellington: New Zealand Electronic Text Centre, 2007), https://nzetc.victoria.ac.nz/tm/scholarly/tei-BucViki.html, p. 23. The extent to which Moriori arrival histories may have been influenced by those of Taranaki Māori before they were recorded remains unclear, and this is a factor to be mindful of in assessing this information.
4. Margaret Orbell, *The Illustrated Encyclopedia of Māori Myth and Legend* (Christchurch: Canterbury University Press, 1995), pp. 51–52.
5. James Herries Beattie, *Traditional Lifeways of the Southern Maori*, ed. Atholl Anderson (Dunedin: Otago University Press in association with Otago Museum, 1994), pp. 445–47, 569; Te Rangi Hīroa, *Coming of the Maori*, pp. 14, 16; Elsdon Best, *Forest Lore of the Maori* (Wellington: E.C. Keating, 1977), pp. 85–86; Bruce Biggs, 'The languages of Polynesia', *Current Trends*

in Linguistics, vol. 8, 1971, p. 498; Ross Clark, 'Moriori and Maori: The linguistic evidence', in *The Origins of the First New Zealanders*, ed. Douglas G. Sutton (Auckland: Auckland University Press, 1994), p. 132; Ray Harlow, 'Regional variation in Maori', *New Zealand Journal of Archaeology*, vol. 1, 1979, pp. 123–38; B.F. Leach et al., 'The origin of prehistoric obsidian artefacts from the Chatham and Kermadec Islands', *New Zealand Journal of Archaeology*, vol. 8, 1986, pp. 143–70; Elizabeth Matisoo-Smith, 'More than just old bones: On the contribition of biological anthropology to New Zealand archaeology', in *Change Through Time: 50 years of New Zealand archaeology*, eds Louise Furey & Simon Holdaway (Auckland: New Zealand Archaeological Association, 2004), p. 245; Elizabeth Matisoo-Smith et al., 'Patterns of prehistoric human mobility indicated by mitochondrial DNA from the Pacific rat', *PNAS*, vol. 95, no. 25, 1998; 'Prehistoric mobility in Polynesia: MtDNA variation in *Rattus exulans* from the Chatham and Kermadec Islands', *Asian Perspectives*, vol. 38, no. 2, 1999, pp. 193–94; Alexander Shand, 'The early history of the Morioris', *TPNZI*, vol. 37, 1904, pp. 145, 148; 1911, pp. 101, 117, 184, 189; Henry D. Skinner, *The Morioris of Chatham Islands* (Honolulu: Bishop Museum, 1923); James West Stack, *South Island Maoris: A sketch of their history and legendary lore* (Christchurch; Wellington; Dunedin; Auckland: Whitcombe & Tombs, 1898), p. 29; W.T.L. Travers, 'Notes of the traditions and manners and customs of the Mori-oris', *TPNZI*, vol. 9, 1876, p. 18; Muru Walters, *An Examination of the Literary Evidence for the Existence of Discrete Groups of Moriori in the Chatham Islands in the 19th Century* (Dunedin: Dept of Anthropology, University of Otago, 1977), p. 18; H.W. Williams, 'Some notes on the language of the Chatham Islands', *TPNZI*, vol. 51, 1919, p. 415; Herbert W. Williams, 'The Maruiwi myth', *JPS*, vol. 46, no. 183, 1937, p. 116.

6. Malee Buranarugsa & Foss Leach, 'Coordinate geometry of Moriori crania', *Man and Culture in Oceania*, vol. 9, 1993, pp. 38–39; *contra* Geoffrey Irwin, *The Prehistoric Exploration and Colonisation of the Pacific* (Cambridge; New York: Cambridge University Press, 1992), p. 215; Rhys Richards, *Moriori: Origins, lifestyles and language* (Wellington: Paremata Press, 2018), p. 27; S. Percy Smith, *Hawaiki: The original home of the Maori, with a sketch of Polynesian history* (Christchurch: Whitcombe & Tombs, 1904), p. 44; J.W. Williams, 'Notes on the Chatham Islands', *Journal of the Anthropological Institute of Great Britain and Ireland*, vol. 27, 1898, p. 345.
7. Rhys Richards, *Manu Moriori: Human and bird carvings on live kopi trees on the Chatham Islands* (Wellington: Paremata Press, 2007), p. 57.
8. Helen Leach, *1,000 Years of Gardening in New Zealand* (Wellington: A.H. & A.W. Reed, 1984), p. 11; see also Atholl Anderson, *The First Migration: Māori origins 3000BC–AD1450* (Wellington: Bridget Williams Books, 2016), pp. 99–101.
9. Teone Taare Tīkao, in Beattie, *Traditional Lifeways*, pp. 51–52.
10. Te Rangi Hīroa, *Coming of the Maori*, p. 37; Orbell, *Illustrated Encyclopedia*, p. 150; Melenaite Taumoefolau, 'From *Sau `Ariki to Hawaiki', *JPS*, vol. 105, no. 4, 1996, pp. 394–96; Tīkao, in Beattie, *Traditional Lifeways*, p. 51; Williams, 'Notes on the language', p. 415; Williams, 'The Maruiwi myth', *JPS*, vol. 46, no. 183, 1937, pp. 109–16.
11. Douglas Sutton, 'Polynesian coastal hunters in the subantarctic zone: A case for the recognition of convergent cultural adaptation' (PhD thesis, University of Otago, 1979), p. 44.

CHAPTER 1: TAONGA PŪORO NAMES AND WHAKAPAPA

1. H.W. Williams, *Dictionary of the Maori Language* (Wellington: Government Printer, 1971).
2. Richard Nunns & Allan Thomas, *Te Ara Puoro: A journey into the world of Māori music* (Nelson: Craig Potton Publishing, 2014), p. 15.
3. Sebastian Lowe & Alistair Fraser, 'Connecting with inner landscapes: Taonga pūoro, musical improvisation and exploring acoustic Aotearoa/New Zealand', *Journal of New Zealand and Pacific Studies*, vol. 6, no. 1, 2008, p. 7. The Māori term taonga pūoro came into widespread use from the early 1980s and miheke oro – the Moriori equivalent – was coined by musician Ajay Peni and language specialist Kiwa Hammond in 2019. If there was an umbrella term for Moriori musical instruments that existed in pre-contact times, it was not recorded.
4. Nunns & Thomas, *Ara Puoro*, p. 69.
5. Samuel Timoti Robinson, *Tohunga: The revival* (Auckland: Reed Books, 2005), p. 45.
6. Elsdon Best, *Games and Pastimes of the Maori* (Wellington: Whitcombe & Tombs, 1925), p. 163. Poi work along the same lines. In Taranaki, poi that have a diamond design on the bottom are called te karu ō te atua (the eye of god) poi, and are used to send incantations to the gods. The design is intended to let the gods see that the incantations are coming. If used correctly, the incantation is more likely to be successful (Ngāmoni Huata, *The Rhythm and Life of Poi* (Auckland: HarperCollins, 2000), p. 32). The visual effect of this design is best displayed when the poi is played slowly and has a long string (Karyn Paringatai, 'Poia mai taku poi: Unearthing the knowledge of the past' (MA thesis, University of Otago, 2004), pp. 86, 88, 90). Poi manu are poi used to keep time during the recitation of karakia. In South Taranaki, poi matakite are prophetical poi songs (Kopeka Hawe, in McLean, *Maori Music* (Auckland: Auckland University Press, 1996), p. 138; Paringatai, 'Poia mai', pp. 156, 158, 162–63, 166).
7. Brian Flintoff, *Taonga Pūoro: Singing treasures* (Nelson: Craig Potton, 2004), p. 12. If puoro (singing) rather than pūoro is used to refer to musical instruments, then there is a direct connection between this term and the act of the atua singing the world into existence. It is important to note that te atua translates as 'the god' (singular) rather than 'the gods' (plural), which is a significant mistranslation in Flintoff's text. Tiramōrehu converted to the Wesleyan faith in 1843 (Evison, n.d.), so the spiritual beliefs expressed here are almost certainly influenced by his conversion to Christianity.
8. See Nunns & Thomas, *Ara Puoro*; Robinson, *Tohunga*, pp. 243–48.
9. Arapeta Awatere, in McLean, *Maori Music*, p. 235. Interestingly, in peacetime in Tahiti, ʻOro is the god of fine arts; he is also founder of the Arioi (or Areoi) cult, whose members were talented performers.
10. McLean, *Maori Music*, pp. 235, 376.
11. Rangiiria Hedley, in Harold Atwood Anderson, 'A confluence of streams: Music and identity in Aotearoa/New Zealand', (PhD diss., University of Maryland, 2008), p. 200.
12. As with Māori, the world of musical instruments for Moriori was inseparable from their deities (etchu) and, by extension, particular elements of the natural world. It is almost certain that Moriori regarded their instruments as being profoundly sacred, and as having esoteric power.
13. Flintoff, *Taonga Pūoro*; Huata, *Rhythm and Life*, pp. 32–33; Jerome Kavanagh, 'Hue', in *Introduction to Taonga Puoro*, video, SOUNZ Centre for NZ Music, www.youtube.com/watch?v=DNCVspOv2Y4&t=2s; Jo'el Komene, 'Kōauau auē, e auau tō au e: The kōauau in Te Ao Māori' (MA thesis, University of Waikato, 2009), pp. 171, 174; Toby Mills, 'Taonga pūoro: A gift of sound',

in *Toi Puoro: Taonga puoro* (Wellington: Tawera Productions, 1994–99), p. 6; Paringatai, 'Poia mai', pp. 14–15; Rangiiria Hedley, in 'Papatuanuku – earth rhythms', https://otago.etv.org.nz/tv/vod/view/30122; Ruby Solly, 'How to make an ukutangi', www.kauaeraro.com/matauranga/ukutangi; Awhina Tamarapa & Ariana Tikao, 'Mai te Pō, ki te Ao: The reclamation of taonga puoro as a living treasure', in *Searches for Tradition: Essays on New Zealand music, past and present*, eds Michael Brown & Samantha Owens (Wellington: Victoria University Press, 2017), p. 140.

14. Atwood Anderson, 'Confluence', p. 200; Augustus Hamilton, *Maori Art* (London: Holland Press, 1972), p. 374; Nunns & Thomas, *Ara Puoro*, pp. 96, 100, 136. Taonga pūoro practitioner Jerome Kavanagh (Mōkai Pātea, Ngāti Maniapoto, Ngāti Kahungunu) uses pūrerehua to clear the path prior to cleansing himself in the ocean, or to clear the air and reset things when an indoor meeting has become heated. See Jerome Kavanagh, 'Porotiti and pūrerehua', *Introduction to Taonga Puoro*, video, SOUNZ Centre for NZ Music, www.youtube.com/watch?v=LSdXLyWYgQg
15. Elsdon Best, *The Maori*, vol. 1 (Wellington: Polynesian Society, 1924), pp. 99–102.
16. Robinson, *Tohunga*, pp. 163–64.
17. Flintoff, *Taonga Pūoro*, p. 6; Hirini Melbourne, *Toiapiapi: He huinga o ngā kura puoro a te Māori* (Wellington: Shearwater, 2016), p. 55; Robinson, *Tohunga*, p. 153.
18. Elsdon Best, 'Notes on Maori musical instruments' (unpublished manuscript held in Alexander Turnbull Library, Wellington, MS-Papers-0072-19B, 1923), p. 34; David Miller, 'The insect people of the Maori', *JPS*, vol. 61, 1952, pp. 28, 40; Bradford Haami, 'Ngārara – reptiles', Te Ara – the Encyclopedia of New Zealand, https://teara.govt.nz/en/ngarara-reptiles/print
19. See H.T. Whatahoro (trans. S. Percy Smith), 'The lore of the whare-wānanga: Introduction', www.sacred-texts.com/pac/lww/lww0.htm
20. Nunns & Thomas, *Ara Puoro*, pp. 51, 55, 65.
21. Robinson, *Tohunga*, p. 153.
22. Richard Nunns, 'Taonga puoro and Peka Mākarini's bugle', in *Kia Rōnaki: The Māori performing arts*, eds Rachael Ka`ai-Mahuta, Tania Ka`ai & John Moorfield (Auckland: Pearson, 2013), p. 189.
23. Harko Brown, *Ngā Taonga Tākaro II: The matrix* (Mt Maunganui: Physical Education New Zealand, 2016), pp. 34–35.
24. 'Rua-torino' was also the name of a mākutu rite whereby a victim's soul was enticed to eat an offering while they were asleep, thereby destroying their soul and leading to physical death a few days afterwards (Robinson, *Tohunga*, p. 261). There is no evidence that the instrument tōrino was used in this rite, though that is unsurprising given the sacred nature of this practice.
25. Nunns & Thomas, *Ara Puoro*, p. 32.
26. Te Rangi Hīroa [Sir Peter Buck], *The Coming of the Maori* (Wellington: Whitcombe & Tombs; Maori Purposes Fund Board, 1966), p. 466.
27. Johannes C. Andersen, *Maori Music with its Polynesian Background* (New Plymouth: Thomas Avery & Sons, 1934), pp. 29–30; James Herries Beattie, *Traditional Lifeways of the Southern Maori*, ed. Atholl Anderson (Dunedin: Otago University Press in association with Otago Museum, 1994), pp. 135, 259, 343–44; Elsdon Best, *Forest Lore of the Maori* (Wellington: E.C. Keating, 1977), pp. 308–16; Komene, 'Kōauau', p. 111.
28. Brown, *Tākaro II*, p. 127; Huata, *Rhythm and Life*, pp. 32–33; Johnston, cited in Paringatai, 'Poia mai', p. 131.
29. Johannes C. Andersen, *Maori Life in Ao-tea* (Christchurch: Whitcombe & Tombs, 1907), p. 367.
30. Mrs Teihana, in Huata, *Rhythm and Life*, pp. 37–38.

31. McLean, *Maori Music*, p. 126.
32. Te Rangi Hīroa, *Coming of the Maori*, p. 364.
33. Kopeka Hawe, in McLean, *Maori Music*, p. 138; Paringatai, 'Poia mai', pp. 156, 158, 162–63, 166.
34. Elsdon Best, 'The diversions of the whare tapere: Some account of the various games, amusements, and trials of skill practised by the Maori in former times', *TPNZI*, vol. 34, 1901, pp. 42–43.
35. The words of this karakia are given by Best, *Games and Pastimes*, p. 163.
36. Robinson, *Tohunga*, p. 166.
37. Flintoff, *Taonga Pūoro*, p. 61.
38. Tuta Nihoniho, in Best, *Games and Pastimes*, p. 163; Nunns & Thomas, *Ara Puoro*, pp. 100, 133.
39. Margaret Orbell, *A Concise Encyclopedia of Māori Myth and Legend* (Christchurch: Canterbury University Press, 1998), pp. 119–20.
40. Hamilton, *Maori Art*, p. 374.
41. Robinson, *Tohunga*, p. 153; see also Kavanagh, 'Porotiti and pūrerehua'.
42. Jill Hindle, 'Renaissance in Birdland: The preservation of traditional Maori instrumental music', in Richard Nunns (1993–98), 'Research papers' (unpublished manuscript held in Alexander Turnbull Library, Wellington, MS-Papers-8544-33, 1996), p. 14.
43. Solly, 'How to make an ukutangi'.
44. Komene, 'Kōauau', pp. 58, 112, 153.
45. For histories of particular kōauau hoariri, see Andersen, *Maori Music*, pp. 239–42; Keith Kennedy, 'The ancient four-note musical scale of the Maoris', *Mankind*, vol. 1, p. 13; Komene, 'Kōauau', pp. 111–14, 146–48; Richard Moyle, *The Sounds of Oceania: An illustrated catalogue of the sound producing instruments of Oceania in the Auckland Institute and Museum* (Auckland: Auckland Institute and Museum, 1989), p. 12; Paul Tapsell, *Māori Treasures of New Zealand* (Auckland: David Bateman, 2006), pp. 47–50, 96–100, 102.
46. James Cowan, 'The Maori signal gong: Stories of the wooden pahu' (unpublished manuscript held in the Alexander Turnbull Library, Wellington, MS papers 11310-187, n.d.), p. 1; Best, *Games and Pastimes*, pp. 154, 160, 165.
47. McLean, *Maori Music*, p. 179; Nunns & Thomas, *Ara Puoro*, p. 94. The second term is alternatively spelt putura putura: see Sachs in Sibyl Marcuse, *Musical Instruments: A comprehensive dictionary* (New York: W.W. Norton, 1975), p. 425.
48. Another term that likely refers to a trumpet's signalling function is putare. This instrument was made from tutu, and its entire length was bound with harakeke root – the binding toward one end forming the bell mouth (Potts, cited in Best, *Games and Pastimes*, p. 155). Putare is not in Williams' dictionary; though tare refers to 'send', which is appropriate for this instrument.
49. Best, *Games and Pastimes*, p. 160. Koea means 'brilliant, beautiful', which is appropriate for the long wooden trumpet the name pertains to, but is not perhaps as apt as kāeaea or kāea.
50. Atwood Anderson, 'Confluence', p. 220, defines pūkāea as 'the sound of news'.
51. Nunns & Thomas, *Ara Puoro*, p. 143.
52. Best, 'Notes', p. 26; Cowan, 'Signal gong', p. 1; Jill Hindle, 'Renaissance in Birdland: The preservation of traditional Maori instrumental music' (unpublished manuscript held in the Alexander Turnbull Library, Wellington, MS-Papers-8544-33, 1996), p. 15; M. Martin, 'Maori music' (unpublished manuscript held in the Alexander Turnbull Library, Wellington, MS-Papers-8544-32, n.d.), p. 159; Alfred K. Newman, 'On the musical notes and other features of the long Maori trumpet', *TPNZI*, vol. 38, 1905, p. 136.
53. Tregear, cited in Newman, 'Musical notes', p. 136.

54. In te reo Māori, tumutumu means 'stump, post'; tumu is a term also used for 'quarter-staff, pike, pole, stake'. While these meanings could refer to the shape or perhaps material of the instrument, it is more likely that its name is connected to its use. Kōauau could also be 'used to help memorise knowledge retained in oral tradition': Jeremy Cloake, 'Taonga puoro', www.jeremycloake.com/taonga-puoro
55. Best, *The Maori*, vol. 1, p. 102.
56. McLean, *Maori Music*, p. 176.
57. Rere (part of the term pūrerehua) can also have the same meaning as pī.
58. Kōwhai Ngutu Kākā, in Thomas McDonnell, *A Maori History: Being a native account of the Pakeha–Maori wars in New Zealand* (Auckland: H. Brett, 1887), p. 498.
59. According to other narratives, Tūmatauenga (or Tāne or Tiki/Tikiauaha) were responsible for creating the first human being: a man – in some versions called Tiki (or Tikiauaha) – who was progenitor of the human race (Best, *The Maori*, vol. 1, p. 121; Te Rangi Hīroa, *Coming of the Maori*, pp. 451–52).
60. Karanga weka may or may not be a name used historically, though it aptly describes the voice of a birdcaller held in the British Museum (Flintoff, *Taonga Pūoro*, p. 40).
61. At Kāwhia in the Tainui rohe, korowhiti is the name given to the large pōhutukawa, Tangi-te-korowhiti, to which the ancestral Tainui canoe was tied in Kāwhia harbour. The flutes named korowhiti were played to express sorrow and pain upon the death of a loved one, to farewell the deceased, and to announce a death (Komene, 'Kōauau', pp. 35–36, 39, 104, 130, 165; Napi Waaka, in Nunns & Thomas, *Ara Puoro*, pp. 58, 62–63, 78, 135–36; Tamarapa & Tikao, 'Mai te Pō', p. 148).
62. Hamilton, *Maori Art*, p. 388.
63. Komene, 'Kōauau', pp. 34, 110–11; Hamilton, *Maori Art*, p. 405. Similarly, in the Murihiku region, when the point of a toro (spear) made from mānuka was being fire-hardened, a whistling noise (toi) was regarded as a very good omen for the spear's user. Tao whio was a term used for a whistling dart or spear. See Beattie, *Traditional Lifeways*, p. 102; Nunns & Thomas, *Ara Puoro*, p. 147. See also Robinson, *Tohunga*, p. 191.
64. Ronald Spencer Ngata, 'Understanding matakite: A kaupapa Maori study on the impact of matakite/intuitive experiences on wellbeing' (PhD thesis, Massey University, 2014), pp. 84–85.
65. Komene, 'Kōauau', p. 110.
66. Similarly, kure (found in the name pākure, tapping rods) perhaps relates to kūrē, meaning 'cry'. Whakataki is possibly a southern (Kāi Tahu) form of whakatangi (Nunns & Thomas, *Ara Puoro*, p. 150).
67. Robert L. Thorne, '(Re)constructing the kōauau: Traditional and modern methods in the making of kōauau rākau'(MA thesis, Massey University, 2012), pp. 84, 86, 114–16, 123–25. For further information about the connection between shells and birds, and ocean and forest, see Brown, *Tākaro II*, p. 88; Jerome Kavanagh, 'Te kū and rōria', *Introduction to Taonga Puoro*, video, SOUNZ Centre for NZ Music, www.youtube.com/watch?v=0vexiEHXAHA
68. Nunns & Thomas, *Ara Puoro*, p. 97.
69. Flintoff, *Taonga Pūoro*, p. 52.
70. The term kaowaowaow [kōauau] was used to describe 'a small flute' in 1773 – the first instance of this term appearing in print: see Sydney Parkinson, *A Journal of a Voyage to the South Seas, in His Majesty's Ship, the* Endeavour (London: Caliban Books, 1984), p. 127.
71. Komene, 'Kōauau', p. 4.
72. It was also used in Hawai`i and the Marquesas. In Hawai`i, this was called i`i and was characteristic of particular forms of oli (chant). In Aotearoa, it was called oriori (a cognate of oli), and took the form of alternate vowels (generally u-e, but perhaps also a-u) in waiata of the Waikato area

(Mervyn McLean, *Weavers of Song: Polynesian music and dance* (Auckland: Auckland University Press / Honolulu: University of Hawai`i Press, 1999), pp. 31, 406).

73. Komene, 'Kōauau', pp. 32, 34–35.
74. Margaret Orbell, *The Illustrated Encyclopedia of Māori Myth and Legend* (Christchurch: Canterbury University Press, 1995), p. 37.
75. Hindle, 'Renaissance', p. 14.
76. Hirini Melbourne, cited in Komene, 'Kōauau', p. 35.
77. In a related note, the image of a lizard (mokomoko) carved on one kōauau made from human thigh bone and held in the British Museum may be symbolic of death and misfortune (lizards are considered symbols of Whiro, god of darkness and evil), or may represent a kaitiaki connected with that kōiwi. See Terence Barrow, *The Decorative Arts of the New Zealand Maori* (Wellington: A.H. & A.W. Reed, 1964), p. 72; Te Awekotuku, cited in Komene, 'Kōauau', pp. 78–79. It is worth noting that lizards were servants of Moko (ruler of lizards) according to Mangaian (Cook Islands) legend (Paringatai, 'Poia mai', pp. 58–59).
78. The flute's accession number is 08617; it was purchased from Acland Wansey in 1899; and its precise measurements are 251 millimetres long, 18.25 millimetres wide and 14.56 millimetres high.
79. www.taiuru.maori.nz/word-list-te-reo-moriori/; POLLEX.
80. There is doubt over whether Māori, before European contact, used the term nguru to denote a musical instrument. There is a description matching this instrument, 'resembling a child's ninepin in shape' or 'a tobacco pipe', from 1770 (Cook and Banks, in Andersen, *Maori Music*, pp. 9, 263), but the instrument is not named. When the instrument first appears by name in the written record, it is termed kōauau: see Richard Taylor, *Te Ika a Maui or New Zealand and its Inhabitants* (London: Wertheim & MacIntosh, 1855), fig. 50a. Hamilton (*Maori Art*) was the first to print the name nguru, in 1901.
81. Ngunguru, similarly, refers to 'noise'. This type of flute was played to notify the first arrival of people at a place subsequently named Te Ngunguru a Manaia, near Whanganui (George Graham, cited in Andersen, *Maori Music*, p. 262).
82. William Baucke, 'Maori music: Flutes and flautists', *New Zealand Herald Supplement*, 15 November 1924.
83. Johannes C. Andersen, 'Maori musical instruments', *Art in New Zealand*, vol. 2, 1929, p. 99.
84. Flintoff, *Taonga Pūoro*, p. 30.
85. Hohō, a cognate term, is also given as the name for the 'lowest range of pitches possible on a kōauau': see Te Aka Māori Dictionary, maoridictionary.co.nz/search?idiom=&phrase=&proverb=&loan=&histLoanWords=&keywords=hoho
86. Nunns & Thomas, *Ara Puoro*, pp. 70, 76.
87. Te Rangi Hīroa, 'Historical Maori artifacts', *New Zealand Journal of Science and Technology*, vol. 9, 1927, pp. 37–38.
88. Iehu Nukunuku, in Best, *Games and Pastimes*, p. 129.
89. George Graham, in Andersen, *Maori Music*, p. 273.
90. Robinson, *Tohunga*, pp. 21, 38, 151, 280, 301–2, 308–9. For information on the cosmic vine and on how the development of a human baby mirrors the creation of the universe (and vice versa), see Robinson, *Tohunga*, pp. 19–29, 306–13.
91. Kākara was the term used by Te Arawa and Tūhoe (Best, *Forest Lore*, pp. 167, 170, 175). It seems to be a localisation of the term tātara, with the t replaced by k.
92. See Richard Nunns, 'Tarakimere', *He Ara Pūoro*, RNZ, 2 February 2012, www.rnz.co.nz/audio/player?audio_id=2508859
93. A leaf (for example, of karamū, manono or taupata) could be folded along its rib, its shiny side facing inwards, and then blown

into. The leaf is pinched near the top and bottom, creating a reed between the two sets of fingers, which is blown into. The subtle tension exerted between the fingers controls the sound (John Vercoe, cited in Nunns & Thomas, *Ara Puoro*, p. 149).

94. Ngāti Porou people used two different types of clappers, both made from the short, thick base of a harakeke leaf. Pākēkē were made by completely separating the leaf into two halves; these were held in each hand and clapped together. With pākōkō, the two halves were only separated to within a few centimetres of the butt end. One half was then bent outwards and downwards. When waved up and down, the loose half struck the rigid half (Tuta Nihoniho, in Best, *Games and Pastimes*, p. 173). Renowned weaver Erenora Puketapu-Hetet (Te Āti Awa), who grew up at Waiwhetū marae near Lower Hutt, referred to a similar instrument, noting that the take (the hard base of a harakeke leaf) could be split through to make a clapper for children to use: see Erenora Puketapu-Hetet, *Maori Weaving* (Auckland: Longman, 2000), p. 11. Pākēkē (flax clappers) have been differentiated from pākōkō (wooden clappers): see Rachael Ka`ai-Mahuta, Tania Ka`ai & John Moorfield, eds, *Kia Rōnaki: The Māori performing arts* (Auckland: Pearson, 2013), p. 310.
95. Best, 'Diversions of the whare tapere', p. 48.
96. There are several definitions for pō, but none of them seems pertinent to this instrument.
97. Best, *Games and Pastimes*, p. 153.
98. Given as pūtātere (instead of pūtētere) by Gilbert Mair (cited in Andersen, *Maori Music*, p. 287), but this may have been a typo rather than a spelling variation. Huata (*Rhythm and Life*, p. 35) gives a very different definition of tētere, noting that it was a 'drum' used to accompany poi songs about the arrival of the first waka in Taranaki.
99. Letters to George Grey, 1862 (Unpublished letters held in Auckland Libraries Heritage Collections, GNZMMS144), pp. 75–76.
100. Best, *Games and Pastimes*, p. 128.
101. Wairore is likely an abbreviation of takawairore. This term does not have a separate entry in Williams' dictionary, though it is noted in his definition of takawairore.
102. Taraere is not listed in Williams' dictionary, and there is also no entry for ere. This term could be a modified version of tararī.
103. Among Ngāti Porou, pōtaka kukume were carved from a single piece of wood, and consisted of a top with a spindle. A cord was wound from the top of the spindle's shaft downwards to its base. A small stick distinctively shaped like a shepherd's crook was hooked by the left hand over the cord held in the right hand, and slid along the cord until it rested sideways against the base of the top's shaft. With a finger curled around the shaft to keep it in position, the operator pulled the cord vigorously with their right hand. The stick may or may not have been a pre-European feature of this type of humming top (Tuta Nihoniho, in Best, *Games and Pastimes*, p. 88).
104. Robinson, *Tohunga*, p. 23.
105. Komene, 'Kōauau', p. 111; Nunns & Thomas, *Ara Puoro*, pp. 32, 37. In some traditions (e.g. Tainui), it is Tāwhaki instead of Tāne who ascends the heavens and receives the three kete.
106. Another meaning of pā is to 'act in concert', which could refer to these instruments being played in ensembles (Mair, cited in Andersen, 'Musical instruments', p. 92). This is another instance where one term can have two different but equally applicable meanings.
107. Best, *Games and Pastimes*, pp. 88–89. A variation of this type of top had a hole near the top of its spindle: 'The top itself, as a rule most elaborately carved and inlaid with paua shell, measured about six inches by three and a quarter inches in diameter. In addition, there was a spindle protruding from the exact centre of the top. This was about three

and a quarter inches long and had a hole bored through the side at the extreme tip. In operation a cord was threaded through the hole and tied to the branch of a tree so that the top was suspended at about chest level. A shorter cord was then wound round the base of the spindle and pulled against a kip – a small piece of wood which acted as a fulcrum with such force that it would cause the top to spin very swiftly. It would spin so swiftly, in fact, that the cord by which the top was suspended would wind itself round the spindle, and in winding itself, would cause the top to climb upwards, on the cord itself. Of course, the winner of the contest was the one whose top climbed highest.' See Hemi Bennett, 'Games of the old time Maori', *Te Ao Hou*, vol. 24, 1958, p. 52.

108. Best, 'Diversions of the whare tapere', p. 56.

109. This prefix also features in the names of instruments that are descendants of Tāwhirimātea – pūmamae, pūrēhua, pūrerehua, pūrorohu – which is appropriate given that hau refers to both wind and breath. Pua (gourd whistle) is not in Williams' dictionary, but also relates to pū.

110. Grey, cited in Komene, 'Kōauau', pp. 27–29.

111. Nunns & Thomas, *Ara Puoro*, p. 133. Reflexes of the Proto Oceanic *upi/*ipu (blow), or compounds containing it, often refer to the playing of wind instruments or the instruments themselves (for example, in Papuan Tip, Meso-Melanesian, Southeast Solomonic and Fijian languages) (Ross, Pawley & Osmond, *Lexicon*, pp. 107–8). This source bears no apparent connection to ipu kōrero, however.

112. See Richard Nunns, 'Poi (raupō, ipu kōrero, poi piu)', *He Ara Pūoro*, RNZ, 2 February 2012, www.rnz.co.nz/audio/player?audio_id=2508994.

113. Flintoff, *Taonga Pūoro*, p. 57.

114. John White, cited in Andersen, *Maori Music*, pp. 257–58.

115. Wera means 'hot or burnt'. This may indicate the use of burnt decorations on this instrument, though there is no historical record to support this supposition (Milton Brown, cited in Nunns & Thomas, *Ara Puoro*, pp. 68, 149).

116. Melbourne, *Toiapiapi*, p. 21.

117. Ki, in tarakimere, means 'on'.

118. Another name for these shells is pūpūtātara. In that case, Williams does not note that this name was used for conch trumpets, but that may have been an error of omission as it is very similar to other names used for conch trumpets. Jerome Kavanagh reserves the term pūmoana for shell trumpets that have no wooden mouthpieces, while pū was a Waitaha term for such trumpets: 'Pūtātara, pū moana & pūpu', *Introduction to Taonga Puoro*, video, SOUNZ Centre for NZ Music, www.youtube.com/watch?v=mZbE2lxh4qo. Jeremy Cloake distinguishes between instruments made using Pacific triton shells (pūmoana) and endemic conch shells (tātara) (Cloake, 'Taonga puoro').

119. Harko Brown, 'Traditional Maori games', 2006, https://wavesouthcanterbury.co.nz/media/4693/tmgharkobrown160120.pdf

120. Harko Brown, *Ngā Taonga Tākaro: Māori sports and games* (Auckland: Penguin Books, 2008), p. 54; Brown, *Tākaro II*, pp. 48, 61, 126–27.

121. Mahina-ina Kaui, in Awhina Tamarapa & Ariana Tikao, 'Mai te Pō, ki te Ao: The reclamation of taonga puoro as a living treasure', in *Searches for Tradition: Essays on New Zealand music, past and present*, eds Michael Brown & Samantha Owens (Wellington: Victoria University Press, 2017), p. 151.

122. Kō is also the first syllable in terms for bamboo elsewhere in East Polynesia (the Marquesas, Mangareva and Hawai`i), and in West Polynesia (Tonga, Sāmoa, Tokelau, East Futuna). These terms reconstruct to the Fijic term kofe. The Proto Oceanic *kopi, referring to bamboo or bamboo flutes, is the source of Gumawanan, Luangiuan and Niuean terms for wind instruments (ko-kopi,

kohe and kofe, respectively) (Ross, Pawley & Osmond, *Lexicon*, p. 108; see also Mervyn McLean, *Music, Lapita, and the Problem of Polynesian Origins* (Auckland: Mervyn McLean, 2014), pp. 45–46. Kō, in West Polynesian (Tonga, Niue, East Futuna, East `Uvea) and Polynesian outlier (West Futuna) languages, also refers to the barking of dogs, reconstructing to the Fijic koro or Polynesian kō (POLLEX).

123. Best, *Games and Pastimes*, pp. 141, 143; Komene, 'Kōauau', pp. 103–4; Nunns & Thomas, *Ara Puoro*, pp. 58–59. Hue puruhau can also be used to ease labour, particularly during contractions to help the mother regulate her breathing, according to Jerome Kavanagh, 'Hue', in *Introduction to Taonga Puoro*, video, SOUNZ Centre for NZ Music, www.youtube.com/watch?v=DNCVspOv2Y4). In many versions of the Māori creation narrative, when Tāne separated his primordial parents, Ranginui and Papatūānuku, his brother Tāwhirimātea was angry and unleashed powerful winds and storms. Amid the chaos, Hinepūtehue emerged and breathed in all of the wind, anger and hatred. This caused her body to become rounded from holding in so much wind. Her swollen body relates to that of pregnant women, making the hue puruhau an appropriate taonga to use during childbirth. For the same reasons, kōauau were also played to alleviate illness and distress in babies, to relieve their pain while teething, and to promote physical and mental healing after the birth (John White, cited in Best, *Games and Pastimes*, p. 143; Komene, 'Kōauau', p. 105). Similarly, pākuru accompanied whakawai (a soothing song used during the application of tā moko). See Hamilton, *Maori Art*, p. 398; Komene, 'Kōauau', pp. 104–5; Nunns & Thomas, *Ara Puoro*, p. 60.

124. Komene, 'Kōauau', p. 104.

125. Mair, cited in Andersen, *Maori Music*, p. 253; see also Robinson, *Tohunga*.

126. Richard Nunns, 'Maori Flute Series: The koauau', *Flute Focus*, vol. 4, October 2005, p. 33.

127. Ray Harlow, 'Borrowing and its alternatives in Māori', in *Borrowing: A Pacific perspective*, eds Jan Tent & Paul Geraghty (Canberra: Pacific Linguistics Research School of Pacific and Asian Studies, 2004), p. 148.

128. In Te Ika a Māui flax oboes were used, but they were known by different names, for example, kōrari (Tai Tokerau) and tētere (Tainui and Whanganui). The same kinds of instruments were used by Ngāti Tūwharetoa (Arawa) and Tūhoe (Mataatua) (Andersen, *Maori Music*, pp. 291, 293; Gordon Kapa and Paihere Brown, in Nunns & Thomas, *Ara Puoro*, p. 135).

129. Teone Taare Tīkao, in Beattie, *Traditional Lifeways*, p. 258.

130. See, for example, Te Rangi Hīroa's (*Coming of the Maori*, p. 262) description of a Ngāti Huia pōrutu. For Manawatū, the name pōrutu was used instead of pūtōrino: see Beatrice Ashton, 'The koauau player', *Te Ao Hou*, vol. 2, 1952, p. 55.

131. Beattie, *Traditional Lifeways*, pp. 78–79, 258–59, 483–84; C. Campbell, 'Typescript of Remainders volume on Murihiku, by Herries Beattie' (unpublished manuscript, held in Hocken Library, Dunedin, MS-2450, 1989), p. 33.

132. Te Rangi Hīroa, *Coming of the Maori*, p. 262; John White, in Andersen, *Maori Music*, p. 257; Nunns & Thomas, *Ara Puoro*, p. 68; Best, *Games and Pastimes*, pp. 142–44. Instruments like this, made from tutu/tupakihi, were used by children in Te Ika a Māui. A similar North Island instrument, with three fingerholes on top, made in two pieces, was made from kōiwi tangata (human bone).

133. Beattie, *Traditional Lifeways*, p. 78; Edward Tregear, *The Maori Race* (Whanganui: A.D. Willis, 1904), p. 66.

CHAPTER 2: THE IWITANGA AND ROHE DIFFERENCES OF TAONGA PŪORO

1. Ian Barber, 'Culture change in northern Te Wai Pounamu' (PhD thesis, University of Otago, 1994), p. 490.
2. Richard Nunns, in Hirini Melbourne, *Toiapiapi: He huinga o ngā kura puoro a te Māori* (Wellington: Shearwater, 2016), p. 19.
3. Nunns, in Melbourne, *Toiapiapi,* p. 19.
4. Huata Holmes, in Richard Nunns & Allan Thomas, *Te Ara Puoro: A journey into the world of Māori music* (Nelson: Craig Potton Publishing, 2014), pp. 44, 104, 149.
5. Samuel Timoti Robinson, *Tohunga: The revival* (Auckland: Reed Books, 2005), p. 85.
6. James Herries Beattie, *Traditional Lifeways of the Southern Maori*, ed. Atholl Anderson (Dunedin: Otago University Press in association with the Otago Museum, 1994), p. 76. A similar instrument was a type of pūrerehua that was fastened to a pou (pole) with a pin, and activated by the wind. See Elsdon Best, 'Maori notebook No 7' (unpublished manuscript held in the Alexander Turnbull Library, Wellington, qMS-0183, 1897), p. 260.
7. M.M. Trotter, 'Excavations at Katiki Point, North Otago', *Records of the Canterbury Museum*, vol. 8, no. 3, 1967, pp. 237, 242, fig. 4.2.
8. W.J. Phillipps, 'Maori bird calls or whistles', *Ethnos*, vol. 15, nos 3–4, 1950, p. 205.
9. Phillipps, 'Bird calls', pp. 201–4.
10. Nunns & Thomas, *Ara Puoro*, pp. 93, 144.
11. Beattie, *Traditional Lifeways*, p. 78.
12. Ibid., pp. 79–80.
13. For a performance using a reconstruction of this instrument, see Richard Nunns, 'Te taonga pūoro: The traditional instruments of the Māori', in Hirini Melbourne, Richard Nunns & Aroha Yates Smith, *Te Hekenga-ā-Rangi* (Auckland: Rattle Records, 2003). For an image of this instrument, see Brian Flintoff, *Taonga Pūoro: Singing treasures: The musical instruments of the Māori* (Nelson: Craig Potton Publishing, 2004), p. 89. This instrument is very different in form and use from instruments named pākuru found elsewhere (Mataatua, Tairāwhiti, Takitimu and Te Upoko o te Ika).
14. Flintoff, *Taonga Pūoro*, p. 88; Teone Taare Tīkao, in Beattie, *Traditional Lifeways*, p. 259.
15. Beattie, *Traditional Lifeways*, pp. 79–80, 259, 484.
16. Chapman, cited in Alfred K. Newman, 'On the musical notes and other features of the long Maori trumpet', *TPNZI*, vol. 38, 1905, p. 135.
17. Tregear, cited in Beattie, *Traditional Lifeways*, p. 79. A similar, transitional instrument – a type of kazoo – is described as being made from two glass bottle necks – one of which slid inside the other, cushioned with tissue paper (see Richard Nunns, 'Kazoo', *He Ara Pūoro*, RNZ, 2 February 2012, www.rnz.co.nz/audio/player?audio_id=2508882).
18. Nunns & Thomas, *Ara Puoro*, pp. 60–61; Robinson, *Tohunga*, p. 245.
19. Stack, in Johannes C. Andersen, *Maori Music with its Polynesian Background* (New Plymouth: Thomas Avery, 1934), p. 213.
20. Hohepa Te Rake's description does not mention the instrument's name. See Hohepa Te Rake, in Ettie Rout, *Maori Symbolism* (New York: Harcourt, 1926), pp. 75–76.
21. Andersen, *Maori Music*, pp. 212–13; Nathaniel B. Emerson, *Unwritten Literature of Hawaii: The sacred songs of the hula* (Washington: Government Printing Office, 1909), pp. 147–48; Hans Fischer, *Sound-producing Instruments in Oceania: Construction and playing technique, distribution and function* (Port Moresby: Institute of Papua New Guinea Studies, 1986), pp. 73–75; Rout, *Symbolism*, p. 75.
22. Hohepa Te Rake, in Rout, *Maori Symbolism*, pp. 75–76. Whale or albatross gut could also be used to make kū strings (see Jerome Kavanagh, 'Te kū and rōria', in *Introduction*

to Taonga Puoro: Porotiti and *pūrerehua*, video, SOUNZ Centre for NZ Music, www.youtube.com/watch?v=0vexiEHXAHA).

23. Flintoff, *Taonga Pūoro*, p. 83. This instrument is held in Te Papa's collection (accession number: ME000466).
24. Nunns & Thomas, *Ara Puoro*, pp. 54–55, 92.
25. Poukai Waiari, in Nunns & Thomas, *Ara Puoro*, p. 147.
26. Flintoff, *Taonga Pūoro*, p. 71; Whitu Waiariki, in Nunns & Thomas, *Ara Puoro*, pp. 59–60, 143. Kōauau can be used in much the same way, instilling in infants important information about their whakapapa and ngā mahi a ngā tūpuna (traditions) (Jo'el Komene, 'Kōauau auē, e auau tō au e: The kōauau in Te Ao Māori', MA thesis, University of Waikato, 2009, p. 124).
27. Tuta Nihoniho, in Best, *Games and Pastimes*, p. 166.
28. Best, *Games and Pastimes*, p. 170.
29. Thomas E. Donne, *The Maori: Past and present* (London: Seeley Service & Co., 1927), p. 60; Nunns & Thomas, *Ara Puoro*, p. 44. Grey also refers to human bones being used as percussion instruments: see George Grey, *Mythology and Traditions of the New Zealanders* (London: George Willis, 1854), p. 56.
30. Robinson, *Tohunga*, pp. 218–19.
31. Crowe, cited in Harko Brown, *Ngā Taonga Tākaro II: The matrix* (Mt Maunganui: Physical Education New Zealand, 2016), p. 78; Tuta Nihoniho, in Best, *Games and Pastimes*, p. 175.
32. Brown, *Tākaro II*, pp. 34–35.
33. Anon, *Songs from the Past, He Waiata Onamata* (Auckland: Te Reo Rangatira Trust, 1998), p. 47; Iehu Nukunuku, in Best, *Games and Pastimes*, p. 158.
34. Komene, 'Kōauau', pp. 139–40.
35. In Brown, *Tākaro II*, p. 38. The use of water as a percussion instrument is also found in Vanuatu and the Solomon Islands, though there it involves groups of women performing while immersed in water. Any similarities here are simply due to independent invention. In a related note, another instance of musicians deriving their sounds from bodily movement occurred during the playing of traditional Māori sports and games. According to Melbourne (in Brown, *Tākaro II*, p. 35), flute players would 'tune in' to the tempo of a game and collectively improvise music to the movements and wairua of the contestants.
36. Mauri Tirikatene, in Nunns & Thomas, *Ara Puoro*, pp. 33, 151.
37. Wooden pahu of various types belong exclusively to Te Ika a Māui. In the Banks Peninsula area, after pā were introduced, two pieces of wood struck together were used instead. These were used to alert people in a pā or kāika to an impending attack during wartime. A similar instrument, two sticks struck together, was a boys' game and was also sometimes used to accompany young people's singing (Teone Taare Tīkao, in Beattie, *Traditional Lifeways*, pp. 258–59).
38. Te Mata Hāpuku pā was located on the west side of Wairewa Lake Forsyth near its outlet, between the Kaitorete Spit and Horomaka.
39. Roger Fyfe, 'A wooden trumpet, pūkaea, from Te Mata Hapuka Pa, Canterbury, New Zealand', *New Zealand Journal of Archaeology* 23, 2001, pp. 151–159; 'Two tetere', p. 326; Sally Mekalik, 'Te Mata Hapuka pukaea' (unpublished manuscript, held in Alexander Turnbull Library, Wellington, MS-Papers-8544-33, 1996); Awhina Tamarapa & Ariana Tikao, 'Mai te Pō, ki te Ao: The reclamation of taonga puoro as a living treasure', in *Searches for Tradition: Essays on New Zealand music, past and present*, eds Michael Brown & Samantha Owens (Wellington: Victoria University Press, 2017), p. 151.
40. Georg Forster, *A Voyage Round the World*, eds Nicholas Thomas & Oliver Breghof

(Honolulu: University of Hawai`i Press, 2000), p. 129.

41. Mervyn McLean, *Maori Music* (Auckland: Auckland University Press, 1996), p. 25.
42. Janet Davidson, *The Prehistory of New Zealand* (Auckland: Longman Paul, 1984), p. 93. Post butts from the Moa Bone Point Cave site were dated to 1304±62 and 1310±25. The shell species was *Struthiolaria.* See D.R. Simmons, 'Suggested periods in South Island prehistory', *Records of the Auckland Institute and Museum*, vol. 10, 1973), p. 5; Julius von Haast, cited in H.D. Skinner, 'Archaeology of Canterbury: Moa-bone Point Cave', *Records of the Canterbury Museum*, vol. 2, 1923, p. 101. The artefacts from Otago are held in Tūhura Otago Museum (accession numbers: D32.363 and D65.986). Otago Museum is also home to the remains of another shell trumpet, made from a different type of shell, found at Long Beach: see Otago Museum, *Kāi Tahu Taoka: Treasures from the Otago Museum* (Auckland: Reed Books, 2006), p. 47.
43. James Herries Beattie, *Māori Place-names of Otago* (Christchurch: Cadsonbury, 2001), p. 82.
44. Andersen, *Maori Music*, p. 276. Another account gives a different version of whose hands the instrument passed through. It may be the pūtōrino now in Auckland Museum (ethnology number: 6400), which by some accounts was acquired in 1923 from Mr J. Martin's next of kin. W.A. Taylor, *Lore and History of the South Island Maori* (Christchurch: Bascands, n.d.), pp. 65–66.
45. Henare Toka, in Mervyn McLean, 'An investigation of the open tube Maori flute or kooauau', *JPS*, vol. 77, no. 3, 1968, pp. 214, 217–18, 231; Kiwi Amohau, in Andersen, *Maori Music*, pp. 232–33.
46. Iehu Nukunuku, in Best, *Games and Pastimes,* pp. 135–36.
47. Nunns & Thomas, *Ara Puoro,* p. 82.
48. McLean, 'An investigation of the open tube Maori flute or kooauau', p. 226.
49. Best, *Games and Pastimes,* pp. 129, 142, 151; Flintoff, *Taonga Pūoro,* p. 77; McNab, *Historical Records*, p. 479.
50. Te Kahupuka, in Beattie, *Traditional Lifeways*, p. 483.
51. Robert McNab, *Historical Records of New Zealand*, vol. 2 (Wellington: Government Printer, 1914), p. 479. This fits with information given by White (cited in Komene, 'Kōauau', p. 50), who describes a short flute with three holes as a 'pūtōrino'.
52. Teone Taare Tīkao, in Beattie, *Traditional Lifeways*, pp. 258–59.
53. Beattie, *Traditional Lifeways*, p. 78; Best, 'Maori notebook', p. 6.
54. Best (*Games and Pastimes*, pp. 129–30) was unsure if pūhoho was a northern name for the instrument.
55. Te Rangi Hīroa [Sir Peter Buck], 'Historical Maori artifacts', *New Zealand Journal of Science and Technology* 9, 1927, pp. 37–38; Iehu Nukunuku, in Best, *Games and Pastimes*, pp. 129–30.
56. Nunns & Thomas, *Ara Puoro*, p. 140. In 1769, M. de Surville and P. de l'Horne described an instrument like pererau as follows: '[It] has the shape of an olive, but much bigger and longer – that is to say, it may be 2 in. long, and hollow all its length, with a hole in the middle. They produce with this instrument five or six distinct sounds'. See Robert McNab, *Historical Records of New Zealand*, vol. 2 (Wellington: Government Printer, 1914), p. 335.
57. Richard Nunns, 'Ororuarangi', *He Ara Pūoro*, RNZ, 2 February 2012, www.rnz.co.nz/audio/player?audio_id=2508857
58. Komene, 'Kōauau', p. 58.
59. The text of one such song is provided by Tuta Nihoniho, in Best, *Games and Pastimes*, p. 134. Nunns & Thomas (*Ara Puoro*, p. 78) use tūteure as a synonym for kōauau.
60. Tuta Nihoniho, in Best, *Games and Pastimes*, p. 135.
61. Taraire wood, mataī bark or whalebone could be used (see Richard Nunns, 'Tarakimere',

He Ara Pūoro, RNZ, 2 February 2012, www.rnz.co.nz/audio/player?audio_id=2508859).

62. Gordon Kapa and Paihere Brown, in Nunns & Thomas, *Ara Puoro*, p. 147. Another key informant was Tupari Te Whata (see Nunns, 'Tarakimere').
63. Ada Haig, in Nunns & Thomas, *Ara Puoro*, pp. 36, 133; see also Joel Samuel Polack, *Manners and Customs of the New Zealanders*, vol. 1 (London: Madden, 1840), p. 101.
64. Teone Taare Tīkao, in Beattie, *Traditional Lifeways*, p. 258.
65. Nunns uses the term hoputea for this type of instrument, made from a small whelk. Hopu can mean 'surprise', and teatea has a related meaning: 'apprehensive, afraid'. Whakai i tama were similar, though the shell used was larger. Nunns does not specify the type of shell used, but notes that, for both instruments, the pitch could be altered by the player inserting their finger inside the unworked open end of the shell (Nunns & Thomas, *Ara Puoro*, p. 97; Richard Nunns, 'Hoputea and whakai i tama', *He Ara Pūoro*, RNZ, 2 February 2012, www.rnz.co.nz/audio/player?audio_id=2508867). Different types of shell could also be used to make whakai-o-tama (note the spelling variation). Half of a *Spisula aequilateralis* (marine bivalve mollusc; surf clam) shell, labelled whakai-o-tama, is from the Herries Beattie collection in the Otago Museum (D63.31) (Museum of New Zealand Te Papa Tongarewa, 'Whakai-o-tama', https://collections.tepapa.govt.nz/object/920080). Another half of a shell, this time of *Mactra ovata*, is also labelled whakai-o-tama (D.63.30) (Artnet, www.artnet.com/artists/fiona-pardington/d63-30-whakai-o-tama-temuka-tuaki-rapaki-mactr-aa-Ix6LeN5KiDfr54rGWP8NQ2).
66. Beattie, *Traditional Lifeways*, pp. 78–80, 259–60; Mahina-ina Kaui, in Tamarapa & Tikao, 'Mai te Pō', p. 151.
67. George Graham, in Andersen, *Maori Music*, p. 296.
68. Nunns & Thomas, *Ara Puoro*, p. 36.
69. Iuta Nihoniho, in Best, *Games and Pastimes*, p. 158. An example of a gourd trumpet in the British Museum has a small bone mouthpiece (see Richard Nunns, 'Pū hue', *He Ara Pūoro*, RNZ, 2 February 2012, www.rnz.co.nz/audio/player?audio_id=2508869).
70. Melbourne, *Toiapiapi*, p. 30.
71. Whitu Waiaki, in Nunns & Thomas, *Ara Puoro*, p. 37.
72. Nunns & Thomas, *Ara Puoro*, p. 37. These rituals perhaps took place at mauri sites in the forest: see Elsdon Best, *Forest Lore of the Maori* (Wellington: E.C. Keating, 1977), pp. 7–15; Melbourne, *Toiapiapi*, p. 30.
73. Richard Nunns, 'Poi āwhiowhio and tuarōria (with nīkau leaf)', *He Ara Pūoro*, RNZ, 2 February 2012, www.rnz.co.nz/audio/player?audio_id=2508846
74. Tawai Taunoa, in Nunns & Thomas, *Ara Puoro*, p. 37.
75. Te Rangi Hīroa [Sir Peter Buck], *The Coming of the Maori* (Wellington: Whitcombe & Tombs; Maori Purposes Fund, 1966), p. 503.
76. Johannes C. Andersen, 'Maori music', *TPNZI*, vol. 54, 1924, p. 691; James Cowan, 'The Maori signal gong: Stories of the wooden pahu' (unpublished manuscript held in Alexander Turnbull Library, Wellington, MS papers 11310-187, n.d.), p. 1.
77. Cowan, 'Signal gong', p. 2; George Grey, cited in Best, *Games and Pastimes*, p. 165.
78. John Morgan, in McLean, *Maori Music*, p. 168.
79. Nunns & Thomas, *Ara Puoro*, pp. 63, 102. The neighbouring rohe of Te Arawa also had a signal language for pahu (Hohepa Te Rake, in Rout, *Symbolism*, pp. 144–45).
80. Best, *Games and Pastimes*, pp. 166–67.
81. Gilbert Mair, 'Inward correspondence J-N (Letters to Elsdon Best)' (unpublished manuscript held in Alexander Turnbull Library, Wellington, MS Papers 007204, 1900). Writing in general terms of this type of pahu, Andersen ('Maori music', p. 691)

says that they were made from hollow, living trees. A tongue 6.1–9.1 metres long was cut out of the trunk. Three or four different notes could be produced by striking the tongue at a higher or lower position.

82. Nunns & Thomas, *Ara Puoro*, p. 63.
83. Andersen, *Maori Music*, p. 211; Elsdon Best, *The Maori*, vol. 2 (Wellington: Polynesian Society, 1924), pp. 83–84; Edward Tregear, *The Maori Race* (Whanganui: A.D. Willis, 1904), p. 55.
84. William Colenso, 'Contributions towards a better knowledge of the Maori race', *TPNZI*, vol. 13, 1880, p. 79.
85. Te Rangi Hīroa, *Coming of the Maori*, p. 239.
86. Best, *Forest Lore*, pp. 167, 170, 175; Nunns & Thomas, *Ara Puoro*, pp. 34, 134. Names used elsewhere include: patete (Waitaha) and rore (Waikato). See Teone Taare Tīkao, in Beattie, *Traditional Lifeways*, p. 342.
87. Sebastian Lowe & Alistair Fraser, 'Connecting with inner landscapes: Taonga pūoro, musical improvisation and exploring acoustic Aotearoa/New Zealand', *Journal of New Zealand and Pacific Studies*, vol. 6, no. 1, 2008, p. 12.
88. Te Kahupuka and Teone Taare Tīkao, in Beattie, *Traditional Lifeways*, pp. 258–59, 483.
89. Rua McCallum, *He Kete Taoka* (Dunedin: Komiti Taoka Tuku Iho & Hughes Lithographics Ltd, 2008), p. 164.
90. Lowe & Fraser, 'Inner landscapes', p. 15; Robert L. Thorne, '(Re)constructing the kōauau: Traditional and modern methods in the making of kōauau rākau' (MA thesis, Massey University, 2012), pp. 91, 93, 97, 100.
91. Beattie, *Traditional Lifeways*, p. 126.
92. Nunns, in Thorne, '(Re)constructing kōauau', pp. 97, 99–100; Nunns & Thomas, *Ara Puoro*, p. 78. A possible one-off instrument, from an unnamed location, was a kelp trumpet. It is described as 'a large pūkāea that was made from the long, already hollow stipe of a kelp that ended with a flared structure (possibly the holdfast) that formed the distal bell': Thorne, '(Re) constructing kōauau', p. 133.
93. Thorne, '(Re)constructing kōauau', pp. 10, 76, 87–101, 126–35.
94. Richard Nunns, 'Maori Flute Series: The koauau', *Flute Focus* 4, October 2005, p. 33.
95. George Te Au, in Nunns & Thomas, *Ara Puoro*, p. 143; Phillip Smith, in Lowe & Fraser, 'Inner landscapes', p. 12.
96. Lowe & Fraser, 'Inner landscapes', p. 12.
97. Beattie, *Traditional Lifeways*, pp. 77–78.
98. Nunns & Thomas, *Ara Puoro*, p. 102. I've been privileged in being allowed to play a pounamu xylophone, pahu and tuning fork made by the late pounamu expert Russell Beck, and can attest to the incredible tones and resonance of these taonga.
99. Flintoff, *Taonga Pūoro*, p. 61; Nunns & Thomas, *Ara Puoro*, pp. 22, 34, 101, 132.
100. Richard Walter, Chris Jacomb & Sreymony Bowron-Muth, 'Colonisation, mobility and exchange in New Zealand prehistory', *Antiquity* 84, 2010, pp. 501, 508–9, 511.
101. Flintoff, *Taonga Pūoro*, p. 61; Melbourne, *Toiapiapi*, p. 55; Nunns & Thomas, *Ara Puoro*, p. 98.
102. Best, *Games and Pastimes*, p. 166; Cowan, 'Signal gong', p. 2; Nunns & Thomas, *Ara Puoro*, pp. 102–4. Richard Nunns ('Taonga puoro and Peka Mākarini's bugle', in *Kia Rōnaki: The Māori performing arts*, eds Rachael Ka`ai-Mahuta, Tania Ka`ai & John Moorfield (Auckland: Pearson, 2013), p. 183) also records stone pahu being used in the Waikato area. Similar stone instruments (though not suspended, as in the Māori examples) were used in Micronesia (Ponape, Kosrae), Papua New Guinea and Mangareva (Fischer, *Sound-producing Instruments*, p. 12).
103. Hamilton, cited in McLean, *Maori Music*, p. 370; Margaret Orbell, *The Illustrated Encyclopedia of Māori Myth and Legend* (Christchurch: Canterbury University Press, 1995), p. 87.

104. Victor F. Fisher, 'The material culture of Oruarangi, Matatoki, Thames. 4: Musical instruments', *Records of the Auckland Institute and Museum*, vol. 2, no. 2, 1937, pp. 111–15; Louise Furey, *Oruarangi: The archaeology and material culture of a Hauraki pa* (Auckland: Auckland Institute and Museum, 1996), pp. 125, 128, figs. 74 and 75; 'Clay – a lesser known medium for Maori artefacts', *Records of the Auckland Museum*, vol. 50, 2015, pp. 22, 24, 29; Roger Fyfe, 'Rediscovering two tetere, flax trumpets in Canterbury Museum', in *Ngā Kete a Rēhua Inaugural Māori Research Symposium Te Waipounamu 2008*, eds Rawiri Taonui & Hamuera Kahi (Christchurch: Aotahi School of Māori and Indigenous Studies, Te Whare Wānanga o Waitaha, 2008), p. 326; F.W. Shawcross & J.E. Terrell, 'Paterangi and Oruarangi Swamp pas', *JPS*, vol. 75, no. 4, 1966, p. 427.
105. Wendy J. Harsant, 'Excavations at Oue Pa, N43/35, South Auckland', *Records of the Auckland Institute and Museum* 18, 1981, pp. 78–79.
106. Furey, *Oruarangi*, p. 123; Komene, 'Kōauau', p. 142.
107. See Louise Furey, 'Clay – a lesser known medium for Māori artefacts', *Records of the Auckland Museum*, vol. 50, 2015, pp. 21–31.
108. Ruby Solly, 'How to make an ukutangi', www.kauaeraro.com/matauranga/ukutangi.
109. Flintoff, *Taonga Pūoro*, p. 52.
110. Flintoff, *Taonga Pūoro*, p. 52; Nunns & Thomas, *Ara Puoro*, p. 98.
111. It can be difficult even for trained ornithologists to tell which marine bird species was used for a flute; descriptions in museum catalogues often reflect this unsureness.
112. Examples dating from the 16th century have been found at Otara (False Island), Little Papanui and Pūrākaunui. In the early 18th and 19th centuries, kōiwi toroa flutes are more prolific in the archaeological record of lower eastern South Island coastal sites (those of Little Papanui, Pene Bay in Pahia, Long Beach, Whareakeake (Murdering Beach), Tarewai Point, Kaikai Beach and Karitāne). See Beattie, *Traditional Lifeways*, pp. 77, 79; C. Campbell, 'Typescript of Remainders volume on Murihiku, by Herries Beattie' (unpublished manuscript, held in Hocken Library, Dunedin, MS-2450, 1989), p. 33; Davidson, *Prehistory*, p. 93; Helen Leach & G.E. Hamel, 'The place of Taiaroa Head and other Classic Maori sites in the prehistory of East Otago', *Journal of the Royal Society of New Zealand*, vol. 8, no. 3, 1978, p. 249; Helen M. Leach & Jill Hamel, 'Archaic and Classic Maori relationships at Long Beach, Otago: The artefacts and activity areas', *New Zealand Journal of Archaeology*, vol. 3, 1981, pp. 112, 127; Lockerbie, cited in Simmons, 'Suggested periods', pp. 3–4, 51, table 12; McLean, 'Open tube', pp. 214–15; Mervyn McLean, 'A chronological and geographical sequence of Maori flute scales', *Man*, vol. 17, 1982, p. 129; Murray Thacker, 'Excavations at Pa Bay, Banks Peninsula', *New Zealand Archaeological Association Newsletter*, vol. 4, no. 1, 1960, p. 11; M.M. Trotter, 'Excavations at Katiki Point, North Otago', *Records of the Canterbury Museum*, vol. 8, no. 3, 1967, pp. 237, 242, fig. 4.1; Walter et al., 'Colonisation', p. 507.
Most flutes recovered from archaeological sites in the area have been designated as belonging to a 'late' period – the South Island aspect of the 'Classic' period of Māori culture. In the Murihiku region, this period dates to c. 1800–1820; and in Waitaha, it dates from c. 1550 to 1820. Simmons, 'Suggested periods', p. 55.
113. Beattie, *Traditional Lifeways*, p. 78; Tregear, *Maori Race*, p. 66.
114. Davidson, *Prehistory*, p. 93; Richard Moyle, *The Sounds of Oceania: An illustrated catalogue of the sound producing instruments of Oceania in the Auckland Institute and*

Museum (Auckland: Auckland Institute and Museum, 1989), p. 11; D.R. Simmons, 'Suggested periods', table 12.

115. Leach & Hamel, 'Taiaroa Head', p. 245; Lowe & Fraser, 'Inner landscapes', p. 12. The first historical record of these birds' presence at Taiaroa Head dates to 1917; the first egg recorded there was in 1920, and the first successful rearing of a chick in 1937.

116. Lowe & Fraser, 'Inner landscapes', p. 16. Flutes made from toroa bones were found at Rarotoka (Centre Island) in Foveaux Strait, at a 'late' Māori site: see McLean, 'Sequence of flute scales', pp. 129, 135; Simmons, 'Suggested periods', table 12.

117. Komene, 'Kōauau', p. 140.

118. Flintoff, *Taonga Pūoro*, p. 30; Leach & Hamel, 'Taiaroa Head', p. 245.

119. Leach & Hamel, 'Taiaroa Head', p. 250; Walter et al., 'Colonisation', p. 502; in 1350–1550 according to Atholl Anderson, *When All the Moa Ovens Grew Cold: Nine centuries of changing fortune for the southern Maori* (Dunedin: Otago Heritage Books, 1983), p. 24.

120. B.F. Leach, 'The Ngai-tahu migration: The Norman conquest of the South Island', *New Zealand Archaeological Association Newsletter*, vol. 21, no. 1, 1978, p. 19. The former arrived around 1500 or from the late 1500s: see Stack, cited in I.W. Keyes, 'The Ngatimamoe: The Western Polynesian-Melanesoid sub-culture in New Zealand', *JPS*, vol. 76, no. 1, 1967, p. 51; Te Maire Tau & Atholl Anderson (eds), *Ngāi Tahu: A migration history* (Wellington: Bridget Williams Books, 2008), p. 27.

121. Anderson, *Moa Ovens*, pp. 31–32, 37; Barber, *Culture Change*, pp. 466–67, 495; Andrew Alexander Brown, 'Material culture traditions of prehistoric Murihiku' (MA thesis, University of Otago, 2011), p. 28.

122. Anderson, cited in Brown, *Material Culture*, p. 42.

123. George Graham, in Andersen, *Maori Music*, p. 248.

124. Best, *Games and Pastimes*, pp. 88–90; Nunns & Thomas, *Ara Puoro*, pp. 141–42.

125. William Barrett Marshall, *A Personal Narrative of Two Visits to New Zealand in His Majesty's Ship* Alligator *A.D. 1834* (London: Nisbet, 1836), p. 24.

126. Keri Hulme, 'He pūoro', *Karaka*, vol. 54, 2012, p. 5.

127. Terence Barrow, *Traditional and Modern Music of the Maori* (Wellington; Sydney: Seven Seas, 1965), p. 18; Flintoff, *Taonga Pūoro*, pp. 65–66; John White, cited in Best, *Games and Pastimes*, pp. 142–44; William Baucke, cited in Mary Martin, 'Maori music' (unpublished manuscript, held in Alexander Turnbull Library, Wellington, MS-Papers-8544-32, n.d.), p. 149.

128. John White, cited in Best, *Games and Pastimes*, p. 130.

129. Komene, 'Kōauau', p. 45.

130. Florence Keene, cited in Komene, 'Kōauau', pp. 44–45. This story was originally related by Miss S.C. Matthews.

131. Nunns & Thomas, *Ara Puoro*, p. 82.

132. Savage, cited in Andersen, *Maori Music*, pp. 66–67.

133. Napi Waaka, in Nunns & Thomas, *Ara Puoro*, p. 58.

134. Robinson, cited in Komene, 'Kōauau', p. 105; Komene, 'Kōauau', pp. 36, 38. Pōrutu were also used for this purpose in Murihiku.

135. Komene, 'Kōauau', p. 32.

136. David Miller, 'The insect people of the Maori', *JPS*, vol. 61, 1952, p. 3.

137. Best, *Games and Pastimes*, pp. 155, 165.

138. Best, *Games and Pastimes*, p. 89; Robinson, *Tohunga*, p. 198.

139. Jeremy Cloake, 'Taonga puoro', www.jeremycloake.com/taonga-puoro. During playing, sometimes the porotiti disc will suddenly and seemingly inexplicably jump to either the left or the right rather than remain balanced in the centre. I cannot help but wonder if those movements were regarded as tohu by tohunga.

140. McLean was sceptical of these instruments' ability to communicate human speech. However, they were not intended to act as megaphones. Rather, these tapu instruments communicated intimate, secret verbal (sung, chanted, spoken) messages to another person. See Mervyn McLean, *The N.Z. Nose Flute: Fact or fallacy?*, *Working papers in anthropology, archaeology, linguistics, Maori Studies*, No. 18, Anthropology Dept, University of Auckland, 1972.
141. Nunns & Thomas, *Ara Puoro*, p. 56.
142. Tom Kupenga, in Nunns & Thomas, *Ara Puoro*, pp. 106, 136.
143. Nunns & Thomas, *Ara Puoro*, pp. 56–58.
144. Te Rangi Hīroa, 'Historical Maori artifacts', *New Zealand Journal of Science and Technology*, vol. 9, 1927, pp. 35, 37–38.
145. Either Tūtānekai or Tiki is said to have played kōauau or pūtōrino, or both instruments (Andersen, *Maori Music*, pp. 237–38; Komene, 'Kōauau', p. 43).
146. George Grey, *Polynesian Mythology and Ancient Traditional History of the New Zealand Race* (Auckland: H. Brett, 1885), p. 147. In another narrative from the same area, on Mokoia Island the sounds of kōauau could be heard from Pukeroa, a hill above Ōhinemutu (Mair, cited in Andersen, 'Maori music', p. 695).
147. Murdoch Riley, *Māori Love Legends – and Other True Stories* (Paraparaumu: Viking Sevenseas, 2003), pp. 5–8.
148. James Cowan, cited in Komene, 'Kōauau', pp. 117–19. The translation is Cowan's, with some amendments by Komene.
149. Makereti, *The Old Time Maori* (Auckland: New Women's Press, 1986), p. 94.
150. In Andersen, *Maori Music*, pp. 232–33.
151. Maui Pomare & James Cowan, *Legends of the Maori*, vol. 1 (Auckland: Southern Reprints, 1987), pp. 301–3.
152. Both versions of this tale are recounted in Komene, 'Kōauau', p. 49. For the words of Kōmako's waiata kōauau, see Komene, 'Kōauau', pp. 115–17. Hare Hongi (aka Henry Stowell) may have known the rangi for this waiata; marks placed over the vowels and some of his hyphens in his text may have been intended as mnemonic aids.
153. Best, *Games and Pastimes*, pp. 143–44.
154. For various retellings of this story see Orbell, *Illustrated Encyclopedia*, p. 82. Karipa Te Whetu, 'Kame-tara and his ogre wife', *JPS*, vol. 6, no. 3, 1897, pp. 97–106. Te Whetu's version was transmitted to Taranaki in the 1820s by Ngāmotu (New Plymouth) chief Te Wharepōuri. The tale was brought from the tropics by the ancestors of Māori and Moriori, as a version has been recorded in Manihiki, an atoll north of Rarotonga. In Orbell's version, Kametara's second wife was a tipua – translated here as 'demon' rather than 'ogre'.
155. Komene, 'Kōauau', pp. 36–37.

CHAPTER 3: DISCOVERING NEW VOICES

1. Elsdon Best, 'The diversions of the whare tapere: Some account of the various games, amusements, and trials of skill practised by the Maori in former times', *TPNZI*, vol. 34, 1901, p. 48; Edward Tregear, *The Maori Race* (Whanganui: A.D. Willis, 1904), p. 53.
2. Te Rangi Hīroa [Sir Peter Buck], *Arts and Crafts of the Cook Islands* (Honolulu: Bernice P. Bishop Museum, 1944), p. 259.
3. W.O. Oldman, *Catalogue of Ethnographical Specimens* (London, 1908).
4. Richard Nunns, 'Rore/Tātara', *He Ara Pūoro*, RNZ, 2 February 2012, www.rnz.co.nz/audio/player?audio_id=2508993
5. The Penrhyn term pararā is a cognate.
6. Another cognate term, tātara, is a similar case; it was possibly used for the long wooden trumpet as well as a dog rattle in Whanganui.
7. Mervyn McLean, *Weavers of Song: Polynesian music and dance* (Auckland: Auckland University Press; Honolulu: University of Hawai`i Press, 1999), pp. 59–60, 350.
8. POLLEX.

9. Information on this game was gathered by Elsdon Best from Ropata Wahawha; and details of how it was played are provided in: Harko Brown, *Ngā Taonga Tākaro: Māori sports and games* (Auckland: Penguin Books, 2008), p. 54.
10. Similarly, in some cases, strings of tuangi (New Zealand cockle), *Turritella* or kākahi (freshwater mussel) shells were fastened to the head or neck of a kite, and these rattled as the kite was agitated by the wind. It is unclear where this practice occurred, or whether these shells (or the kites with shells attached) were given a particular name: see Elsdon Best, *Games and Pastimes of the Maori* (Wellington: Whitcombe & Tombs, 1925), p. 73.
11. Harko Brown, *Ngā Taonga Tākaro II: The matrix* (Mt Maunganui: Physical Education New Zealand, 2016), p. 61.
12. Best, *Games and Pastimes*, p. 170; Mervyn McLean, *Music, Dance and Polynesian Origins: The evidence from POc and PPn* (Auckland: Archive of Maori and Pacific Music, University of Auckland, 2010), pp. 24–26.
13. Richard Nunns & Allan Thomas, *Te Ara Puoro: A journey into the world of Māori music* (Nelson: Craig Potton Publishing, 2014), pp. 101–2.
14. Patrick V. Kirch & Roger C. Green, *Hawaiki, Ancestral Polynesia: An essay in historical anthropology* (Cambridge: Cambridge University Press, 2001), p. 191; McLean, *Music, Dance*, p. 91; McLean, *Music, Lapita, and the Problem of Polynesian Origins* (Auckland: Mervyn McLean, 2014), pp. 44–45; Malcolm Ross, Andrew Pawley & Meredith Osmond, *The Lexicon of Proto Oceanic: The Culture and Environment of Ancestral Oceanic Society*, vol. 1 (Canberra: Australian National University, 1998), p. 110.
15. Best, *Games and Pastimes*, p. 170; McLean, *Weavers of Song*, pp. 461–62; McLean, *Music, Lapita*, pp. 45, 101; Ross, Pawley & Osmond, *Lexicon*, p. 110. Pahu also refers to 'bang' or 'to thump' in Niue and Tonga, respectively, reconstructing to *(v/b)asu (POLLEX).
16. Te Rangi Hīroa, *Coming of the Maori*, p. 254.
17. Te Rangi Hīroa, *Arts and Crafts*, p. 457.
18. SOUNZ Centre for New Zealand Music, '*Introduction to Taonga Puoro* – Q & A session with Jerome Kavanagh', www.youtube.com/watch?v=2HQQwgahTEU
19. Best, *Games and Pastimes*, pp. 165–66, 170; Mair, in Andersen, *Maori Music*, p. 202; John Morgan, in Mervyn McLean, *Maori Music* (Auckland: Auckland University Press, 1996), p. 168; Teone Taare Tīkao, in James Herries Beattie, *Traditional Lifeways of the Southern Maori*, ed. Atholl Anderson (Dunedin: Otago University Press in association with Otago Museum, 1994), p. 258; Andrew P. Vayda, *Maori Warfare* (Wellington: Polynesian Society Inc., 1960), p. 56. Log idiophones in `Uvea were used for the same purpose; in Tonga, they were used to intimidate the enemy prior to an attack.
20. Andersen, *Maori Music*, p. 70. Pahu in Nukuhiva (Marquesas) were also used to incite the warriors prior to battle.
21. Best, *Games and Pastimes*, p. 166; James Cowan, 'The Maori signal gong: Stories of the wooden pahu' (unpublished manuscript held in Alexander Turnbull Library, Wellington, MS papers 11310-187, n.d.), p. 2; McLean, *Weavers of Song*, pp. 25, 59, 114. Also in West Polynesia: Sāmoa, Tonga and `Uvea (McLean, *Weavers of Song*, p. 220; Te Rangi Hīroa, in Andersen, *Maori Music*, p. 163).
22. Hans Fischer, *Sound-producing Instruments in Oceania: Construction and playing technique, distribution and function* (Port Moresby: Institute of Papua New Guinea Studies, 1986), p. 66; McLean, *Weavers of Song*, pp. 24, 58, 84–85, 292, 300; Richard Moyle, *Polynesian Sound-producing Instruments* (Princes Risborough, UK: Shire

Ethnography, 1990), p. 8. Pahu were also used in the Northern Cooks, Hawai`i and Mangareva to accompany dance (McLean, *Weavers of Song*, pp. 150–51, 178, 210, 234, 240, 246).

23. Beaglehole, cited in McLean, *Weavers of Song*, p. 302.
24. Cowan, 'Signal gong', p. 2; George Grey, cited in Best, *Games and Pastimes*, p. 165.
25. Ernest S. Dodge, *Hawaiian and Other Polynesian Gourds* (Ku Pa`a Publishing, Honolulu, 1995), pp. 44–45; Fischer, *Sound-producing Instruments*, pp. 13–14; McLean, *Weavers of Song*, pp. 282–83.
26. Andersen, *Maori Music*, pp. 202–3; Best, *Games and Pastimes*, pp. 166–68, 170–71; Thomas E. Donne, *The Maori: Past and present* (London: Seeley Service & Co, 1927), pp. 79–80; Fischer, *Sound-producing Instruments*, pp. 21, 28, 37.
27. Fischer, *Sound-producing Instruments*, p. 29.
28. Mair, cited in Johannes C. Andersen, *Maori Music with its Polynesian Background* (New Plymouth: Thomas Avery, 1934), p. 197; John White, *Maori Customs and Superstitions, being the Subject of Two Lectures Delivered at the Mechanics' Institute in Auckland, During the Year 1861* (Christchurch: Kiwi Publishers, 1999), p. 175.
29. Anderson, 'Origins', p. 40; McLean, *Maori Music*, pp. 170–71.
30. Te Rangi Hīroa, *Coming of the Maori*, p. 255.
31. In Sāmoa and Tonga, this instrument consisted of a wooden base with a fitted slat that rattled when struck (Andersen, *Maori Music*, pp. 79, 160, 164). Apart from this type of sounding board and the slab form of Māori pahu being flat, these instruments are dissimilar.
32. Fischer, *Sound-producing Instruments*, pp. 11–13; McLean, *Weavers of Song*, p. 353; Moyle, *Polynesian Sound-producing Instruments*, p. 23.
33. Wooden bowls are also struck in the Yonggom area of the Western Province, Papua: see Don Niles, 'Papuan region of Papua New Guinea: Musical instruments', in *The Garland Encyclopedia of World Music*, vol. 9, eds Adrienne L. Kaeppler & J.W. Love (New York; London: Garland Publishing, 1998), p. 490.
34. A variety of names are used in West Polynesia, the Polynesian outliers, and in East Polynesia (POLLEX; McLean, *Weavers of Song*, pp. 151–52, 221, 240, 246, 302; Moyle, *Polynesian sound-producing instruments*, p. 31).
35. Raymond Firth, 'Tikopia', in *The Garland Encyclopedia of World Music*, vol. 9, eds Adrienne L. Kaeppler & J.W. Love (New York; London: Garland Publishing, 1998), p. 853.
36. Fischer, *Sound-producing Instruments*, p. 37; Hohepa Te Rake, in Ettie Rout, *Maori Symbolism* (New York: Harcourt, 1926), p. 145; McLean, *Weavers of Song*, pp. 197, 221, 353.
37. Māori tōkere could be clappers or a type of flute (Best, *Games and Pastimes*, p. 170). Of other names for clappers (see Appendix 2), only tokerangi resembles tōkere.
38. McLean, *Music, Dance*, pp. 53–54.
39. Edwin G. Burrows, *Western Polynesia: A study of cultural differentiation* (Dunedin: University Book Shop Ltd, 1970); Jon Tikivanotau Jonassen, 'Southern Cook Islands: Instrumental music', in *The Garland Encyclopedia of World Music*, vol. 9, eds Kaeppler & Love (New York; London: Garland Publishing, 1998), pp. 898–99. Toere was the name of the tallest, smallest and highest-pitched skin-headed drums in Tahiti; so the term was used for skin-headed drums as well as log idiophones: see Ellis, cited in McLean, *Weavers of Song*, p. 23.
40. This name was also given to the deathwatch beetle, which makes a tapping or ticking sound.
41. Huata, *Rhythm and Life*, p. 101.
42. Nunns & Thomas, *Ara Puoro*, p. 133.
43. Fischer, *Sound-producing Instruments*, p. 137.

44. Williams, in Andersen, *Maori Music*, p. 272.
45. Nunns & Thomas, *Ara Puoro*, p. 94.
46. Fischer, *Sound-producing Instruments*, p. 137.
47. Conch trumpets with the tip removed for blowing, but without the addition of a bamboo mouthpiece, were reportedly used in West and East Polynesia (Fischer, *Sound-producing Instruments*, pp. 136–37; Te Rangi Hīroa, *Arts and Crafts*, p. 268; McLean, *Weavers of Song*, pp. 266, 306–7). In Nukuhiva (Marquesas), a candlenut could be inserted and used as a mouthpiece instead: see Edward S.C. Handy, *The Native Culture in the Marquesas* (Honolulu: Bernice P. Bishop Museum, 1923), p. 313. Fischer, *Sound-producing Instruments*, pp. 135–36 also notes the use of small gourds or coconuts as mouthpieces in the Marquesas.
48. Te Rangi Hīroa, *Coming of the Maori*, pp. 257–58.
49. Fischer, *Sound-producing Instruments*, p. 127.
50. Georg Buschan, *Illustrierte Völkerkunde in Zwei Bänden* (Stuttgart: Strecker & Schröder, 1923), p. 93.
51. The trumpet is more likely to originate in the Marquesas, the bell being identical to the bells of trumpets from there. In similar fashion, Sāmoan instruments made from coconut palm, 'fa`aili niu vao' or 'puroraiti', are sometimes labelled trumpets in the literature, but are actually flutes (Richard Moyle, 'Samoan musical instruments', *Ethnomusicology*, vol. 18, no. 1, 1974, p. 65, p. 69).
52. Moulin, 'Kapatuhe', p. 136. End-blown conical wooden trumpets also occur in the West Sepik area of Papua New Guinea, from Bewani southward to Green River (Niles, 'Papuan region', p. 547). They are rare among the Iatmul: see Gordon Donald Spearritt, 'Iatmul', in *The Garland Encyclopedia of World Music*, vol. 9, eds Kaeppler & Love (New York; London: Garland Publishing, 1998), p. 556.
53. Fischer, *Sound-producing Instruments*, p. 130.
54. Handy, *Native Culture*, p. 313.
55. Colenso, cited in Elsdon Best, *The Maori*, vol. 2 (Wellington: Polynesian Society, 1924), p. 159; Tregear, *Maori Race*, p. 65.
56. Fischer, *Sound-producing Instruments*, pp. 131–32, 134–35; Richard Moyle, *The Sounds of Oceania: An illustrated catalogue of the sound producing instruments of Oceania in the Auckland Institute and Museum* (Auckland: Auckland Institute and Museum, 1989, p. 39.
57. Moulin, 'Kapatuhe', p. 137. Colenso ('Contributions', p. 80) notes the use of one such phrase, 'to roro, to roro' ('your blood, your blood') in response to an insult (pokokohua ma). Maui Pomare (in Andersen, *Maori Music*, pp. 291–92) gives the text of another kanga pūkaea (pūkaea curse).
58. George French Angas, *Savage Life and Scenes in Australia and New Zealand*, vol. 2 (London: Smith, Elder, 1847), pp. 151–52; Best, *Games and Pastimes*, pp. 155, 165.
59. George Graham, in Andersen, *Maori Music*, p. 296; Thomas Moser, *Mahoe Leaves* (Whanganui: H.I. Jones & Son, 1888), p. 51; Edward Tregear, *Maori Race*, p. 65; Tuta Nihoniho, in Best, *Games and Pastimes*, p. 158.
60. Chapman, cited in Alfred K. Newman, 'On the musical notes and other features of the long Maori trumpet', *TPNZI*, vol. 38, 1905, p. 135.
61. Banks, cited in Andersen, *Maori Music*, p. 5.
62. Fischer, *Sound-producing Instruments*, p. 87.
63. Jean-Michel Beaudet, 'New Caledonia: Musical instruments', in *The Garland Encyclopedia of World Music*, vol. 9, eds Adrienne L. Kaeppler & J.W. Love (New York; London: Garland Publishing, 1998), p. 680; Richard Feinberg, 'Anuta', in *The Garland Encyclopedia of World Music*, vol. 9, eds Adrienne L. Kaeppler & J.W. Love (New York; London: Garland Publishing, 1998), p. 860; Fischer, *Sound-producing Instruments*, p. 78.
64. Beattie, *Traditional Lifeways*; Best, *Forest Lore*, pp. 303–5.

65. Flintoff, *Taonga Pūoro*, p. 29.
66. Bengt Anell, *Hunting and Trapping Methods in Australia and Oceania* (Lund, Sweden: Hakan Ohlssons Boktryckeri, 1960), pp. 33–34; Henry D. Skinner & William Baucke, *The Moriors* (Honolulu: Bishop Museum, 1928), p. 22.
67. Flintoff, *Taonga Pūoro*, p. 30.
68. Bernice Pauahi Bishop Museum, Hawai`i (accession number: 08617). A similar artefact comes from a Moriori archaeological site at Lake Huro, Rēkohu; although archaeologist Ian Barber (pers. comm., 3 June 2020) thinks this artefact is most likely not a flute, but rather a needle.
69. The proximal ends of panpipes in Tonga (mimiha), Sāmoa and the Philippines also had bevelled edges like that used for pūmotomoto: see Ernest Dodge & Edwin Brewster, 'The acoustics of three Maori flutes', *JPS*, vol. 54, no. 1, 1945, p. 44.
70. Fischer, *Sound-producing Instruments*, pp. 90–92.
71. There may, however, be a physical connection with a Hawaiian instrument. A small number of pūtōrino had two bores, joined at the top and bottom to form a single bore at each end (pūtōrino kakau rua). This resembles a sole account of a small double nose flute from Hawai`i (Byron, cited in Andersen, *Maori Music*, p. 218).
72. Grey, cited in Andersen, *Maori Music*, p. 239.
73. Anon, *A Journal of a Voyage Round the World in …* Endeavour *in the Years 1768, 1769, 1770 and 1771* (London: Becket & Hondt, 1771), p. 108; J.C. Beaglehole (ed.), *The Journals of Captain James Cook: The Voyage of the Endeavour 1768–1771*, vol. 1 (Cambridge: Cambridge University Press, 1955), p. 285; J.C. Beaglehole (ed.), *The Endeavour Journal of Joseph Banks 1768–1771* (Sydney: Angus & Robertson, 1962), p. 30.
74. In the far north, Raukataura's flute was once the cocoon of the casemoth, but she later went to live in this cocoon. Since losing her flute, her music takes the form of sudden, unintelligible sounds in the forest. Raukataura is alternatively spelt Raukatauri, Hine Raukatauri or Rakataura. Raukataura was the original name of the goddess, used in the north of Te Ika a Māui (Tai Tokerau); her name changed to Raukatauri elsewhere. The goddesses of the arts of pleasure – including flute playing, for Tūhoe and Ngāti Kahungunu – were Takatakaputea and Marereotonga. Among other iwi, these goddesses were the sisters Raukatauri and Raukatamea, respectively. See Best, cited in Augustus Hamilton, *Maori Art* (London: Holland Press, 1972), p. 372; Jo'el Komene, 'Kōauau auē, e auau tō au e: The kōauau in Te Ao Māori', MA thesis, University of Waikato, 2009, pp. 29, 32; Richard Nunns & Allan Thomas, 'The search for the sound of the pūtōrino: "Me te wai e utuutu ana"', *Yearbook for Traditional Music* 37, 2005, p. 72; Orbell, *Illustrated Encyclopedia*, pp. 151–53; White, cited in Karyn Paringatai, 'Poia mai taku poi: Unearthing the knowledge of the past' (MA thesis, University of Otago), 2004, p. 29.
75. Komene, 'Kōauau', pp. 32–33.
76. Orbell, cited in Nunns & Thomas, 'Sound of the pūtōrino', p. 72. In the Tuamotus, names for these sisters include Katouri and Katomea (Longstaff, cited in Paringatai, 'Poia mai', p. 62).
77. Flintoff, *Taonga Pūoro*, p. 65; Orbell, *Illustrated Encyclopedia*, p. 152. Other sources name Raukataura the daughter or sister of Tinirau, or the sister of Rupe and Māui (Komene, 'Kōauau', pp. 29, 32; Paringatai, 'Poia mai', p. 19).
78. Jonassen, 'Southern Cook Islands', p. 901.
79. Te Rangi Hīroa, cited in Andersen, *Maori Music*, p. 164; Peter Crowe, 'Nose flute music of Fiji', *Domodomo*, vol. 1, no. 2, 1995, pp. 6–8; Fischer, *Sound-producing Instruments*, p. 108.

80. Johannes C. Andersen, *Maori Life in Ao-tea* (Christchurch: Whitcombe & Tombs, 1907), p. 143; Te Rangi Hīroa, *Coming of the Maori*, p. 261; Flintoff, *Taonga Pūoro*, pp. 14, 24, 65, 74; Jerome Kavanagh, 'Pūtōrino ā Raukatauri', *Introduction to Taonga Puoro: Porotiti and pūrerehua*, video, SOUNZ Centre for NZ Music, www.youtube.com/watch?v=Wi85Xgdysbo. The Pākehā scientific explanation is that she attracts a mate by scent rather than by sound (Nunns & Thomas, 'Sound of the pūtōrino', p. 73).
81. According to taonga pūoro player, maker and educator Bob Bickerton (pers. comm. April 2023), Māori arts advocate Te Aue Davis (1925–2010, Ngāti Maniapoto, Ngāti Uekaha and Ngāti Te Kanawa) recalled her grandmother waking her up one night when she was a child to listen to the song of the casemoths in the trees outside.
82. Nunns & Thomas, 'Sound of the pūtōrino', p. 72.
83. Cook, cited in Komene, 'Kōauau', p. 32; Nunns & Thomas, *Ara Puoro*, pp. 42, 50, 55–58, 76.
84. If so, this aspect of the pūtōrino's voice is similar to the spirit voices of Papua New Guinea sacred flutes (Fischer, *Sound-producing Instruments*, pp. 93–94, 97–99).
85. Ibid., pp. 75–76.
86. Flintoff, *Taonga Pūoro*, p. 77; Mauri Tirikatene, in Nunns & Thomas, 'Sound of the pūtōrino', pp. 70–71, 76.
87. Terence Barrow, *Traditional and Modern Music of the Maori* (Wellington; Sydney: Seven Seas, 1965), pp. 35–36, 38; Andersen, *Maori Music*, p. 238.
88. Komene, 'Kōauau', p. 34; Hirini Melbourne, *Toiapiapi: He huinga o ngā kura puoro a te Māori* (Wellington: Shearwater, 2016), p. 47; Nunns & Thomas, 'Sound of the pūtōrino', pp. 71, 73; Robert L. Thorne, '(Re) constructing the kōauau: Traditional and modern methods in the making of kōauau rākau' (MA thesis, Massey University, 2012), pp. 105–6. Wheke is also a term for 'a very small centipede': see David Miller, 'The insect people of the Maori', *JPS*, vol. 61, 1952, p. 53. Jerome Kavanagh explains that the central mangai relates to the hole the young bag-moth caterpillars chew through their mother's cocoon, and that blowing across that hole references their voices: Pūtōrino ā Raukatauri', *Introduction to Taonga Puoro*, www.youtube.com/watch?v=Wi85Xgdysbo. This reference to offspring links to ideas of fertility and procreation.
89. Iehu Nukunuku, in Best, *Games and Pastimes*, pp. 129–30.
90. The Ngāti Kahungunu version of the tale of Tinirau and Kae refers to tō and tōrehe in addition to pūtōrino (Best, *Games and Pastimes*, p. 153). From their context in this narrative, it appears that tō and tōrehe were types of musical instrument, though tō is described solely by Brown (*Tākaro II*, p. 39) and tōrehe is described nowhere. Tō and tōrehe may have been alternative names for pūtōrino, or different but related instruments, as shown in the etymology of their names. One definition of tō is 'moisten, wet'; while a meaning of the related term totō is 'gush forth, spring up'. Tō also relates to conception, which aligns with meanings and uses elsewhere ascribed to pūtōrino. None of the definitions of tōrehe or rehe directly apply to a musical instrument, though tore means 'cut, split' – which would be apt for a flute made in two halves and then bound together, as are pūtōrino.
91. Fischer, *Sound-producing Instruments*, pp. 87–88.
92. POLLEX.
93. Fischer, *Sound-producing Instruments*, pp. 87, 95–97.
94. Ibid., p. 131.
95. Ibid., pp. 86, 102–3.
96. As well as in the Polynesian outliers (Anuta, Tikopia), and the Solomons (Small Malaita and Ulawa).
97. POLLEX.

98. Hans Fischer, 'Polynesische musikinstrumente: Innerpolynesische Gliederung – ausserpolynesische Parallelen', *Zeitschrift für Ethnologie*, vol. 86, no. 2, 1961, p. 294; Melbourne, *Toiapiapi*, p. 57; McLean, *Maori Music*, p. 192. The natural shape of sperm whale teeth meant they were ideal for being made into nguru in Aotearoa. Whale teeth were highly valued and were used as indicators of high social status, which may be one reason why nguru (either made from whale teeth, or echoing their shape) were often worn around the neck by chiefs. The use of sperm whale teeth as ornaments has also been noted in the Marquesas and Mangareva, as well as in Aotearoa and Rēkohu (Te Rangi Hīroa, *Coming of the Maori*, p. 287).
99. See Joan Maingay, 'Notes on a *nguru* from Kauri Point swamp', *NZ Archaeological Association Newsletter*, vol. 27, no. 2, 1984, pp. 79–82. There are also historical accounts of similar instruments. One nguru was 'formed from a gourd, and instead of being blown, was softly crooned into' – a description appropriate to a definition given by Williams for the term nguru: murmur: see William Baucke, 'Maori music: Flutes and flautists', *New Zealand Herald Supplement*, 15 November 1924. Hue with elongated necks could be used to make 'toy nguru or pu' : see George Graham, in Andersen, *Maori Music*, p. 296.
100. Ernest Dodge & Edwin Brewster, 'The acoustics of three Maori flutes', *JPS*, vol. 54, no. 1, 1945, p. 59.
101. Andersen, *Maori Music*, p. 250.
102. Fischer, *Sound-producing Instruments*, pp. 103–7, 111–12; Tepaki Mokotupu, in McLean, *Weavers of Song*, pp. 61, 360. The bamboo mouth 'flute' (more correctly, free single-reed aerophone) called kī or pū hakahau, as well as the mouth-blown vivo found in the Marquesas, are similar (McLean, *Weavers of Song*, p. 265). A mouth flute named 'mamapu' was played in Sāmoa, and was either side- or end-blown – though this may have been introduced in post-European contact times (Te Rangi Hīroa, in Andersen, *Maori Music*, pp. 164–65). A mouth flute tradition characterised Melanesia, where they were likely introduced from Micronesia (or from Polynesia in the case of New Caledonia) (McLean, *Music, Dance*, p. 94; McLean, *Music, Lapita*). End-blown flutes blown in a manner somewhat similar to kōauau have been reported from Papua New Guinea. The flute's upper opening is placed in front of the player's lower lip, and their airstream is directed into the tube with the upper lip pushed forward. The air is blown in sideways, with the flute typically held somewhat to one side. Like Māori kōauau, these flutes are described as having typically three but as many as four or five fingerholes, but are much longer than kōauau (around 50cms) (Fischer, *Sound-producing Instruments*, pp. 88–89).
103. McLean, *Maori Music*, pp. 193–94, 373–74.
104. In West Polynesia, both ends were generally closed, and the flutes could be played from either end; whereas in East Polynesia (as in Aotearoa) only one end was closed, with the nose hole located near the closed end (Andersen, *Maori Music*, pp. 30, 105, 241; Best, *Games and Pastimes*, pp. 148–53; McLean, *Weavers of Song*, p. 359). Though many kōauau in museum collections, particularly bird bone examples, have holes very near one end like Tūteranginoti's flute, these are often very small and are holes for suspension cords; they have no detectable effect on pitch when used as fingerholes, and would need to be larger in order to function as nose-blowing holes.
105. Beattie, *Traditional Lifeways*, p. 78. The piercing of the nasal septum by Tūhoe was probably introduced by Kāti Mamoe: see Skinner, cited in I.W. Keyes, 'The Ngatimamoe: The Western Polynesian-Melanesoid sub-culture in New Zealand', *JPS*, vol. 76, no. 1, 1967, p. 70.

106. Komene, 'Kōauau', p. 100; Nunns & Thomas, *Ara Puoro*, pp. 46–49, 89. Nose playing from the upturned end soothed babies to sleep, and mouth playing from the end with the large bore was used from when the lid of a person's coffin was closed until the time it was laid in the urupā during tangihanga: Jerome Kavanagh, 'Nguru – nose flutes', *Introduction to Taonga Puoro*, www.youtube.com/watch?v=FtQPOIylDrQ.

107. Kiwi Amohau, in Andersen, *Maori Music*, p. 233. One kōauau, 1799.2.18, is described as 'making a sound only when the nostrils breathe in': see Te Rangi Hīroa, in Jan Söderstrom, *A. Sparrman's Ethnographical Collection from James Cook's Second Expedition (1772–1775)* (Stockholm: The Ethnological Museum of Sweden, 1939), pp. 54–56; Anders Sparrman, *A Voyage Round the World with Captain James Cook in H.M.S.* Resolution (Great Britain: Golden Cockerel Press, 1944), p. 56.

108. Iehu Nukunuku, in Best, *Games and Pastimes*, pp. 135–36.

109. Nunns & Thomas, *Ara Puoro*, pp. 46–49.

110. Written as hōpo or hopo, and pronounced hōp' (Shand, 'Moriori people', p. 81; Skinner & Baucke, *The Morioris*, p. 18).

111. By the 1890s the only type of instrument remembered by Moriori elders was a type of flute equivalent to Māori kōauau. Moriori had 'no musical instrument, although they knew traditionally of the Koauau, or flute of the Maoris, the use of which, however, was neglected'; see: Alexander Shand, 'The Moriori people of the Chatham Islands: Their traditions and history', *JPS*, vol. 3, no. 2, 1894, p. 76. It is not known which term Moriori used to describe this instrument, though Moriori language expert Kiwa Hammond coined the term miheke rē hopo for such flutes in 2019: Kiwa Hammond, pers. comm., Kōpinga marae, 2019.

112. Skinner asserts that the fourth hole was added 'because the spacing of the first three did not produce the required notes' and, if so, 'we may suppose that one of the first three was plugged when the fourth was in use'. See Henry D. Skinner, *The Morioris of Chatham Islands* (Honolulu: Bishop Museum, 1923), p. 121. There is, however, no valid reason to suppose that this flute, in its current form, is not anything other than what it was intended to be. Skinner appears to be assuming that, as most Māori kōauau had three fingerholes, the same should be expected of Moriori flutes of the same type.

113. Jenny Cave, *Experimental Analysis of Bird Bone Artefacts from the Waihora Site, Chatham Island* (Dunedin: Anthropology Dept, University of Otago, 1977), p. 40.

114. Douglas G. Sutton, 'Polynesian coastal hunters in the subantarctic zone: A case for the recognition of convergent cultural adaptation' (PhD thesis, University of Otago, 1979), pp. 149, 230–31.

115. Henry D. Skinner & William Baucke, *The Morioris* (Honolulu: Bishop Museum, 1928), pp. 31–32.

116. Frank A. Simpson, *Chatham Exiles: Yesterday and to-day at the Chatham Islands* (Wellington: A.H. & A.W. Reed, 1950), p. 28. See also Henry D. Skinner, *The Morioris of Chatham Islands* (Honolulu: Bishop Museum, 1923), p. 63.

117. Christina Jefferson, *Dendroglyphs of the Chatham Islands: Moriori designs on karaka trees* (Wellington: Polynesian Society, 1956), pp. 373, 380, 424–45; Tom Lanauze, pers. comm., August 2019; Justin Maxwell, 'The Moriori: The integration of arboriculture and agroforestry in an East Polynesian society' (PhD thesis, University of Otago, 2014), pp. 88–89; Hough, cited in Rhys Richards, *Manu Moriori: Human and bird carvings on live kopi trees on the Chatham Islands* (Wellington: Paremata Press, 2007), pp. 37–38; Skinner, *The Morioris*, pp. 62–63; Skinner & Baucke, *Morioris*, p. 22; J.W. Williams, 'Notes on the Chatham Islands', *Journal of the Anthropological Institute of Great Britain and Ireland* 27, 1898, p. 345.

118. Alexander Shand, 'The early history of the Morioris', *TPNZI*, vol. 37, 1904, p. 151. Susan Thorpe (pers. comm., March 2023) uses an alternative spelling of this deity's name: Heauoro. She states that he is one of the most important Moriori etchu, and is referred to in connection with war. The pou north of Te Awa Pātiki, one of the most sacred and important Moriori sites, is named Ko Ro Puke o Heauoro. Thorpe notes that heiau and heau are terms used in Hawai`i to denoted a temple.
119. Skinner & Baucke, *Morioris*, p. 38.
120. This term, with the same or similar meanings, is also found in Tahiti, Rarotonga, Penrhyn and Rapa Nui; it reconstructs to the East Polynesian tofu, meaning 'point out, indicate' (POLLEX).

CHAPTER 4: ECHOES OF THE ANCESTORS

1. For information about Oceanic musical instruments, I've drawn on early historical accounts and scholarly research, instruments housed in museum collections, and linguistic research on instrument names. Research related to Polynesian migration and trade has also informed this discussion.
2. See, for example: Melinda S. Allen, 'New ideas about late Holocene climate variability in the Central Pacific', *Current Anthropology*, vol. 47, no. 3, 2006, pp. 521–35; Atholl Anderson, 'Chapter 1: Ancient origins', in *Tangata Whenua: A history*, eds Atholl Anderson, Judith Binney & Aroha Harris (Wellington: Bridget Williams Books, 2015); Thomas S. Dye, 'Dating human dispersal in Remote Oceania: A Bayesian view from Hawai`i', *World Archaeology*, vol. 47, no. 4, 2015, p. 668; Tom Higham & Martin Jones, 'Chronology and settlement', in *Change Through Time: 50 years of New Zealand archaeology*, eds Louise Furey & Simon Holdaway (Auckland: New Zealand Archaeological Association, 2004), pp. 215–34; Michael Knapp et al., 'Complete mitochondrial DNA genome sequences from the first New Zealanders', *PNAS*, vol. 109, no. 45, 2012, pp. 18350–54.

    Some scholars favour the early to mid 14th century: see Chris Jacomb et al., 'High-precision dating and ancient DNA profiling of moa (*Aves: Dinornithiformes*) eggshell documents a complex feature at Wairau Bar and refines the chronology of New Zealand settlement by Polynesians', *Journal of Archaeological Science* 50, 2014, p. 29; Richard Walter et al., 'Mass migration and the Polynesian settlement of New Zealand', *Journal of World Prehistory*, vol. 30, no. 4, 2017, pp. 351–76; Elizabeth Matisoo-Smith, 'The human landscape: Population origins, settlement and impact of human arrival in Aotearoa/New Zealand', in *Landscape and Quaternary Environmental Change in New Zealand*, ed. J. Schulmeister (Paris: Atlantis Press, 2017), p. 306.

    Others posit slightly earlier dates: see Atholl Anderson, *The First Migration: Māori origins 3000BC–AD1450* (Wellington: Bridget Williams Books, 2016), pp. 52–53; Ian Goodwin, Stuart Browning & Atholl J. Anderson, 'Climate windows for Polynesian voyaging to New Zealand and Easter Island', *PNAS*, vol. 111, no. 41, 2014, p. 14719; Mara A. Mulrooney et al., 'High-precision dating of colonization and settlement in East Polynesia', *PNAS*, vol. 108, no. 23, 2011, pp. 192–94; Janet Wilmshurst, Terry Hunt, Carl Lipo & Atholl Anderson, 'High-precision radiocarbon dating shows recent and rapid initial human colonisation of East Polynesia', *PNAS*, vol. 108, no. 5, 2011, pp. 1817–18.

    Rēkohu is, at present, believed to have been settled around the same time as Aotearoa – perhaps as early as the 13th century, but definitely by around 1450–1650. See Anderson, *First Migration*, pp. 53–54; Ian Barber, Justin Maxwell &

Fiona Petchey, 'A radiocarbon investigation of Moriori forest use on Rēkohu (Chatham Island), southwestern Polynesia', *Journal of Archaeological Science: Reports* 10, 2016, p. 105; Geoffrey Irwin, *The Prehistoric Exploration and Colonisation of the Pacific* (Cambridge; New York: Cambridge University Press, 1992), pp. 114–15; Justin Maxwell & Ian Smith, 'A re-assessment of settlement patterns and subsistence at Point Durham, Chatham Island', *Archaeology in Oceania*, vol. 50, no. 3, 2015, pp. 162–74.

3. Roger C. Green, 'Changes over time: Recent advances in dating human colonisation of the Pacific Basin area', in *The Origins of the First New Zealanders*, ed. Douglas G. Sutton (Auckland: Auckland University Press, 1994), p. 43; Richard Walter, 'The Cook Islands – New Zealand connection', in *The Origins of the First New Zealanders*, ed. Douglas G. Sutton (Auckland: Auckland University Press, 1994), p. 228. Mervyn McLean, *Were Lapita Potters Ancestral to Polynesia?* (Auckland: Archive of Maori and Pacific Music, University of Auckland, 2008), p. 53.
4. Andrew Crowe, 'New Zealand place names shared with Central East Polynesia', *Rapa Nui Journal*, vol. 28, no. 1, 2014, p. 9.
5. John Gibb, 'Old stone blocks linked to Tahiti', *Otago Daily Times*, 5 April 2019, p. 17; Karen Greig et al., 'Ancient DNA evidence for the introduction and dispersal of dogs (*Canis familiaris*) in New Zealand', *Journal of Pacific Archaeology*, vol. 9, no. 1, 2018, p. 5; Ray Harlow, 'Māori dialectology and the settlement of New Zealand', in *The Origins of the First New Zealanders*, ed. Douglas G. Sutton (Auckland: Auckland University Press, 1994), p. 114; Dilys Johns, Geoffrey Irwin & Yun Sung, 'An early sophisticated East Polynesian voyaging canoe discovered on New Zealand's coast', *PNAS*, vol. 111, no. 41, 2014, pp. 14728–33; Elizabeth Matisoo-Smith et al., 'Patterns of prehistoric human mobility indicated by mitochondrial DNA from the Pacific rat', *PNAS*, vol. 95, no. 25, 1998, pp. 15145–50.
6. In a related note, there is a linguistic similarity that links the spaces where musical instruments, among other entertainments, were performed. Travelling groups of entertainers, known as Arioi, were observed in Tahiti by early European observers. This name relates to the Māori whare karioi (travelling whare tāpere, or house of entertainment), as well as the Cook Islands `are karioi. `Are tapere existed on Mangareva. See Johannes C. Andersen, *Maori Music with its Polynesian Background* (New Plymouth: Thomas Avery, 1934), p. 17; Karyn Paringatai, 'Poi mai taku poi: Unearthing the knowledge of the past' (MA thesis, University of Otago, 2004), pp. 27–28.
7. William R. Dickinson, 'Impact of mid-Holocene hydro-isostatic highstand in regional sea level on habitability of islands in Pacific Oceania', *Journal of Coastal Research*, vol. 19, no. 3, 2003, p. 495; Marshall Weisler & Roger Green, 'Rethinking the chronology of colonization of southeast Polynesia', in *Polynesians in America: Pre-Colombian Contacts with the New World*, eds Terry Jones et al. (Lanham, New York, Toronto, Plymouth, UK: Altamira, 2011), p. 226.
8. Allen, 'New ideas'; Howard A. Bridgman, 'Could climate change have had an influence on the Polynesian migrations?', *Paleogeography, Paleoclimatology, Paleoecology*, vol. 41, 1983, pp. 193–206; C.J. Burrows & D.E. Greenland, 'An analysis of the evidence for climatic change in New Zealand in the last thousand years: Evidence from diverse natural phenomena and from instrumental records', *JRSNZ*, vol. 9, no. 3, 1979, pp. 321–73; Andrew Crowe, *Pathway of the Birds: The voyaging achievements of Māori and their Polynesian ancestors* (Auckland: David Bateman, 2018), pp. 227–28; Patrick J. Grant, 'Late Holocene histories of climate,

geomorphology and vegetation, and their effects on the first New Zealanders', in *The Origins of the First New Zealanders*, ed. Douglas G. Sutton (Auckland: Auckland University Press, 1994), p. 182; Higham & Jones, 'Chronology', p. 229; Geoff J. Irwin, 'Voyaging and settlement', in *Vaka Moana: Voyages of the ancestors*, ed. K.R. Howe (Auckland: David Bateman, 2006), p. 91; Helen Leach & B.F. Leach, 'Environmental change in Palliser Bay', in *Prehistoric man in Palliser Bay*, eds B.F. Leach & H.M. Leach (Wellington: National Museum of New Zealand, 1979), pp. 229–40; Patrick D. Nunn et al., 'Times of plenty, times of less: Last-millennium societal disruption in the Pacific Basin', *Human Ecology*, vol. 35, no. 4, 2007, pp. 385–401; Barry V. Rolett, 'Voyaging and interaction in ancient East Polynesia', *Asian Perspectives*, vol. 41, no. 2, 2002, pp. 182–94; Douglas G. Sutton, 'Polynesian coastal hunters in the subantarctic zone: A case for the recognition of convergent cultural adaptation' (PhD thesis, University of Otago), 1979, p. 238.

9. Some research points toward contact with, or migration from, the Marquesas: see Jeff Evans, *The Discovery of Aotearoa* (Auckland: Reed, 1998), p. 25; Roger C. Green, 'Linguistic subgrouping within Polynesia: The implications for prehistoric settlement', *JPS*, vol. 75, no. 1, 1966, pp. 31–32; Michael Pietrusewsky, 'The physical anthropology of Polynesia: A review of some cranial and skeletal studies', in *Oceanic Culture History: Essays in honour of Roger Green*, ed. Roger C. Green & Janet Davidson (Dunedin: New Zealand Journal of Archaeology Special Publication, 1996), pp. 347–48; Konrad Wagner, *The Craniology of the Oceanic Races* (Oslo: Jacob Dybwad, 1937), pp. 128–29, 131, 133). However, researchers have found absolutely no evidence of Aotearoa's Pacific rat population having originally come from the Marquesas: see Matisoo-Smith et al., 'Patterns of prehistoric human mobility'. Pacific rats cannot swim for long distances and do not interbreed, making them an excellent species to study as a proxy for human migrations.
10. K. Ann Horsburgh & Mark McCoy, 'Dispersal, isolation, and interaction in the islands of Polynesia: A critical review of archaeological and genetic evidence', *Diversity*, vol. 9, no. 37, 2017, p. 11; Marshall Weisler, 'Hard evidence for prehistoric interaction in Polynesia', *Current Anthropology*, vol. 39, no. 4, 1998.
11. Ray Harlow, 'Borrowing and its alternatives in Māori', in *Borrowing: A Pacific perspective*, eds Jan Tent & Paul Geraghty (Canberra: Pacific Linguistics Research School of Pacific and Asian Studies, 2004), p. 146.
12. Kenneth David Collerson & Marshall I. Weisler, 'Stone adze compositions and the extent of ancient Polynesian voyaging and trade', *Science* 317, 2007, pp. 1907–11; see also Irwin, *Prehistoric Exploration*, p. 165.
13. Goodwin et al., 'Climate windows', p. 14718.
14. Weisler ('Introduction', p. 11) favours the first of these options, arguing that the development of two-piece fishhooks in Hawai`i, Aotearoa and Rapa Nui, for example, was an example of convergent evolution versus diffusion.
15. Mervyn McLean, *Were Lapita Potters*, p. 9. The musical systems of marginal East Polynesia share some common traits, including: narrowness of range (typically within an interval of a perfect fourth or less), few notes (generally two to four), small melodic leaps (mostly major and minor seconds, and minor thirds), and trailing cadences (endings). Traits such as smallness of range and microtonality are shared characteristics of pre-European contact Māori and Tahitian music. See Andersen, *Maori Music*, pp. 4–5, 10; Johann Reinhold Forster, *Observations Made During a Voyage Round the World*, eds Nicholas Thomas, Harriet Guest & Michael Dettelbach (Honolulu: University

of Hawai`i Press, 1996), p. 285; McLean, *Weavers of Song*, pp. 30–31.

16. Haplogroup IIIa (a genetic population specific to Remote Oceania that shares a common paternal or maternal ancestor).
17. Elizabeth Matisoo-Smith & J.H. Robins, 'Origins and dispersals of Pacific peoples: Evidence from mtDNA phylogenies of the Pacific rat', *PNAS*, vol. 101, no. 24, 2004, pp. 9167–72.
18. For a summary of key differences between East and West Polynesian musical traits, see McLean, *Weavers of Song*, p. 453.
19. POLLEX.
20. See Ernst Dieffenbach, *Travels in New Zealand*, vol. 2 (Christchurch: Capper, 1843), p. 56. Similarly, an early missionary in the north talks about 'tossing the poi, a ball about the size of a good cricket-ball': see William Yate, *An Account of New Zealand* (London: Seeley & Burnside, 1835), p. 113.
21. Beattie, *Traditional Lifeways*, pp. 80–81.
22. William Colenso, 'Contributions towards a better knowledge of the Maori race', *TPNZI*, vol. 13, 1880, p. 59.
23. Te Rangi Hīroa [Sir Peter Buck], *Ethnology of Mangareva* (Honolulu, Hawai`i: Bernice P. Bishop Museum, 1938), pp. 185–86; Paringatai, 'Poia mai', pp. 40, 42, 57, 60, 62–64, 115.
24. Ngata, cited in Mervyn McLean, *Maori Music* (Auckland: Auckland University Press, 1996), p. 129. Long-stringed poi are referred to as being older than short-stringed poi in Murihiku, Canterbury, and in Whakarewarewa, Rotorua. See Beattie, *Traditional Lifeways*, pp. 80–81, 260; Guide Rangi and Kiriwaitangini Maniapoto, in Ngāmoni Huata, *The Rhythm and Life of Poi* (Auckland: HarperCollins, 2000), p. 61.
25. James Herries Beattie, *Traditional Lifeways of the Southern Maori*, ed. Atholl Anderson (Dunedin: Otago University Press in association with Otago Museum, 1994), pp. 47, 80–81; Harko Brown, *Ngā Taonga Tākaro: Māori sports and games* (Auckland: Penguin Books, 2008), pp. 54, 73; Harko Brown, *Ngā Taonga Tākaro II: The matrix* (Mt Maunganui: Physical Education New Zealand, 2016), pp. 48; 127; Riley, cited in Paringatai, 'Poia mai', p. 95. Historian Arthur Thomson captures this transition from long- to short-stringed poi, noting the string being 'shortened and lengthened' during the game. Arthur S. Thomson, *The Story of New Zealand: Past and present, savage and civilised* (London: Murray, 1859), p. 196.
26. Beattie, *Traditional Lifeways*, p. 81. Poi are mentioned in a version of the tale of Tinirau and Kae recorded by an informant from the Otago Heads – a narrative that travelled with the ancestors of Māori from tropical Polynesia, although it's unknown at what point poi were included in the narrative (Beattie, *Traditional Lifeways*, p. 562).
27. Haddon, and Hardy & Elkington, in Elsdon Best, *Games and Pastimes of the Maori* (Wellington: Whitcombe & Tombs, 1925), pp. 58–59.
28. Edwin G. Burrows, 'Native music of the Tuamotus', *Bishop Museum Bulletin*, vol. 109, 1933, p. 37; Williams, cited in Paringatai, 'Poia mai', p. 67.
29. Paringatai, 'Poia mai', pp. 60–61, 64, 66.
30. Thomson, *The Story of New Zealand*, p. 196. Long-stringed poi were used in games in other ways in Aotearoa: see Beattie, *Traditional Lifeways*, pp. 80–81, 484; Best, *Games and Pastimes*, pp. 54–57.
31. A Tongan game could also be a possible precursor. Ferdon (cited in Paringatai, 'Poia mai', p. 51) describes it as involving a 61 centimetres long piece of string with a hard, round seed about the size of a musketball attached to each end. The string was held at the midpoint, and the aim of the game was to twirl the seeds without them striking each other. A remarkably similar Māori game is described by Beattie (*Traditional Lifeways*, p. 70): 'stone swinging, was to tie two stones in flax strings and swing both

with one hand, each stone going in the opposite direction to the other'. Such games may relate to the Cook Islands stone sling (maka), which made a haunting humming sound when swung through the air, and accompanied songs about war. See Jon Tikivanotau Jonassen, 'Southern Cook Islands: Instrumental music', in *The Garland Encyclopedia of World Music*, vol. 9, eds Adrienne L. Kaeppler & J.W. Love (New York; London: Garland Publishing, 1998), p. 901.

32. Beattie, *Traditional Lifeways*, p. 562; Longstaff, cited in Paringatai, 'Poia mai', pp. 61–62.
33. West Polynesian terms for juggling are different from pei/poi. See J.W. Love, 'Sāmoa', in *The Garland Encyclopedia of World Music*, vol. 9, eds Adrienne Kaeppler & J.W. Love (New York; London: Garland Publishing, 1998), p. 804; Paringatai, 'Poia mai', pp. 52–54; Vula Saumaiwai, 'Fijian *meke*', in *Talking About Oral Traditions*, ed. Saimone Vatu (Suva: Fiji Museum, 1976), p. 42.
34. POLLEX. The same is possibly true for Moriori, where the term poi means 'leap, jump' – though no concrete evidence of Polynesian juggling traditions having been transferred to Rēkohu has survived. Poi, a direct match for the Māori term, was used on Pukapuka (Northern Cook Islands), although there it was a child's guessing game that had nothing to do with juggling (Beaglehole, cited in Paringatai, 'Poia mai', pp. 55–56). In almost all of East Polynesia, poi is a type of dish where food such as taro and breadfruit is mixed with water and mashed to a pulp (Paringatai, 'Poia mai', p. 71).
35. Te Rangi Hīroa, cited in Paringatai, 'Poia mai', p. 57.
36. Te Rangi Hīroa [Sir Peter Buck], *Arts and Crafts of the Cook Islands* (Honolulu: Bernice P. Bishop Museum, 1944), p. 260. As in the Southern Cooks, the fruit of the candlenut tree was used in the Marquesas, and in Mangareva – where another name for pei was kita`irama. Kita`i means 'to keep a number of balls in the air; to throw high', while rama refers to the green fruit of the candlenut tree. Rama were often used as a source of light. These fruits are not found in Aotearoa, but memory of them persists in the use of the term rama to mean 'torch or other artificial light.'
37. *Hoheria populnea* bark was used in Te Tau Ihu o te Waka and in Murihiku to make poi (Beattie, *Traditional Lifeways*, pp. 47, 80–81, 476).
38. Best, *Games and Pastimes*, pp. 55–57. The clay balls discussed by Louise Furey ('Clay – a lesser known medium for Maori artefacts', *Records of the Auckland Museum*, vol. 50, 2015, pp. 21–31) may possibly have been juggled, though they may just have likely have been used in various games otherwise involving stones. See also Harko Brown, *Ngā Taonga Tākaro: Māori sports and games* (Auckland: Penguin Books, 2008), pp. 57–59; *Ngā Taonga Tākaro II: The Matrix* (Mt Maunganui: Physical Education New Zealand, 2016), pp. 43–44.
39. Beattie, *Traditional Lifeways*, p. 254.
40. POLLEX.
41. William Mariner, cited in Paringatai, 'Poia mai', p. 47. Moyle (cited in Paringatai, 'Poia mai', p. 48) says it was performed by girls rather than women.
42. Paringatai, 'Poia mai', p. 50.
43. Moyle, cited in Paringatai, 'Poia mai', pp. 49, 65–66.
44. Edward S.C. Handy, *The Native Culture in the Marquesas* (Honolulu: Bernice P. Bishop Museum, 1923); Linton, cited in Paringatai, 'Poia mai', pp. 64, 66.
45. Te Rangi Hīroa, *Ethnology of Mangareva*, p. 107–8.
46. Colocott, cited in Paringatai, 'Poia mai', p. 48; Adrienne L. Kaeppler, 'Tonga', in *The Garland Encyclopedia of World Music*, vol. 9, eds Adrienne L. Kaeppler & J.W. Love (New

York; London: Garland Publishing, 1998), p. 787.

47. Hohaia et al., cited in Paringatai, 'Poia mai', pp. 162–63; Huata, *Rhythm and Life*, p. 35.
48. Mervyn McLean & Margaret Orbell, *Traditional Songs of the Maori* (Auckland: Auckland University Press, 2004), pp. 44–49.
49. Stewart Culin, 'Hawaiian Games', *American Anthropologist*, vol. 1, no. 2, 1899, p. 220; Ernest S. Dodge, *Hawaiian and Other Polynesian Gourds* (Ku Pa`a Publishing, Honolulu, Hawai`i, 1995), pp. 56–57, plate XXIId. A similar name, pokakakaka, was used in the Southern Cooks for lamellaphones made from coconut-leaflet midribs (Te Rangi Hīroa, *Arts and Crafts*, p. 262).
50. Hans Fischer, *Sound-producing Instruments in Oceania: Construction and playing technique, distribution and function* (Port Moresby: Institute of Papua New Guinea Studies, 1986), pp. 80–81; McLean, *Weavers of Song*, p. 240.
51. Culin, 'Hawaiian Games', p. 220; McLean, *Weavers of Song*, pp. 307–8.
52. POLLEX.
53. Fischer, *Sound-producing Instruments*, p. 81.
54. An object made from whalebone is described as being 15 or 19 centimetres long. It was found by Abner Clough in an old Moriori burial ground among the sandhills on the shore near a place called Ōkawa, near Kaingaroa. The notch in the centre of the narrow end may have been caused by cord wearing through a hole. Horizontal notches near the narrow end may have been intended to help secure binding in place, or may be purely decorative. Dendy identifies this artefact as a bullroarer, an identification supported by Susan Thorpe of the Hokotehi Moriori Trust (pers. comm., August 2019). Skinner believed it may have been a pendant or a toy – perhaps a stylised representation of a patu, though Moriori pendants discussed by Skinner tend to be shorter – around 9 centimetres long. See Arthur Dendy, 'On some relics of the Moriori race', *TPNZI*, vol. 34, 1901, pp. 131–32; Henry D. Skinner, *The Morioris of Chatham Islands* (Honolulu: Bishop Museum, 1923), plate VIII.
55. Tuta Nihoniho, in Elsdon Best, 'Notes on Maori musical instruments' (unpublished manuscript held in Alexander Turnbull Library, Wellington, MS-Papers-0072-19B, 1923), pp. 34–35. Best, *Games and Pastimes*, p. 163; Fischer, *Sound-producing Instruments*, p. 81.
56. Brian Flintoff, *Taonga Pūoro: Singing treasures* (Nelson: Craig Potton Publishing, 2004), p. 61; Nunns & Thomas, *Ara Puoro*, pp. 22, 34, 101, 132.
57. Simpson, cited in Fischer, *Sound-producing Instruments*, p. 82.
58. Augustus Hamilton, *Maori Art* (London: Holland Press, 1972), p. 374; Nunns & Thomas, *Ara Puoro*, pp. 100, 136.
59. Fischer, *Sound-producing Instruments*, p. 82.
60. A variety of names were used. For example, Cook Islands leaf whizzers were called pātangitangi or wakatangitangi (Te Rangi Hīroa, *Arts and Crafts*, p. 262; McLean, *Weavers of Song*, pp. 63, 89, 133, 212). The term pinao was used in the Marquesas: Jane Freeman Moulin, *Music of the Southern Marquesas Islands* (Auckland: Archive of Maori and Pacific Music, 1994), p. 20.
61. POLLEX.
62. McKern, cited in Richard Moyle, *Tongan Music* (Auckland: Auckland University Press, 1987), p. 108. In addition to Aotearoa, places where a bow was used as part of the instrument include Espiritu Santo (Vanuatu) and Papua New Guinea (Fischer, *Sound-producing Instruments*, p. 86).
63. Fischer, *Sound-producing Instruments*, pp. 126–27; Te Rangi Hīroa, *Ethnology of Mangareva*, p. 183; Te Rangi Hīroa, *Arts and Crafts*, p. 259; Richard Moyle, *The Sounds of Oceania: An illustrated catalogue of the sound producing instruments of Oceania in the Auckland Institute and Museum* (Auckland:

Auckland Institute and Museum, 1989), p. 25.

64. The term refers to whip tops in Rapa. In Pukapuka (Northern Cooks), the cognate pōteka is used for spinning tops. In Rarotonga, and elsewhere in East Polynesia, the term has meanings closer to the term's East Polynesian reconstruction: POLLEX.
65. Ibid.
66. McLean, *Weavers of Song*, p. 357; Mervyn McLean, *Music, Lapita, and the Problem of Polynesian Origins* (Auckland: Mervyn McLean, 2014), pp. 51–52.
67. Neville Keith Drew, 'Music of Fiji' (BA thesis, University of Queensland Conservatorium, 1979), p. 58; Nathaniel B. Emerson, *Unwritten Literature of Hawaii: The sacred songs of the hula* (Washington: Government Printing Office, 1909), pp. 116, 144–45; Fischer, *Sound-producing Instruments*, p. 16; McLean, *Weavers of Song*, pp. 89, 221, 354.
68. A 1778 account from Hawai`i mentions an instrument somewhat similar to the Māori pākuru: a stick around 61 centimetres long was held in one hand 'as we do a fiddle', and this was struck with a smaller stick 'resembl[ing] a drumstick'. Another account, from 1816, notes: 'the women have pieces of wood which they strike in time one upon the other': see Andersen, *Maori Music*, pp. 46, 103. Māori pākuru were made from a piece of mataī around 46 centimetres long and 2.5 centimetres in diameter (equivalent to the length of the forearm), slightly flat in the centre, and tapering a little at each end. The ends were carved, and the middle left smooth. It was suspended on the thumb of the left hand by a piece of string tied to each end of it, so that one end should be a little within the teeth when the mouth was partially open. The performer held in their right hand, interlaced between the three middle fingers, another piece of mataī around 25.5 centimetres long and as thick as a man's middle finger: they struck this against the other piece gently while breathing words of the chant, producing higher or lower tones by closing or opening the lips. See Charles Te Ahukaramū Royal, 'Te Whare Tapere: Towards a model for Māori performance art' (PhD dissertation, Victoria University, 1998), p. 114; John White, *The Ancient History of the Maori, His Mythology and Traditions*, vol. 2 (Wellington: George Didsbury, 1887), pp. 130–31.
69. Helen Reeves Lawrence, 'Northern Cook Islands', in *The Garland Encyclopedia of World Music*, vol. 9, eds Adrienne L. Kaeppler & J.W. Love (New York; London: Garland Publishing, 1998), p. 906.
70. McLean, *Weavers of Song*, p. 263; Jane Freeman Moulin, 'Gods and mortals: Understanding traditional function and usage in Marquesan musical instruments', *JPS*, vol. 106, no. 3, 1997, p. 255.
71. Andersen, *Maori Music*, pp. 143, 207; Ellis, cited in Best, *Games and Pastimes*, p. 173.
72. Best, *Games and Pastimes*, p. 174; McLean, *Weavers of Song*, pp. 356–58; Moulin, 'Gods and mortals', p. 255.
73. Fischer, *Sound-producing Instruments*, p. 48; Teone Taare Tīkao, in Beattie, *Traditional Lifeways*, p. 259.
74. In the Marquesas, this type of use may postdate the introduction of metal Jew's harps, whereby lamellaphones assumed the speaking function of other instruments: see Jane Freeman Moulin, 'Kapatuhe: Exploring word-based performance on Marquesan musical instruments', *The Galpin Society Journal* 55, 2002, p. 143.
75. Te Rangi Hīroa [Sir Peter Buck], *The Coming of the Maori* (Wellington: Whitcombe & Tombs; Maori Purposes Fund Board, 1966), p. 364; Mrs Ngata, in Andersen, *Maori Music*, p. 299. Pākuru could be used the same way. In the Arawa rohe, these instruments were used to perform rangi pākuru: the words (for example, about love) were breathed over the longer of the two rods (Mair, 'Inward correspondence').

Both lamellaphones and percussion rods were quite quiet and intimate, and therefore perfect for communicating private words of love.

76. Fischer, *Sound-producing Instruments*, pp. 47–50; McLean, *Weavers of Song*, pp. 153, 264–65; Moulin, 'Kapatuhe', pp. 142, 144.
77. Moulin, 'Kapatuhe', p. 156.
78. Edwin G. Burrows, *Western Polynesia: A study of cultural differentiation* (Dunedin: University Bookshop Ltd., 1970), p. 51, distribution diagram 14; Fischer, *Sound-producing Instruments*, p. 74. This instrument was also reported from Polynesian outlier Mungiki.
79. Gold, in McLean, *Weavers of Song*, p. 63.
80. Fischer, *Sound-producing Instruments*, p. 74.
81. Andersen, *Maori Music*, p. 213; Fischer, *Sound-producing Instruments*, p. 73.
82. Te Rangi Hīroa, *Coming of the Maori*, p. 268.
83. Fischer, *Sound-producing Instruments*, pp. 70–71; Stack, cited in Andersen, *Maori Music*, p. 213.
84. Moulin (*Southern Marquesas Islands*, p. 16) notes that, according to a Fatu Hiva elder, tita`apu were around 457 millimetres long, making them similar in length to Hawaiian examples, though still longer than Māori ones.
85. Andersen, *Maori Music*, pp. 151, 212; Fischer, *Sound-producing Instruments*, pp. 73–74.
86. Best, *Games and Pastimes*, pp. 164–65.
87. John White, cited in Best, 'Notes', p. 29.
88. Tuta Nihoniho, in Best, 'Notes', p. 29; Thomson, cited in Best, *Games and Pastimes*, p. 166.
89. John G. Wood, *The Natural History of Man*, vol. 2 (New York: Routledge, 1880), p. 138.
90. This is 73 centimetres long, and is held in Te Papa (accession number: ME000466). For a photograph, see: Flintoff, *Taonga Pūoro*, p. 83.
91. Richardson, cited in Best, *Games and Pastimes*, p. 165.
92. Burrows, *Western Polynesia*, p. 50, distribution diagram 14; Fischer, *Sound-producing Instruments*, pp. 18–22, 33–34. Likewise, bamboo slit gongs in Ureparapara (Banks Islands, northern Vanuatu) were placed on a stand made from two tree forks (Fischer, *Sound-producing Instruments*, p. 17).
93. Fischer, *Sound-producing Instruments*, p. 35.
94. Te Rangi Hīroa, *Coming of the Maori*, pp. 253–54; Te Rangi Hīroa, *Arts and Crafts*, p. 459.
95. Beattie, *Traditional Lifeways*, pp. 77–78.
96. McLean, *Maori Music*, p. 370.
97. Best, *Games and Pastimes*, p. 170.
98. MacGregor, cited in McLean, *Weavers of Song*, p. 89.
99. Best, *Games and Pastimes*, p. 170; Richard Moyle, *Polynesian Sound-producing Instruments* (Princes Risborough, UK: Shire Ethnography, 1990), pp. 31–32. Instruments consisting solely of rolled mats, which may also have provided inspiration for this type of Māori pākuru, are used in Sāmoa (fala), `Uvea and Futuna (fala or tāfala), Tokelau (fala or moega), Fiji, Rotuma and Tuvalu. None of the West Polynesian terms for these struck mats resembles pākuru, however.
100. POLLEX.
101. McLean, *Weavers of Song*, p. 197; Richard Moyle, 'Samoan musical instruments', *Ethnomusicology*, vol. 18, no. 1, 1974, p. 65. They are also found in the Polynesian outliers.
102. McLean, *Weavers of Song*, pp. 351–52.
103. Parkinson, cited in McLean, *Weavers of Song*, p. 27; Louis Bougainville, *A Voyage round the World … in 1766, 1767, 1768, and 1769*, trans. John Reinhold Forster (London: J. Nourse & T. Davies, 1772), pp. 247, 270–71; Fischer, *Sound-producing Instruments*, p. 44; Forster, *Observations*, p. 334; Douglas L. Oliver, *Ancient Tahitian Society* (Hawai`i: University of Hawai`i Press, 1974), pp. 328, 331. Seashell clappers were also used in Tonga (Fischer, *Sound-producing Instruments*, p. 7; McLean, *Weavers of Song*, p. 354).

104. Fischer, *Sound-producing Instruments*, pp. 6–7.

105. Emerson, *Unwritten Literature*, p. 147. The term `ili`ili is also used for lithophones in Sāmoa, but in that case Moyle (*Polynesian Sound-producing Instruments*, p. 28) believed it may have been a local and comparatively recent invention, as there are no references to this instrument in the historical literature.

106. Fischer, *Sound-producing Instruments*, pp. 6–7, 44. Pebble castanets were also used in the Marianas, and bamboo clappers were used on Gaua (Banks Islands).

107. Mary E. Lawson Burke, 'Marshall Islands', in *The Garland Encyclopedia of World Music*, vol. 9, eds Adrienne L. Kaeppler & J.W. Love (New York; London: Garland Publishing, 1998), pp. 753–54; Lamont Lindstrom, 'Southern area', in *The Garland Encyclopedia of World Music*, vol. 9, eds Adrienne L. Kaeppler & J.W. Love (New York; London: Garland Publishing, 1998), p. 708; Mac Marshall, Larry Gabriel & Joakim Manniwel Peter, 'Chuuk', in *The Garland Encyclopedia of World Music*, vol. 9, eds Adrienne L. Kaeppler & J.W. Love (New York; London: Garland Publishing, 1998), p. 737; Barbara B. Smith, 'The music and dance of Micronesia: Musical instruments', in *The Garland Encyclopedia of World Music*, vol. 9, eds Adrienne L. Kaeppler & J.W. Love (New York; London: Garland Publishing, 1998), p. 716.

108. Moyle, *Polynesian Sound-producing Instruments*, p. 38.

109. Jonassen, 'Southern Cook Islands', p. 899.

110. Laval, cited in Te Rangi Hīroa, *Ethnology of Mangareva*, p. 399.

111. Instruments like this were also used in New Caledonia: Dan Bendrups, *Singing and Survival: The music of Easter Island* (New York: Oxford University Press, 2019), p. 23.

112. POLLEX. *tumutumu means 'top' in PPN (Kirch & Green, *Hawaiki*, p. 165).

113. Jo'el Komene, 'Kōauau auē, e auau tō au e: The kōauau in te ao Māori' (MA thesis, University of Waikato, 2009), p. 198.

114. Andersen, *Maori Music*, p. 195.

115. Brigham, cited in Best, *Games and Pastimes*, p. 160. Dodge (*Polynesian Gourds*, p. 45) notes that these instruments may sometimes have been blown with the mouth.

116. Dodge, *Polynesian Gourds*, p. 45; Fischer, *Sound-producing Instruments*, p. 123.

117. Andersen, *Maori Music*, p. 295; Best, *Games and Pastimes*, pp. 158–60; James Edge-Partington, 'Tahitian group', in *An Album of the Weapons, Tools, Ornaments, Articles of Dress etc. of the Natives of the Pacific Islands*, vol. 1 (Manchester, 1890), p. 19.

118. Vida Chenoweth, 'Eastern Highlands Province', in *The Garland Encyclopedia of World Music*, vol. 9, eds Adrienne L. Kaeppler & J.W. Love (New York; London: Garland Publishing, 1998), p. 533; Fergus Clunie, 'Fijian musical instruments', *Fiji Heritage*, 1 August 1979; Fischer, *Sound-producing Instruments*, pp. 123–25.

119. Brigham, cited in Best, *Games and Pastimes*, p. 160; Edge-Partington, *Album*, p. 35; Paringatai, 'Poia mai', p. 68.

120. Dodge, *Polynesian Gourds*, pp. 45, 51. An instrument similar to poi āwhiowhio, a whirring nut, is associated with love on the Gazelle Peninsula, Papua New Guinea, and another similar instrument can be found in Malekula (Vanuatu): see Fischer, *Sound-producing Instruments*, pp. 125–26.

121. Tawai Taunoa, in Nunns & Thomas, *Ara Puoro*, p. 37.

122. Similar instruments include the Fijian sici (whistles made from small hollowed-out nuts, with an open bottom and pierced sides, swung on strings) and Tokelauan tagihuhu (hollow-eyed coconuts, thrown to make them wail or moan). See Fergus Clunie, *Yalo i Viti – Shades of Viti: A Fiji Museum catalogue* (Suva: Fiji Museum, 1986), p. 45; Richard Moyle, *Traditional Samoan Music* (Auckland: Auckland University Press in association with the Institute for Polynesian Studies, 1988), p. 53.

123. Hirini Melbourne, *Toiapiapi: He huinga o ngā kura puoro a te Māo*ri (Wellington: Shearwater, 2016), p. 30.

124. Dodge, *Polynesian Gourds*, p. 59; Paringatai, 'Poia mai', pp. 51, 67–68.

125. POLLEX.

126. The same instrument is found on Rapa Nui, though it could have been imported from South America. Similar instruments are also found in Papua New Guinea (Fischer, *Sound-producing Instruments*, p. 43). Coconut leaflet rattles were possibly used in the Northern Cooks, and bundles of dried sago palm pinnules were used as rattles (called *ū sēru*) in Tikopia. See Kauraka Kauraka, 'Manihiki: A local view', in *The Garland Encyclopedia of World Music*, vol. 9, eds Adrienne L. Kaeppler & J.W. Love (New York; London: Garland Publishing, 1998), p. 909; Fischer, *Sound-producing Instruments*, pp. 123–25; McLean, *Weavers of Song*, pp. 89, 246, 355. Undescribed 'dance rattles' were used in Tahiti (McLean, *Weavers of Song*, p. 354).

127. Ada Haig, in Nunns & Thomas, *Ara Puoro*, pp. 36, 133; Fischer, *Sound-producing Instruments*, pp. 42–43.

128. See Best, *Games and Pastimes*, p. 160; Peter Gathercole, 'A Maori shell trumpet at Cambridge', in *Problems in Economic and Social Archaeology*, eds Gale de G. Sieveking et al. (London: Duckworth, 1977), p. 195. Similarly, narratives about named conches having been brought to earth by the king of the spirits or the underworld exist in Hawai`i and Tahiti (Fischer, *Sound-producing Instruments*, pp. 144–45).

129. Gilbert Mair, 'Inward correspondence J-N (Letters to Elsdon Best)' (unpublished manuscript, held in Alexander Turnbull Library, Wellington, MS Papers 007204, 1900). It was made from a conch shell found at Matatā or Te Awa a te Atua. This instrument was played to announce the birth and death of the firstborn male issue of Tūwharetoa's descendants: see Rangiiria Hedley, in Harold Atwood Anderson, 'A confluence of streams: Music and identity in Aotearoa/New Zealand' (PhD dissertation, University of Maryland, 2008), p. 200. However, in the family of Te Heuheu Tukino of Tokaanu, the firstborn child was female. On her mother's order, the trumpet was sounded. Later, a boy was born. He was named Tureiti (too late) as the trumpet had already been sounded; nevertheless he inherited his father's rank and leadership. Later his name was changed to the family name of Te Heuheu Tukino (Te Rangi Hīroa, *Coming of the Maori*, p. 345).

130. Andersen, *Maori Music*, p. 272.

131. Patrick V. Kirch & Roger C. Green, *Hawaiki, Ancestral Polynesia: An essay in historical anthropology* (Cambridge, New York: Cambridge University Press, 2001), p. 192.

132. Mervyn McLean, *Music, Dance and Polynesian Origins: The evidence from POc and PPn* (Auckland: Archive of Maori and Pacific Music, University of Auckland, 2010), pp. 17–19; McLean, *Music, Lapita*, pp. 43–44, 67. More than 20 Pacific cultures used the word pū for trumpet – mainly for shell trumpets: in West Polynesia, Niue, Sāmoa, Tokelau and Tuvalu; in the Polynesian outliers Aniwa, Luangiua, Sikaiana, Tikopia and West Futuna; and, in Eastern Polynesia, Rapa Nui, Hawai`i, the Gambier Islands, the Northern Cooks (Manihiki and Pukapuka) and the Marquesas. An exception was Tonga, where they are known as kele`a. Putatara was the term used for conch trumpets in Mangareva and Hawai`i (Andersen, *Maori Music*, p. 195). Cognates of that term used in Aotearoa include kākara, pūputara, pūtara, pūtaratara and pūtātara. In Mangareva, the terms putara and putaratara were only used for trumpets made from *Cassis* shell, so named for the shell's projecting points (tara) (Te Rangi Hīroa, *Ethnology of Mangareva*, p. 400). Others use the term for shells more generally; a whirlwind; or a pursing of the lips (McLean, *Maori Music*, p. 371).

133. Malcolm Ross, Andrew Pawley & Meredith Osmond, *The Lexicon of Proto Oceanic: The culture and environment of ancestral Oceanic society*, vol. 1 (Canberra: Australian National University, 1998), p. 107.
134. Best, *Games and Pastimes*, p. 160; Gathercole, 'Shell trumpets', pp. 194–96.
135. Letters to George Grey, 1862 (Unpublished letters held in Auckland Libraries Heritage Collections, GNZMMS144), pp. 75–76.
136. Deb Goomes, personal communication, 2023.
137. There is a sole account of a tētere (flax leaf oboe) being used in Aotearoa for a similar purpose. In that instance, the instrument was played to announce a visit by Tūkāroto Matutaera Pōtatau Te Wherowhero Tāwhiao, the second Māori king, to Te Horo (Andersen, *Maori Music*, p. 293).
138. Fischer, *Sound-producing Instruments*, pp. 142–43; McLean, *Weavers of Song*, pp. 26, 200. On Tutuila (Sāmoa), a war god named Tapaai resided in a conch shell trumpet. A sacred conch trumpet in Tikopia (Solomons) 'was believed to be the embodiment of the god Rata' (McLean, *Weavers of Song*, pp. 154, 246). A Hawaiian creation chant links the sound of a conch trumpet called Kahai to the voice of the god Lono. Such beliefs extended to Melanesia. In Vanuatu, there is a relationship between conch trumpets, the god Kwat-Ambat-Tagaro, and pig killings; and in Santa Cruz (Solomon Islands) the conch is blown during sacrifices to Tangiteala or Tangaloa. Likewise, conch trumpets are used in turtle sacrifices at Napuka (Tuamotus) (Fischer, *Sound-producing Instruments*, pp. 139, 141–44).
139. Gill (cited in McLean, *Weavers of Song*, p. 62) says it could only be played by the king and was kept near the entrance of the god house; whereas according to Fischer (*Sound-producing Instruments*, p. 144), only the priest could blow the instrument.
140. McLean, *Weavers of Song*, p. 62.
141. Margaret Orbell, *The Illustrated Encyclopedia of Māori Myth and Legend* (Christchurch: Canterbury University Press, 1995), pp. 56–57.
142. Similarly, the conch trumpet was described as a 'war trumpet' in Kaipara (James Buller, cited in Best, *Games and Pastimes*, p. 174).
143. Best, *Games and Pastimes*, p. 161; Fischer, *Sound-producing Instruments*, pp. 141–43; McLean, *Weavers of Song*, pp. 26, 62, 265, 307.
144. Nunns & Thomas, *Ara Puoro*, p. 96.
145. Samuel Timoti Robinson, *Tohunga: The revival: Ancient knowledge for the modern era* (Auckland: Reed Books, 2005), p. 154.
146. McLean, *Weavers of Song*, pp. 25, 62. This usage has also been reported in Sāmoa, Tuvalu and Tokelau (McLean, *Weavers of Song*, pp. 154, 180, 200).
147. McLean, *Weavers of Song*, pp. 25, 62, 266; also in the Marquesas, Sāmoa, Tonga, `Uvea and Futuna (McLean, *Weavers of Song*, pp. 154–55, 222).
148. Fischer, *Sound-producing Instruments*, pp. 127–28; McLean, *Music, Lapita*, p. 33.
149. Beattie, *Traditional Lifeways*, pp. 78–80, 259, 484; Best, *Games and Pastimes*, pp. 155, 165. Elsewhere in Waitaha, these instruments were sounded as an alarm to alert the residents of a pā to imminent danger. Remarkably, pūkaea blown from the top of Pukeuri Hill, Oamaru, could be heard at the Waitaki rivermouth around 16 kilometres distant. Similarly, in the Whanganui rohe, these instruments were used to deliver military signals. See James Cowan, *The New Zealand Wars*, vol. 2 (Wellington: Government Printer, 1922), pp. 39–41. A truly remarkable survival – an example found in the Moa Bone Point Cave, Redcliffs (Christchurch) in 1872 – was carbon dated to 257±30 BP. See Roger Fyfe, 'Rediscovering two tetere, flax trumpets in Canterbury Museum', in *Ngā Kete a Rēhua Inaugural Māori Research Symposium Te Waipounamu 2008*, eds Rawiri Taonui &

Hamuera Kahi (Christchurch: Aotahi School of Māori and Indigenous Studies, Te Whare Wānanga o Waitaha, 2008), pp. 326–31. It is held in the Canterbury Museum (accession number: MH.43.1).

150. George Graham, in Andersen, *Maori Music*, pp. 292–93.

151. McLean, *Weavers of Song*, pp. 63, 200, 212, 267.

152. POLLEX.

153. Best, *Games and Pastimes*, p. 128.

154. Te Rangi Hīroa, *Ethnology of Mangareva*, p. 399.

155. Green harakeke (the rito, or juvenile flax shoot) was used to make tētere. The leaf tip was wound around the end of the third finger of the left hand, and then wound around and around to the desired length (up to around 0.9–1.2 metres long), then tied with a thin strip of harakeke. Sometimes an arero/tohe (tongue/tonsil) made of kōrari was inserted; slits were split in two adjacent coils of the body, and the tongue was inserted so that its free end – sometimes bifurcated, to resemble an inverted Y – projected into the bore. See Andersen, *Maori Music*, pp. 292–93.

156. Te Rangi Hīroa, *Coming of the Maori*, p. 252.

157. Given as e `wiu by Dieffenbach (*Travels*, pp. 57–58), although the alternative name of poretu is also given for a wooden flute with four fingerholes. This type of flute was occasionally played with the nose. See Wolf, cited in Sibyl Marcuse, *Musical Instruments: A comprehensive dictionary* (New York: W.W. Norton, 1975), p. 419.

158. POLLEX; Pawley, cited in McLean, *Music, Lapita*, p. 50. Vivo was also the name of a bamboo whistle in Mangareva, though Te Rangi Hīroa (cited in McLean, *Weavers of Song*, p. 293) thought it may have been a late introduction. Flutes similar to vivo were played in Mangareva (pu ko`e), the Cooks (ko`e) and the Australs. Marquesas nose flutes could also be called pū ihu, pūhekuheku or pūkohe (Te Rangi Hīroa, *Arts and Crafts*, p. 268; McLean, *Weavers of Song*, pp. 106, 265, 292; Moulin, 'Kapatuhe', p. 135), though Moulin ('Gods and mortals', p. 254) distinguishes between nose flutes (pū ihu) and mouth flutes (pū kohe, vivo).

159. Hio is also used for bamboo flutes in Rapa Nui (McLean, *Music, Dance*, p. 45). Cognate terms are also used in East Polynesia (Hawai`i, Mangareva, Ra`ivavae, Rapa, Rarotonga, the Tuamotus) and West Polynesia (Tokelau) for 'whistle' (POLLEX).

160. Best, *Games and Pastimes*, pp. 142–44.

161. J.C. Beaglehole (ed.), *The Journals of Captain James Cook: The voyage of the* Endeavour *1768–1771*, vol. 1 (Cambridge: Cambridge University Press, 1955), p. 127; Ellis, cited in Andersen, *Maori Music*, p. 148. Some flutes of this type could have a hole on the underside – as was the case of the longer whio and some Tahitian vivo: see Colenso, 'Contributions', p. 80; John Savage, *Some Account of New Zealand* (London: Murray & Constable, 1807), p. 83. Some nguru and kōauau also had a hole on the underside. Flintoff (*Taonga Pūoro*, p. 30) even mentions an example of an ororuarangi that has this feature.

162. Best, *Games and Pastimes*, p. 131.

163. POLLEX. Porutu also refers to a laudatory song in the Gambier Islands (McLean, *Music, Dance*, pp. 80–82, 92).

164. This flute was described by Buller and Mair: see Johannes C. Andersen, 'Maori music', *TPNZI*, vol. 55, 1924, p. 694. White (cited in Best, *Games and Pastimes*, pp. 133–34) instead used the term rehu.

165. Te Rangi Hīroa, *Coming of the Maori*, p. 262.

166. McLean, *Weavers of Song*, pp. 61, 106, 114, 265. In Buller's description, the flute is (unusually) semi-closed near one end and closed at the other. This trait is also noted for New Georgia side-blown flutes (Fischer, *Sound-producing Instruments*, p. 101).

167. Moyle, *Samoan Musical Instruments*, p. 68.

168. Mead and Grove, cited in Komene, 'Kōauau', p. 25.
169. Translated by S. Percy Smith, cited in Komene, 'Kōauau', pp. 38–39. Matorohanga's information was recorded, in English, by J.M. Jury; part or all of which was translated into te reo Māori by Thomas Young, and then translated back into English by Smith. Smith attempted to identify the geographical location of Maui-iti and Maui-nui, but these names are more likely to mean 'ancestral dwelling place' rather than referring to a specific location.
170. Paraphrased from Komene, 'Kōauau', p. 39. For the full version of this story, see Te Rangikaheke, in George Grey, *Polynesian Mythology and Ancient Traditional History of the New Zealand Race* (Auckland: H. Brett, 1885), pp. 91–93. In another example, a kōrero from the Takitimu rohe concerns the longest placename in Aotearoa: Taumatawhakatangihangakoauauotamatea-turipukakapikimaungahoronukupokai-whenuakitanatahu (the summit of the hill where Tamateapokaiwhenua played on his kōauau to his love). The identity of the person Tamatea expressed his love for is not known exactly, but it may have been a female lover – or his brother, who was killed in the battle of Matanui by Ngāti Hine iwi from Tai Tokerau (Andersen, *Maori Music*, p. 234; Komene, 'Kōauau', pp. 40, 44).
171. Similar terms are used elsewhere in East Polynesia: Rotuma (au), Hawai`i (`aoa), and Rapa Nui (`au-`au): POLLEX. In an interesting coincidence, the Proto Austronesian *qauR (bamboo) and Proto Oceanic *kauR (bamboo, bamboo wind instrument) apply to bamboo or bamboo wind instruments in Admiralties, North New Guinea, Meso-Melanesian, Southeast Solomonic and North/Central Vanuatu languages. For example, the Sa`a (Solomon Islands) language term for panpipes is au: Malcolm Ross, Andrew Pawley & Meredith Osmond, *The Lexicon of Proto Oceanic: The culture and environment of ancestral Oceanic society*, vol. 1 (Canberra: Australian National University, 1998), p. 108. There is no apparent link, however, between these terms and kōauau.
172. McLean, *Weavers of Song*, pp. 133, 212. Papaya leaf stalks were also used in this way in West Polynesia (Tonga, Sāmoa, Niue and Tokelau) and New Caledonia (Beaudet, 'New Caledonia', p. 679; Moyle, *Tongan Music*, p. 107). Similarly, the hollow stem of ngahu (*Scaevola taccada*) was used in Manihiki (Reeves Lawrence, 'Northern Cook Islands', p. 906). Materials with pithy interiors were also used to make flutes in Tokelau, Niue and the Marquesas. See McLean, *Weavers of Song*, pp. 200, 211; Jane Freeman Moulin, 'Marquesas Islands', in *The Garland Encyclopedia of World Music*, vol. 9, eds Adrienne L. Kaeppler & J.W. Love (New York; London: Garland Publishing, 1998), p. 896. Like Māori flutes made from pithy cores, those from Niue had their bores formed by burning. See Robert L. Thorne, '(Re)constructing the kōauau: Traditional and modern methods in the making of kōauau rākau' (MA thesis, Massey University, 2012). A flute that is probably Niuean, closely resembling a kōauau, is pictured in D.R. Simmons, *Craftsmanship in Polynesia* (Dunedin: Otago Museum Trust, 1963), fig. 100, p. 44.
173. Jonassen, 'Southern Cook Islands', p. 901; Jenny M. Little, *Report on a Preliminary Study of the Music of Nga Pu Toru* (Auckland: Department of Anthropology, 1989), p. 22.
174. Ernest Dodge and Edwin Brewster, 'The acoustics of three Maori flutes', *JPS*, vol. 54, no. 1, 1945, p. 56.
175. In the pūrākau about Māui catching the winds (Robinson, *Tohunga*, pp. 45–48), he uses hue to contain the winds from the north, south and east. Nowadays, hue puruhau are considered taonga pūoro. The gourd's neck is removed, and the player blows across the opening to create a vibrant

bass sound. The pitch can be changed by the player tilting the hue forwards or backwards, or by raising and lowering a finger inside the opening, while blowing. Dried seeds or beans (or similar) can be placed inside the hue to create a rattling sound, and the hard outer skin of the hue can be struck to create a percussive sound.

176. Ailsa Smith (from the writings of Te Kahui Kararehe of Rahotu, Taranaki), *Songs and Stories of Taranaki: He Tuhituhi Tai Hau-ā-uru* (Christchurch: Macmillan Brown Centre for Pacific Studies, University of Canterbury, 1993), p. 17.
177. Nunns & Thomas, *Ara Puoro*, pp. 37, 132.
178. Elsdon Best, *Tūhoe: The children of the mist* (Auckland: Reed, 2005), p. 899.
179. William Wyatt Gill, *Myths and Songs from the South Pacific* (Hawaii: University Press of the Pacific, 2004), p. 321.
180. Robinson, *Tohunga*, pp. 46, 154, 166.
181. Fischer, *Sound-producing Instruments*, p. 108; McLean, *Weavers of Song*, pp. 265, 305, 359.
182. Te Rangi Hīroa, *Arts and Crafts*, p. 274.
183. Radiguet, cited in Moulin, 'Kapatuhe', p. 139.

APPENDIX 1: NAMES OF INSTRUMENTS

1. For the names of instruments that have subsequently joined the taonga pūoro whānau, see Richard Nunns & Allan Thomas, *Te Ara Puoro: A journey into the world of Māori music* (Nelson: Craig Potton Publishing, 2014).

APPENDIX 2: NAMES OF PLANTS, ANIMALS AND OTHER MATERIALS

1. As noted in Chapter 2, hue could be grown north of Ōtautahi Christchurch, though gourd instruments were probably more commonly found in areas further north. See Sebastian Lowe & Alistair Fraser, 'Connecting with inner landscapes: Taonga pūoro, musical improvisation and exploring acoustic Aotearoa/New Zealand', *Journal of New Zealand and Pacific Studies*, vol. 6, no. 1, 2008, p. 12.
2. Tutu has psychoactive elements, which may link instruments made from this wood with healing. Flutes made from tutu may have been used in connection with healing (setting broken bones and reducing inflammation) – perhaps in conjunction with an incantation called hono (to join). See Te Rangi Hīroa [Sir Peter Buck], *The Coming of the Maori* (Wellington: Whitcombe & Tombs; Maori Purposes Fund Board, 1966), p. 407. According to one tradition, the wood for flutes used in seduction was that of hard-to-reach branches (e.g. those of trees situated on a cliff or above a river). Flutes made from tutu, and perhaps poroporo, may have had sacred uses (e.g. matakite); and instruments made from both materials may have played a role in relieving pain during the application of tā moko. Poroporo flutes may also have been associated with birth control or food (ripe berries were eaten; the leaves were not eaten, but were used to flavour food in hāngi). Various types of trumpet were made from tutu. Tētere could be made from hollowed tutu branches with mouthpieces: see Elsdon Best, *Games and Pastimes of the Maori* (Wellington: Whitcombe & Tombs, 1925), p. 155; Cowan, in Mervyn McLean, *Maori Music* (Auckland: Auckland University Press, 1996), p. 371; Robert L. Thorne, '(Re) constructing the kōauau: Traditional and modern methods in the making of kōauau rākau' (MA thesis, Massey University, 2012), pp. 41–50, 55, 65.
3. Mānuka wood is used in the contemporary revival of pūrerehua (Rangiiria Hedley, in Jo'el Komene, 'Kōauau auē, e auau tō au e: The kōauau in Te Ao Māori' (MA thesis, University of Waikato, 2009),

p. 62), though it 'is not a wood that is listed as commonly used for the contruction of kōauau specifically, or taonga pūoro generally' (Thorne, '(Re)constructing the kōauau', p. 160).

4. A shell of this type was used for pūtātara recovered from the Oruarangi pā site. The small ostrich-foot shell (*Pelicaria vermis*) was perhaps used to make shell trumpets, though it may have been too small. See Johannes C. Andersen, *Maori Music with its Polynesian Background* (New Plymouth: Thomas Avery & Sons, 1934), p. 272; Louise Furey, *Oruarangi: The archaeology and material culture of a Hauraki pa* (Auckland: Auckland Institute and Museum, 1996), p. 121.
5. Large triton shells are not native to Aotearoa, but wash up occasionally on beaches in the northern North Island. Europeans also brought these shells to Aotearoa as trade items. See Elsdon Best, *The Maori*, vol. 2 (Wellington: Polynesian Society, 1924), p. 162; Moyle, in McLean, *Maori Music*, p. 371; Edward Tregear, *The Maori Race* (Whanganui: A.D. Willis, 1904), p. 65.
6. Whale teeth, mainly from sperm whales, were used – especially for making nguru, but also for kōauau. The use of whalebone to make instruments was uncommon, but occasionally pūrerehua and pākuru beaters were made from this material (Best, *Games and Pastimes*, p. 173). A sliver of kauwae upokohue (pilot whale jawbone) was sometimes used to make rōria. Porotiti were sometimes made from the circular discs that form the caps of whale vertebrae. Moa bone was also used to make flutes. See Brian Flintoff, *Taonga Pūoro: Singing treasures* (Nelson: Craig Potton Publishing, 2004), pp. 42, 58, 66.
7. Some poi were adorned with dog hair, pāua shell and/or feathers (Davis in Best, *Games and Pastimes*, p. 55). Those with dog hair ornamentation were known as poi awe. Dog hair was also used to ornament pūtōrino and pūtātara, and a strip of dog skin was sometimes used as a handle or string. Kākāpō feathers were used to decorate pūtātara (for example one that belonged to Ihaka Whanga from Kahutara Point Table Cape) (Best, *Games and Pastimes*, pp. 56, 132, 132c, 160, 162). Gathercole (in McLean, *Maori Music*, p. 180) suggests that these feathers may have been symbolic. One painting shows a pūtātara and a pūkaea with huia feather decoration. The painting was done by J. McDonald, and is dated 1906. The range of the huia was: the Ruahine, Tararua, Puketoi, Rimutaka and Orongorongo ranges, with their offshoots and spurs; the Pukeatua ridge; perhaps the Tinakori range; and Eketahuna. The tail feathers were highly valued, and were traded to Waikato and Taupō. See Johannes C. Andersen, 'Manuscripts of published works, Box 9' (Unpublished manuscript, held in Auckland Museum, MS-7 folder 2, n.d.); Elsdon Best, *Forest Lore of the Maori* (Wellington: E.C. Keating, 1977), p p. 179–81. Occasionally human milk teeth were inserted as decorations on flutes (Te Awekotuku, in Komene, *Kōauau*, pp. 80–81).

Bibliography

Addison, David & Elizabeth Matisoo-Smith, 'Rethinking Polynesians origins: A West Polynesia triple-I model', *Archaeology in Oceania*, vol. 45, no. 1, 2010, pp. 1–12

Allen, Melinda S., 'New ideas about late Holocene climate variability in the Central Pacific', *Current Anthropology*, vol. 47, no. 3, 2006, pp. 521–35

Allen, Melinda S. & Jennifer M. Huebert, 'Short-lived materials, long-lived trees, and Pacific radiocarbon dating: Considerations for 14C sample selection and documentation', *Radiocarbon*, vol. 56, no. 1, 2014, pp. 257–76

Allen, Melinda S. & Andrew McAlister, 'Early Marquesan settlement and patterns of interaction: New insights from Hatiheu Valley, Nuku Hiva Island', *Journal of Pacific Archaeology*, vol. 4, no. 1, 2013, pp. 90–109

Amman, Raymond, 'Side-blown flutes of New Caledonia', in *The Garland Encyclopedia of World Music*, vol. 9, eds Adrienne L. Kaeppler & J.W. Love (New York; London: Garland Publishing, 1998), pp. 401–2

Andersen, Johannes C., *Māori Life in Ao-tea* (Christchurch: Whitcombe & Tombs, 1907)

——, 'An introduction to Maori music', *Transactions and Proceedings of the New Zealand Institute*, vol. 54, 1923, pp. 743–62

——, 'Maori music', *Transactions and Proceedings of the New Zealand Institute*, vol. 55, 1924, pp. 689–700

——, 'Maori musical instruments', *Art in New Zealand*, vol. 2, 1929, pp. 91–101

——, *Maori Music with its Polynesian Background* (New Plymouth: Thomas Avery & Sons, 1934)

——, *Polynesian Literature: Māori poetry (waiata and tangi)* (New Plymouth: Thomas Avery, 1946)

——, 'Manuscripts of published works, Box 9' (unpublished manuscript held in Auckland Museum, Auckland, MS-7 folder 2, n.d.)

Anderson, Atholl, *When All the Moa Ovens Grew Cold: Nine centuries of changing fortune for the southern Maori* (Dunedin: Otago Heritage Books, 1983)

——, 'The chronology of colonization in New Zealand', *Antiquity*, vol. 65, 1991, pp. 767–95

——, 'Origins, settlement, and society of pre-European South Polynesia', in *The New Oxford History of New Zealand*, ed. Giselle Byrnes (Melbourne; Auckland: Oxford University Press, 2009)

——, 'Chapter 1: Ancient origins', in *Tangata Whenua: A history*, eds Atholl Anderson, Judith Binney & Aroha Harris (Wellington: Bridget Williams Books, 2015)

——, *The First Migration: Māori origins 3000BC–AD1450* (Wellington: Bridget Williams Books, 2016)

Anderson, Atholl, Brian Allingham & Ian Smith (eds), *Shag River Mouth: The archaeology of an early southern Maori village* (Canberra: ANH Publications, Australia National University, 1996)

Anderson, Atholl, Judith Binney & Aroha Harris, *Tangata Whenua: An illustrated history* (Wellington: Bridget Williams Books, 2015)

Anderson, Atholl & Tom Higham, 'The age of rat introduction in New Zealand: Further evidence', *New Zealand Journal of Archaeology*, vol. 24, 2004, pp. 135–47

Anderson, A. & B.G. McFadgen, 'Prehistoric two-way voyaging between New Zealand and East Polynesia: Mayor Island obsidian on Raoul Island, and possible Raoul Island obsidian in New Zealand', *Archaeology in Oceania*, vol. 25, 1990, pp. 24–37

Anderson, A. & Yosihiko Sinoto, 'New radiocarbon ages of colonization sites in East Polynesia', *Asian Perspectives*, vol. 41, no. 2, 2002, pp. 242–57

Anell, Bengt, *Hunting and Trapping Methods in Australia and Oceania* (Lund, Sweden: Hakan Ohlssons Boktryckeri, 1960)

Angas, George French, *Savage Life and Scenes in Australia and New Zealand*, vol. 2. (London: Smith, Elder, 1847)

——, *The New Zealanders Illustrated* (London: Thomas McLean, 1847)

Anon., *A Journal of a Voyage Round the World in …* Endeavour *in the Years 1768, 1769, 1770 and 1771* (London: Becket & Hondt, 1771)

Anon., 'Koche, King of Pitt', *Catholic World*, vol. 17, no. 100, 1873, pp. 545–57

Anon., 'Letters to George Grey' (Unpublished letters held in Auckland Libraries Heritage Collections, GNZMMS144, 1862)

Anon., *Songs from the Past, He Waiata Onamata* (Auckland: Te Reo Rangatira Trust, 1998)

Ashton, Beatrice, 'The koauau player', *Te Ao Hou*, vol. 2, 1952, p. 55

Atherton, R.A. et al., 'A molecular investigation into the origin and relationships of karaka/kōpi (*Corynocarpus laevigatus*) in New Zealand', *Journal of the Royal Society of New Zealand*, vol. 45, no. 4, 2015, pp. 212–20

Atherton, Michael, *Musical Instruments and Sound-Producing Objects of Oceania: The Collections of the Australian Museum* (Bern: Peter Lang AG, International Academic Publishers, 2010)

Atwood Anderson, Harold, 'A confluence of streams: Music and identity in Aotearoa/New Zealand', PhD dissertation, University of Maryland, 2008

Barber, Ian, 'Culture change in northern Te Wai Pounamu', PhD thesis, University of Otago, 1994

Barber, Ian, 'Archaeological art debates and Polynesian images in place', *World Archaeology*, vol. 44, no. 3, 2002, pp. 436–51

Barber, Ian, Justin Maxwell & Fiona Petchey, 'A radiocarbon investigation of Moriori forest use on Rēkohu (Chatham Island), southwestern Polynesia', *Journal of Archaeological Science: Reports*, vol. 10, 2016, pp. 96–102

Barrow, Terence, *The Decorative Arts of the New Zealand Maori* (Wellington: A.H. & A.W. Reed, 1964)

——, *Traditional and Modern Music of the Maori* (Wellington; Sydney: Seven Seas, 1965)

Baucke, William, 'Maori music: Flutes and flautists', *New Zealand Herald Supplement*, 15 November 1924

Beaudet, Jean-Michel, 'New Caledonia: Musical instruments', in *The Garland Encyclopedia of World Music*, vol. 9, eds Adrienne L. Kaeppler & J.W. Love (New York; London: Garland Publishing, 1998), pp. 679–82

Beaglehole, J.C. (ed.), *The Journals of Captain James Cook: The Voyage of the* Endeavour *1768–1771*, vol. 1 (Cambridge: Cambridge University Press, 1955)

Beaglehole, J.C. (ed.), *The* Endeavour *Journal of Joseph Banks 1768–1771* (Sydney: Angus & Robertson, 1962)

Beaglehole, J.C. (ed.), *The Journals of Captain James Cook: The Voyage of the* Resolution *and* Discovery *1776–1780*, vol. 3, part 2 (Cambridge: Cambridge University Press, 1967)

Beatson, Peter, 'Richard Nunns: The renaissance of traditional Maori music', *Music in the Air: Song and spirituality*, vol. 16, 2003, pp. 17–33

Beattie, James Herries, 'Traditions and legends collected from the natives of Murihiku (Southland, New Zealand), part VIII (continued)', *Journal of the Polynesian Society*, vol. 26, no. 2, 1917, pp. 75–86

——, 'Traditions and legends collected from the natives of Murihiku (Southland, New Zealand), part VI (continued)', *Journal of the Polynesian Society*, vol. 27, no. 107, 1918, pp. 137–61

——, *Traditional Lifeways of the Southern Maori*,

ed. Atholl Anderson (Dunedin: University of Otago Press in association with Otago Museum, 1994)

——, *Māori Place-names of Otago* (Christchurch: Cadsonbury, 2001)

——, *Tikao Talks* (Christchurch: Cadsonbury, 2004)

Bendrups, Dan, *Singing and Survival: The music of Easter Island* (New York: Oxford University Press, 2019)

Bennett, Hemi, 'Games of the old time Maori', *Te Ao Hou*, vol. 24, 1958, pp. 52–53

Best, Elsdon, 'The Maori' (unpublished manuscript held in Central City Special Collections, Central Library, Auckland, 305.8994 B55 v.2, n.d.)

——, 'Maori notebook no. 7' (unpublished manuscript held in Alexander Turnbull Library, Wellington, qMS-0183, 1897)

——, 'The diversions of the whare tapere: Some account of the various games, amusements, and trials of skill practised by the Maori in former times', *Transactions and Proceedings of the New Zealand Institute*, vol. 34, 1901, pp. 34–69

——, *Ceremonial Performances Pertaining to Birth, as Performed by the Maori of New Zealand in Past Times* (London: Royal Anthropological Institute of Great Britain and Ireland, 1914)

——, 'Some place names of islands of the Society group', *Journal of the Polynesian Society*, vol. 26, no. 3, 1917, pp. 111–15

——, 'Notes on Maori musical instruments' (unpublished manuscript held in Alexander Turnbull Library, Wellington MS-Papers-0072-19B, 1923)

——, *The Maori*, vol. 1 (Wellington: Polynesian Society, 1924)

——, *The Maori*, vol. 2 (Wellington: Polynesian Society, 1924)

——, *Games and Pastimes of the Maori* (Wellington: Whitcombe & Tombs, 1925)

——, 'The story of Ngae and Tutununui: An East Coast version of the Kae-Tutunui myth', *Journal of the Polynesian Society*, vol. 37, 1928, pp. 261–70

——, *Tuhoe: The Children of the Mist*, vol. 1 (Auckland: Reed, 1972)

——, *Forest Lore of the Maori* (Wellington: E.C. Keating, 1977)

——, *Maori Religion and Mythology: Part 2* (Wellington: P.D. Hasselberg, 1982)

——, *Tūhoe: The Children of the Mist* (Auckland: Reed, 2005)

Best, Simon, 'Oruarangi Pa: Past and present investigations', *New Zealand Journal of Archaeology*, vol. 2, 1980, pp. 65–91

Biggs, Bruce, 'The structure of New Zealand Maori', *Anthropological Linguistics*, vol. 3, no. 3, 1961, pp. 1–54

——, 'Reviews: A dictionary of some Tuamotuan dialects of the Polynesian language', *Journal of the Polynesian Society*, vol. 74, no. 3, 1965, pp. 375–89

——, 'The languages of Polynesia', *Current Trends in Linguistics*, vol. 8, 1971, pp. 466–505

——, 'History of Polynesian phonology', *Pacific Linguistics*, series C, no. 61, 1979

——, 'Does Maori have a closest relative?', in *The Origins of the First New Zealanders*, ed. Douglas G. Sutton (Auckland: Auckland University Press, 1994), pp. 19–51

Bolton, Lissant & Jim Specht, *Polynesian and Micronesian Artefacts in Australia: An Inventory of Major Public Collections – Fiji and Western Polynesia*, vol. 3 (Sydney: Australian Museum, 1985)

Bougainville, Louis, *A Voyage round the World … in 1766, 1767, 1768, and 1769*, trans. John Reinhold Forster (London: J. Nourse & T. Davies, 1772)

Bridgman, Howard A., 'Could climate change have had an influence on the Polynesian migrations?', *Paleogeography, Paleoclimatology, Paleoecology*, vol. 41, 1983, pp. 193–206

Brook, F.J., 'Prehistoric predation of the landsnail *Placostylus ambagiosis* Suter (Stylommatophora: Bulimulidae), and evidence for the timing of establishment of rats in northernmost New Zealand', *Journal of the Royal Society of New Zealand*, vol. 30, no. 3, 2000, pp. 227–41

Brown, Andrew Alexander, 'Material culture traditions of prehistoric Murihiku', MA thesis, University of Otago, 2011

Brown, Deidre, *Tai Tokerau Whakairo Rākau: Northland Māori wood carving* (Auckland: Reed, 2003)

——, 'Ko te ringa ki nga rakau a te Pakeha – Virtual taonga Maori and museums', *Virtual Resources*, vol. 24, no. 1, 2008, pp. 59–75

Brown, Deidre & Ngarino Ellis, *Te Puna: Māori art from Te Tai Tokerau Northland* (Auckland: Reed, 2007)

Brown, Dan & George Nicholas, 'Protecting Canadian First Nations and Māori heritage through conventional legal means', paper presented at the New Zealand and Canada: Connections, Comparisons and Challenges conference, held at Wellington, New Zealand, 9–10 February 2010, www.sfu.ca/ipinch/sites/default/files/resources/presentations/brown-nicholas_canada_nz_presentation_paper_feb_2010.pdf

——, 'Protecting indigenous cultural property in the age of digital democracy: Institutional and communal responses to Canadian First Nations and Māori heritage concerns', *Journal of Material Culture*, vol. 17, no. 3, 2012, pp. 307–24

Brown, Harko, 'Traditional Maori games', 2006, https://wavesouthcanterbury.co.nz/media/4693/tmgharkobrown160120.pdf

——*Ngā Taonga Tākaro: Māori sports and games* (Auckland: Penguin Books, 2008)

—— *Ngā Taonga Tākaro II: The matrix* (Mt Maunganui: Physical Education New Zealand, 2016)

Buller, James, *Forty Years in New Zealand* (London: Hodder & Stoughton, 1878)

Buranarugsa, Malee & Foss Leach, 'Coordinate geometry of Moriori crania', *Man and Culture in Oceania*, vol. 9, 1993, pp. 1–43

Burrows, C.J. & D.E. Greenland, 'An analysis of the evidence for climatic change in New Zealand in the last thousand years. Evidence from diverse natural phenomena and from instrumental records', *Journal of the Royal Society of New Zealand*, vol. 9, no. 3, 1979, pp. 321–73

Burrows, Edwin G., *Native Music of the Tuamotus* (Honolulu: Bernice P. Bishop Museum, 1933)

——, *Western Polynesia: A study of cultural differentiation* (Dunedin: University Book Shop Ltd, 1970)

Burton, Alfred H., *The Maori at Home* (Dunedin: Daily Times, 1885)

Buschan, Georg, *Illustrierte Völkerkunde in Zwei Bänden* (Stuttgart: Strecker & Schröder, 1923)

Campbell, C., 'Typescript of "Remainders" volume on Murihiku, by Herries Beattie' (unpublished manuscript held in Hocken Library, Dunedin, MS-2450, 1989)

Cave, Jenny, *Experimental Analysis of Bird Bone Artefacts from the Waihora Site, Chatham Island* (Dunedin: Anthropology Dept, University of Otago, 1977)

Chenoweth, Vida, 'Eastern Highlands province', in *The Garland Encyclopedia of World Music*, vol. 9, eds Adrienne L. Kaeppler & J.W. Love (New York; London: Garland Publishing, 1998), pp. 526–33

——, 'Managalasi: musical instruments', in *The Garland Encyclopedia of World Music*, vol. 9, eds Adrienne L. Kaeppler & J.W. Love (New York; London: Garland Publishing, 1998), p. 503

Christen, K. 'Does information really want to be free? Indigenous knowledge systems and the question of openness', *International Journal of Communication*, vol. 6, 2012, pp. 2870–93

Clark, Geoffrey et al., 'Stone tools from the ancient Tongan state reveal prehistoric interaction centers in the Central Pacific', *Proceedings of the National Academy of Sciences*, vol. 111, no. 29, 2014, pp. 10491–96

Clark, Ross, 'Moriori and Maori: The linguistic evidence', in *The Origins of the First New Zealanders*, ed. D.G. Sutton (Auckland: Auckland University Press, 1994), pp. 123–35

Clarke, Andrew, 'Origins and Dispersal of the Sweet Potato and Bottle Gourd in Oceania: Implications for prehistoric human mobility', PhD thesis, Massey University, 2009

Classen, Constance & David Howes, 'The Museum as sensescape: Western sensibilities and Indigenous artifacts', in *Engaging All the Senses: Colonialism, Processes of Perception and the Status of Artifacts*, eds Elizabeth Edwards, Chris Gosden & Ruth B. Phillips (Oxford; New York: Berg, 2006), pp. 199–222

Cloake, Jeremy, 'Taonga puoro', www.jeremycloake.com/taonga-puoro

Clunie, Fergus, 'Fijian musical instruments', *Fiji Heritage*, 1 August 1979

——, Yalo i Viti – Shades of Viti: A Fiji Museum catalogue (Suva: Fiji Museum, 1986)

Colenso, William, 'Contributions towards a better knowledge of the Maori race', *Transactions of the New Zealand Institute*, vol. 13, 1880, pp. 57–84

Collerson, Kenneth David & Marshall I. Weisler, 'Stone adze compositions and the extent of ancient Polynesian voyaging and trade', *Science*, vol. 317, 2007, pp. 1907–11

Conte, Eric & Patrick V. Kirch (eds), *Archaeological Investigations in the Mangareva Islands, French Polynesia* (Berkeley: University of California, 2004)

Conte, Eric & Guillaume Molle, 'Reinvestigating a key site for Polynesian prehistory: New results from the Hane dune site, Ua Huka (Marquesas)', *Archaeology in Oceania*, vol. 49, no. 3, 2014, pp. 121–36

Cook, James, 'An account of a voyage round the world in the years 1768, 1769, 1770 and 1771', in *An Account of the Voyages Undertaken by the Order of His Present Majesty for Making Discoveries in the Southern Hemisphere* ed. John Hawkesworth (Dublin: Potts, 1775).

Cowan, James, 'The Maori signal gong: Stories of the wooden pahu' (unpublished manuscript held in Alexander Turnbull Library, Wellington, MS papers 11310-187, n.d.)

——, *The New Zealand Wars*, vol. 2 (Wellington: Government Printer, 1922)

——, *The Maori Yesterday and Today* (Wellington: Whitcombe & Tombs, 1930)

——, *Maori Folk Tales of the Port Hills, Canterbury, New Zealand* (Christchurch: Cadsonbury, 1995)

Crowe, Andrew, 'New Zealand place names in South Polynesia', *Rapa Nui Journal*, vol. 26, no. 2, 2012, pp. 43–53

Crowe, Andrew, 'New Zealand place names shared with the Hawaiian archipelago', *Rapa Nui Journal*, vol. 27, no. 1, 2013, pp. 21–36

——, 'New Zealand place names shared with Central East Polynesia', *Rapa Nui Journal*, vol. 28, no. 1, 2014, pp. 5–21

——, *Pathway of the Birds: The voyaging achievements of Māori and their Polynesian ancestors* (Auckland: David Bateman, 2018)

Crowe, Peter, 'Nose flute music of Fiji', *Domodomo*, vol. 1, no. 2, 1995, pp. 6–9

Cruise, Richard, *Journal of a Ten Months' Residence in New Zealand* (Christchurch: Capper, 1824)

Culin, Stewart, 'Hawaiian Games', *American Anthropologist*, vol. 1, no. 2, 1899, pp. 201–47

Davidson, Janet, *The Prehistory of New Zealand* (Auckland: Longman Paul, 1984)

Davidson, Janet et al., 'Connections with Hawaiki: The evidence of a shell tool from Wairau Bar, Marlborough, New Zealand', *Journal of Pacific Archaeology*, vol. 2, no. 2, 2011, pp. 93–102

Dawson, Elliot W., 'An extinct sea eagle in the Chatham Islands', *Notornis*, vol. 9, no. 5, 1961, pp. 171–72

De Lange, Peter J., John W.D. Sawyer & Rebecca Ansell, *Checklist of Indigenous Vascular Plant Species Recorded from Chatham Islands* (Wellington: Dept. of Conservation, 1999)

Dendy, Arthur, 'On some relics of the Moriori race', *Transactions of the New Zealand Institute*, vol. 34, 1901, pp. 123–34

Dickinson, William R., 'Impact of mid-Holocene hydro-isostatic highstand in regional sea level on habitability of islands in Pacific Oceania', *Journal of Coastal Research*, vol. 19, no. 3, 2003, pp. 489–502

Dieffenbach, Ernst, 'An account of the Chatham Islands', *Journal of the Royal Geographical Society London*, vol. 11, 1841, pp. 195–215

——, *Travels in New Zealand*, vol. 2 (Christchurch: Capper, 1843)

Dodge, Ernest S., *Hawaiian and Other Polynesian Gourds* (Honolulu: Ku Pa`a Publishing, 1995)

Dodge, Ernest & Edwin Brewster, 'The acoustics of three Maori flutes', *Journal of the Polynesian Society*, vol. 54, no. 1, 1945, pp. 39–61

Dodson, J.R. & R.M. Kirk, 'The influence of man at a quarry site, Nairn River valley, Chatham Island, New Zealand', *Journal of the Royal Society of New Zealand*, vol. 8, no. 4, 1978, pp. 377–84

Donne, Thomas E., *The Maori: Past and present* (London: Seeley Service & Co., 1927)

Donner, William, 'Sikaiana', in *The Garland Encyclopedia of World Music*, vol. 9, eds Adrienne L. Kaeppler & J.W. Love (New York; London: Garland Publishing, 1998), pp. 844–48

Drew, Neville Keith, 'Music of Fiji', BA thesis, University of Queensland Conservatorium, 1979

Dye, Thomas S., 'Dating human dispersal in Remote Oceania: A Bayesian view from Hawai`i', *World Archaeology*, vol. 47, no. 4, 2015, pp. 661–76

Dyson, Laurel E., Max Henriks & Stephen Grant, *Information Technologies and Indigenous Peoples* (Hershey, PA: Information Science Publishing, 2007)

Edge-Partington, James, *An Album of the Weapons, Tools, Ornaments, Articles of Dress etc. Of the Natives of the Pacific Islands*, vol. 1 (Manchester, 1890–98)

Emerson, Nathaniel B., *Unwritten Literature of Hawaii: The sacred songs of the hula* (Washington: Government Printing Office, 1909)

Emory, Kenneth P. 'Tuamotuan concepts of creation', *Journal of the Polynesian Society*, vol. 49, no. 193, 1940, pp. 69–136

Emory, Kenneth P., 'The Societies', in *The Prehistory of Polynesia*, ed. Jesse D. Jennings (Canberra: Australian National University Press, 1979), pp. 200–21

Evans, Jeff, *The Discovery of Aotearoa* (Auckland: Reed, 1998)

Evans, Mark, 'The Silent Echoes of Chatham Island', in *Refereed papers from the 2nd International Small Island Cultures conference, held at the Museum Theatre, Norfolk Island Museum, Kingston, Norfolk Island, 9–13 February 2006*, ed. Henry Johnson (Sydney: SICRI, 2006), pp. 46–53

Evison, Harry C., 'Tiramōrehu, Matiaha', *Dictionary of New Zealand Biography*, first published in 1990, Te Ara – the Encyclopedia of New Zealand, https://teara.govt.nz/en/biographies/1t100/tiramorehu-matiaha

Feinberg, Richard, 'Anuta', in *The Garland Encyclopedia of World Music*, vol. 9, eds Adrienne L. Kaeppler & J.W. Love (New York; London: Garland Publishing, 1998), pp. 856–61

Finney, Ben, *Voyage of Rediscovery: A cultural odyssey of Polynesia* (Berkeley: University of California Press, 1994)

——, 'Experimental voyaging, oral traditions and long-distance interaction in Polynesia', in *Prehistoric Long-distance Interaction in Oceania: An interdisciplinary approach*, ed. Marshall Weisler (Auckland: New Zealand Archaeological Association, 1997), pp. 38–52

Firth, Raymond, 'Tikopia', in *The Garland Encyclopedia of World Music*, vol. 9, eds Adrienne L. Kaeppler & J.W. Love (New York; London: Garland Publishing, 1998), pp. 853–56

Fischer, Hans, 'Polynesische musikinstrumente: Innerpolynesische Gliederung – ausserpolynesische Parallelen', *Zeitschrift für Ethnologie*, vol. 86, no. 2, 1961, pp. 282–302

——, *Sound-producing Instruments in Oceania: Construction and playing technique, distribution and function*, ed. Don Niles, trans. Philip W. Holzknecht (Port Moresby: Institute of Papua New Guinea Studies, revised edn, 1986)

Fisher, Victor F., 'The material culture of Oruarangi, Matatoki, Thames. 1: Bone ornaments and implements', *Records of the*

Auckland Institute and Museum, vol. 1, no. 5, 1934, pp. 275–86

——, 'The material culture of Oruarangi, Matatoki, Thames. 4: Musical instruments', *Records of the Auckland Institute and Museum*, vol. 2, no. 2, 1937, pp. 111–18

Flintoff, Brian, *Taonga Pūoro: Singing treasures* (Nelson: Craig Potton Publishing, 2004)

Forbes, Henry, *The Chatham Islands and their Story* (London: Chapman & Hall, 1893)

Forster, Georg, *A Voyage Round the World*, eds Nicholas Thomas & Oliver Breghof (Honolulu: University of Hawai`i Press, 2000)

Forster, Johann Reinhold, *Observations Made During a Voyage Round the World*, eds Nicholas Thomas, Harriet Guest & Michael Dettelbach (Honolulu: University of Hawai`i Press, 1996)

Furey, Louise, *Oruarangi: The archaeology and material culture of a Hauraki pa* (Auckland: Auckland Institute and Museum, 1996)

——, 'Material culture', in *Change Through Time: 50 years of New Zealand archaeology*, eds Louise Furey & Simon Holdaway (Auckland: New Zealand Archaeological Association, 2004), pp. 29–54

——, 'Clay – a lesser known medium for Maori artefacts', *Records of the Auckland Museum*, vol. 50, 2015, pp. 21–31

Fyfe, Roger, 'A wooden trumpet, pūkaea, from Te Mata Hapuka Pa, Canterbury, New Zealand', *New Zealand Journal of Archaeology*, vol. 23, 2001, pp. 151–59

——, 'Rediscovering two tetere, flax trumpets in Canterbury Museum', in *Ngā Kete a Rēhua Inaugural Māori Research Symposium Te Waipounamu 2008*, eds Rawiri Taonui & Hamuera Kahi (Christchurch: Aotahi School of Māori and Indigenous Studies, Te Whare Wānanga o Waitaha, 2008), pp. 326–31

Gathercole, Peter, 'A Maori shell trumpet at Cambridge', in *Problems in Economic and Social Archaeology*, eds Gale de G. Sieveking et al. (London: Duckworth, 1977), pp. 187–99

Gibb, John, 'Old stone blocks linked to Tahiti', *Otago Daily Times*, 5 April 2019, p. 17

Gill, William Wyatt, *Myths and Songs from the South Pacific* (Hawaii: University Press of the Pacific, 2004)

Gillet, Grant, 'Indigenous knowledges: Circumspection, metaphysics, and scientific ontologies', *Sites: A Journal of Social Anthropology and Cultural Studies*, vol. 6, no. 1, 2009, pp. 97–115

Glamuzina, Kaye, 'Contemporary music and performance practice in Levuka', MMus thesis, University of Auckland, 1993

——, 'Melanesia, Fiji', in *The New Grove Dictionary of Music and Musicians*, vol. 16, ed. Stanley Sadie (London: Macmillan, 2001), pp. 326–33

Goldsworthy, David, 'Fijian music', in *The Garland Encyclopedia of World Music*, vol. 9, eds Adrienne L. Kaeppler & J.W. Love (New York; London: Garland Publishing, 1998), pp. 774–76

Goodwin, Ian, Stuart Browning & Atholl J. Anderson, 'Climate windows for Polynesian voyaging to New Zealand and Easter Island', *Proceedings of the National Academy of Sciences*, vol. 111, no. 41, 2014, pp. 14716–21

Graber, Christopher & Mira Burri-Nenova (eds), *Intellectual Property and Traditional Cultural Expressions in a Digital Environment* (Cheltenham: Edward Elgar, 2008)

Grant, Patrick J., 'Late Holocene histories of climate, geomorphology and vegetation, and their effects on the first New Zealanders', in *The Origins of the First New Zealanders*, ed. Douglas G. Sutton (Auckland: Auckland University Press, 1994), pp. 164–94

Gray, Russell D. & Fiona M. Jordan, 'Language trees support the express-train sequence of Austronesian expansion', *Nature*, vol. 405, 2000, pp. 1052–54

Green, Roger, 'Linguistic subgrouping within Polynesia: The implications for prehistoric settlement', *Journal of the Polynesian Society*, vol. 75, no. 1, 1966, pp. 6–38

——, 'Changes over time: Recent advances in dating human colonisation of the Pacific Basin area', in *The Origins of the First New Zealanders*, ed. Douglas G. Sutton (Auckland: Auckland University Press, 1994), pp. 19–51

——, 'Sweet potato transfers in Polynesian prehistory', in *The Sweet Potato in Oceania: A reappraisal*, eds Chris Ballard et al. (Australia: Centatime, 2005)

Green, Roger C. & K. Green, 'Classic and early European Maori sites on the Hauraki Plains', *New Zealand Archaeological Association Newsletter*, vol. 6, no. 1, 1963, pp. 27–34

Greenhill, Simon J. & Ross Clark, 'POLLEX-Online: The Polynesian lexicon project online', *Oceanic Linguistics*, vol. 50, no. 2, 2011, pp. 551–59

Greig, Karen et al., 'Ancient DNA evidence for the introduction and dispersal of dogs (*Canis familiaris*) in New Zealand', *Journal of Pacific Archaeology*, vol. 9, no. 1, 2018, pp. 1–10

Grey, George, *Mythology and Traditions of the New Zealanders* (London: George Willis, 1854)

——, *Polynesian Mythology and Ancient Traditional History of the New Zealand Race* (Auckland: H. Brett, 1885)

Gordon-Cumming, Constance F., *At Home in Fiji* (Edinburgh; London: William Blackwood & Sons, 1882)

Haami, Bradford, 'Ngārara – reptiles', Te Ara – the Encyclopedia of New Zealand, https://teara.govt.nz/en/ngarara-reptiles/print

Hamilton, Augustus, *The Art Workmanship of the Maori Race in New Zealand* (Dunedin: Fergusson & Mitchell, 1896)

——, *Maori Art* (London: Holland Press, 1972)

Handy, Edward S.C., *The Native Culture in the Marquesas* (Honolulu: Bernice P. Bishop Museum, 1923)

Harlow, Ray, 'Regional variation in Maori', *New Zealand Journal of Archaeology*, vol. 1, 1979, pp. 123–38

——, 'Māori dialectology and the settlement of New Zealand', in *The Origins of the First New Zealanders*, ed. Douglas G. Sutton (Auckland: Auckland University Press, 1994), pp. 106–22

——, 'Borrowing and its alternatives in Māori', in *Borrowing: A Pacific Perspective*, eds Jan Tent & Paul Geraghty (Canberra: Pacific Linguistics Research School of Pacific and Asian Studies, 2004)

——, *Māori: A linguistic introduction* (Cambridge: Cambridge University Press, 2007)

Harrison, C.J.O. & C.A.Walker, 'An undescribed extinct fish-eagle from the Chatham Islands', *Ibis*, vol. 115, no. 2, 1973, pp. 274–77

Harsant, Wendy J., 'Excavations at Oue Pa, N43/35, South Auckland', *Records of the Auckland Institute and Museum*, vol. 18, 1981, pp. 63–93

Hedley, Rangiiria, in 'Papatuanuku – earth rhythms', https://otago.etv.org.nz/tv/vod/view/30122

Hermann, Aymeric et al., 'Geochemical sourcing of volcanic materials imported into Teti`aroa Atoll shows multiple long-distance interactions in the Windward Society Islands, French Polynesia', *Archaeology in Oceania*, vol. 54, no. 3, 2019, pp. 184–99

Higham, T.F.G. & A.G. Hogg, 'Evidence for late Polynesian colonization of New Zealand: University of Waikato radiocarbon measurements', *Radiocarbon*, vol. 39, 1997, pp. 149–92

Higham, Tom & Martin Jones, 'Chronology and settlement', in *Change Through Time: 50 years of New Zealand archaeology*, eds Louise Furey & Simon Holdaway (Auckland: New Zealand Archaeological Association, 2004), pp. 215–34

Higham, T.F.G. et al., 'Dating the first New Zealanders: The chronology of Wairau Bar', *Antiquity*, vol. 73, 1999, pp. 420–27

Hindle, Jill, 'Renaissance in Birdland: The preservation of traditional Maori instrumental music', in Richard Nunns (1993–1998), 'Research papers' (unpublished manuscript held in Alexander Turnbull Library, Wellington, MS-Papers-8544-33, 1996)

Hīroa, Te Rangi [Sir Peter Buck], 'Historical Maori artifacts', *New Zealand Journal of Science and Technology*, vol. 9, 1927, pp. 35–41

——, *Ethnology of Manihiki and Rakahanga* (Honolulu: Bishop Museum Press, 1932)

——, *Ethnology of Mangareva* (Honolulu: Bernice P. Bishop Museum, 1938)

——, 'Pan-pipes in Polynesia', *Journal of the Polynesian Society*, vol. 50, no. 4, 1941, pp. 173–84

——, *Arts and Crafts of the Cook Islands* (Honolulu: Bernice P. Bishop Museum, 1944)

——, *The Coming of the Maori* (Wellington: Whitcombe & Tombs; Maori Purposes Fund, 1966)

——, *Vikings of the Sunrise* (Wellington: New Zealand Electronic Text Centre, 2007), https://nzetc.victoria.ac.nz/tm/scholarly/tei-BucViki.html

Hocart, Arthur M., *Lau Islands, Fiji* (Honolulu: Bernice P. Bishop Museum, 1929)

Hogg, Alan G. Et al., 'A wiggle-match date for Polynesian settlement of New Zealand', *Antiquity*, vol. 77, 2003, pp. 116–25

Hokotehi Moriori Trust & iPinCH, 'iPinCH case study report: Moriori cultural database', www.sfu.ca/ipinch/project-components/community-based-initiatives/moriori-cultural-database/

Holdaway, Richard, 'Arrival of rats in New Zealand', *Nature*, vol. 384, 1996, pp. 225–26

——, 'A spatio-temporal model for the invasion of the New Zealand archipelago by the Pacific rat *Rattus exulans*', *Journal of the Royal Society of New Zealand*, vol. 29, no. 2, 1999, pp. 91–105

Holdaway, Richard N. et al., 'Optical dating of quartz sediments and accelerator mass spectrometry ^{14}C dating of bone gelatin and moa eggshell: A comparison of age estimates for non-archaeological deposits in New Zealand', *Journal of the Royal Society of New Zealand*, vol. 32, no. 3, 2002, pp. 463–505

Horsburgh, K. Ann & Mark McCoy, 'Dispersal, isolation, and interaction in the islands of Polynesia: A critical review of archaeological and genetic evidence', *Diversity*, vol. 9, no. 37, 2017, pp. 1–21.

Horwood, Michelle & Che Wilson, *Te Ara Tapu: Sacred journeys* (Auckland: Random House, 2008)

Howard, Alan, 'Rotuma', in *The Garland Encyclopedia of World Music*, vol. 9, eds Adrienne L. Kaeppler & J.W. Love (New York; London: Garland Publishing, 1998), pp. 817–23

Howe, K.R., *The Quest for Origins: Who first discovered and settled New Zealand and the Pacific Islands?* (Honolulu: University of Hawai`i Press, 2003)

Huata, Ngāmoni, *The Rhythm and Life of Poi* (Auckland: HarperCollins, 2000)

Hulme, Keri, 'He pūoro', *Karaka,* vol. 54, p. 5

Hurles, M.E. et al., 'Untangling Oceanic settlement: The edge of the knowable', *Trends in Ecology and Evolution*, vol. 18, 2003, pp. 531–40

Irwin, Geoffrey, *The Prehistoric Exploration and Colonisation of the Pacific* (Cambridge; New York: Cambridge University Press, 1992)

——, 'Voyaging and settlement', in *Vaka Moana: Voyages of the ancestors*, ed. K.R. Howe (Auckland: David Bateman, 2006), pp. 54–91

Irwin, Geoff J. & Carl Walrond, 'When was New Zealand first settled? – The date debate', Te Ara – the Encyclopedia of New Zealand, https://teara.govt.nz/en/when-was-new-zealand-first-settled/print

Jacobson, Howard C., *Tales of Banks Peninsula* (Akaroa: Akaroa Mail, 1914)

Jacomb, Chris et al., 'High-precision dating and ancient DNA profiling of moa (*Aves: Dinornithiformes*) eggshell documents a complex feature at Wairau Bar and refines the chronology of New Zealand settlement by Polynesians', *Journal of Archaeological Science*, vol. 50, 2014, pp. 24–30

Jefferson, Christina, *Dendroglyphs of the Chatham Islands: Moriori designs on karaka trees* (Wellington: The Polynesian Society, 1956)

Johns, Dilys, Geoffrey Irwin & Yun Sung, 'An early sophisticated East Polynesian voyaging canoe discovered on New Zealand's coast', *Proceedings of the National Academy of the Sciences*, vol. 111, no. 41, 2014, pp. 14728–33

Jonassen, Jon Tikivanotau, 'Southern Cook Islands: Instrumental music', in *The Garland Encyclopedia of World Music*, vol. 9, eds Adrienne L. Kaeppler & J.W. Love (New York; London: Garland Publishing, 1998), pp. 898–901

Ka`ai-Mahuta, Rachael, 'When opposing world views converge: A review of the early literature pertaining to waiata and haka', in *Kia Rōnaki: The Māori performing arts*, eds Rachael Ka`ai-Mahuta, Tania Ka`ai & John Moorfield (Auckland: Pearson, 2013), pp. 205–18

Ka`ai-Mahuta, Rachael, Tania Ka`ai & John Moorfield, 'He kupu arataki', in *Kia Rōnaki: The Māori performing arts*, eds Rachael Ka`ai-Mahuta, Tania Ka`ai & John Moorfield (Auckland: Pearson, 2013), pp. xiv–xxii

Kaeppler, Adrienne L., 'Tonga', in *The Garland Encyclopedia of World Music*, vol. 9, eds Adrienne L. Kaeppler & J.W. Love (New York; London: Garland Publishing, 1998), pp. 783–95

Kayser, Manfred et al., 'Melanesian and Asian origins of Polynesians: mtDNA and Y chromosome gradients across the Pacific', *Molecular Biology and Evolution*, vol. 23, 2006, pp. 2234–44.

Kahn, Jennifer G., 'Household archaeology and "house societies" in the Hawaiian Archipelago', *Journal of Pacific Archaeology*, vol. 5, no. 2, 2014, pp. 18–29

Kahn, Jennifer G. & Yosihiko Sinoto, 'Refining the Society Islands cultural sequence: Colonisation phase and developmental phase coastal occupation on Mo`orea Island', *Journal of the Polynesian Society*, vol. 126, no. 1, 2017, pp. 33–60

Kauraka, Kauraka, 'Manihiki: A local view', in *The Garland Encyclopedia of World Music*, vol. 9, eds Adrienne L. Kaeppler & J.W. Love (New York; London: Garland Publishing, 1998), pp. 907–9

Kavanagh, Jerome, 'Hue', in *Introduction to Taonga Puoro*, video, SOUNZ Centre for NZ Music, www.youtube.com/watch?v=DNCVspOv2Y4

——, 'Porotiti and pūrerehua', in *Introduction to Taonga Puoro*, video, SOUNZ Centre for NZ Music, www.youtube.com/watch?v=LSdXLyWYgQg

——, 'Pūtātara, pū moana and pūpu', in *Introduction to Taonga Puoro*, video, SOUNZ Centre for NZ Music, www.youtube.com/watch?v=mZbE2lxh4qo

——, 'Te kū and rōria', in *Introduction to Taonga Puoro*, video, SOUNZ Centre for NZ Music, www.youtube.com/watch?v=0vexiEHXAHA

Kennedy, Keith, 'The ancient four-note musical scale of the Maoris', *Mankind*, vol. 1, 1931, pp. 11–14

Keyes, I.W., 'The Ngatimamoe: The Western Polynesian-Melanesoid sub-culture in New Zealand', *Journal of the Polynesian Society*, vol. 76, no. 1, 1967, pp. 47–75

King, Michael, *The Penguin History of New Zealand* (Auckland: Penguin, 2003)

Kirch, Patrick V., *On the Road of the Winds: An archaeological history of the Pacific Islands before European contact* (Berkeley: University of California Press, 2000)

——, 'Controlled comparison and the evolution of Polynesian cultures', in *Natural Experiments of History*, eds J. Diamond & J.A. Robinson (Cambridge, Massachusetts: Harvard University Press, 2010), pp. 15–52

——, 'Peopling of the Pacific: A holistic anthropological perspective', *Annual Review of Anthropology*, vol. 39, 2010, pp. 131–48

——, 'When did the Polynesians settle Hawai`i? A review of 150 years of scholarly inquiry and a tentative answer', *Hawaiian Archaeology*, vol. 12, 2011, pp. 3–26

Kirch, Patrick V., Eric Conte, W. Sharp & C. Nickelsen, 'The Onemea site (Taravai Island, Mangareva) and the human colonization of southeastern Polynesia', *Archaeology in Oceania*, vol. 45, no. 2, 2010, pp. 66–79

Kirch, Patrick V. & Roger C. Green, *Hawaiki, Ancestral Polynesia: An essay in historical anthropology* (Cambridge: Cambridge University Press, 2001)

Kirch, Patrick V. & Jennifer G. Kahn, 'Advances in Polynesian prehistory: A review and assessment of the past decade (1993–2004)', *Journal of Archaeological Research*, vol. 15, 2007, pp. 191–238

Knapp, Michael et al., 'Complete mitochondrial DNA genome sequences from the first New Zealanders', *Proceedings of the National Academy of the Sciences*, vol. 109, no. 45, 2012, pp. 18350–54

Komene, Jo'el, 'Kōauau auē, e auau tō au e: The kōauau in Te Ao Māori', MA thesis, University of Waikato, 2009

Koskinen, Aarne A., 'A preliminary statistical study of Polynesian place names', *Studia Missiologica Fennica II*, no. 8, 1963, pp. 7–11

Lawson Burke, Mary E., 'Marshall Islands', in *The Garland Encyclopedia of World Music*, vol. 9, eds Adrienne L. Kaeppler & J.W. Love (New York; London: Garland Publishing, 1998), pp. 748–54

Leach, B.F., 'The Ngai-tahu migration: The Norman Conquest of the South Island', *New Zealand Archaeological Association Newsletter*, vol. 21, no. 1, 1978, pp. 13–30

——, 'The prehistory of the Southern Wairarapa', *Journal of the Royal Society of New Zealand*, vol. 11, no. 1, 1981, pp. 11–33

Leach, B.F. et al., 'The origin of prehistoric obsidian artefacts from the Chatham and Kermadec Islands', *New Zealand Journal of Archaeology*, vol. 8, 1986, pp. 143–70

Leach, Helen, *1,000 Years of Gardening in New Zealand* (Wellington: A.H. & A.W. Reed:, 1984)

Leach, Helen & G.E. Hamel, 'The place of Taiaroa Head and other Classic Maori sites in the prehistory of East Otago', *Journal of the Royal Society of New Zealand*, vol. 8, no. 3, 1978, pp. 239–51

Leach, Helen & Jill Hamel, 'Archaic and Classic Maori relationships at Long Beach, Otago: The artefacts and activity areas', *New Zealand Journal of Archaeology*, vol. 3, 1981, pp. 109–41

Leach, Helen & B.F. Leach, 'Environmental change in Palliser Bay', in *Prehistoric Man in Palliser Bay*, eds B.F. Leach & H.M. Leach (Wellington: National Museum of New Zealand, 1979), pp. 229–40

Leach, Helen & Chris Stowe, 'Oceania arboriculture at the margins: The case of the karaka (*Corynocarpus laevigatus*) in Aotearoa', *Journal of the Polynesian Society*, vol. 114, no. 1, 2005, pp. 7–27

Lindstrom, Lamont, 'Southern area', in *The Garland Encyclopedia of World Music*, vol. 9, eds Adrienne L. Kaeppler & J.W. Love (New York; London: Garland Publishing, 1998), pp. 702–9

Little, Jenny M., *Report on a Preliminary Study of the Music of Nga Pu Toru* (Auckland: Dept. of Anthropology, University of Auckland, 1989)

Locke, Elsie & Janet Paul, *Mrs Hobson's Album* (Auckland: Auckland University Press, 1989)

Loughnan, Robert A., *Royalty in New Zealand: The visit of their Royal Highnesses the Duke and Duchess of Cornwall and York to New Zealand, 10th to 27th June 1901* (Wellington: Government Printer, 1902)

Love, J.W., 'Sāmoa', in *The Garland Encyclopedia of World Music*, vol. 9, eds Adrienne L. Kaeppler & J.W. Love (New York; London: Garland Publishing, 1998), pp. 795–807

——, 'Struck plaques of Anuta', in *The Garland Encyclopedia of World Music*, vol. 9, eds Adrienne L. Kaeppler & J.W. Love (New York; London: Garland Publishing, 1998), pp. 378–79

Love, J.W. & Neville H. Fletcher, 'Aerophones', in *The Garland Encyclopedia of World Music*, vol. 9, eds Adrienne L. Kaeppler & J.W. Love (New York; London: Garland Publishing, 1998), pp. 392–93

——, 'Chordophones', in *The Garland Encyclopedia of World Music*, vol. 9, eds

Adrienne L. Kaeppler & J.W. Love (New York; London: Garland Publishing, 1998), pp. 386–87
Lowe, D.J. & R.M. Newnham, 'Role of tephra in mitochondrial DNA evidence for the spread of Pacific rats through Oceania dating Polynesian settlement and impact, New Zealand', *PAGES (Past Global Changes) News*, vol. 12, no. 3, 2004, pp. 5–7
Lowe, Sebastian & Alistair Fraser, 'Connecting with inner landscapes: Taonga pūoro, musical improvisation and exploring acoustic Aotearoa/New Zealand', *Journal of New Zealand and Pacific Studies*, vol. 6, no. 1, 2008, pp. 5–20
Magnani, M., A.Guttorm & N. Mangani, 'Three-dimensional, community-based heritage management of indigenous museum collections: Archaeological ethnography, revitalization and repatriation at the Sámi Museum Siida', *Journal of Cultural Heritage*, vol. 31, 2018, pp. 162–69
Maingay, Joan, 'Notes on a *nguru* from Kauri Point swamp', *NZ Archaeological Association Newsletter*, vol. 27, no. 2, 1984, pp. 79–82
——, 'Te Hue: People and a plant', MA thesis, University of Auckland, 1985
Mair, Gilbert, 'Notes on the Chatham Islands and their inhabitants', *Transactions and Proceedings of the New Zealand Institute*, vol. 3, 1870, pp. 311–13
——, 'Inward correspondence J-N (Letters to Elsdon Best)' (unpublished manuscript held in Alexander Turnbull Library, Wellington, MS Papers 007204, 1900)
——, 'The early history of the Morioris with an abstract of a Moriori narrative', *Transactions of the New Zealand Institute*, vol. 37, 1904, pp. 156–71
——, *Reminiscences and Maori Stories* (Auckland: Brett, 1923)
Makereti, *The Old Time Maori* (Auckland: New Women's Press, 1986)
Makoare, Bernard, 'Nga taonga puoro', *Spirit Aotearoa*, vol. 1, 1998, pp. 48–50
Maning, Frederick Edward, *Old New Zealand: A tale of the good old times* (Christchurch; Wellington; Dunedin; Melbourne; London: Whitcombe & Tombs, 1906)
Marck, Jeff, *Topics in Polynesian Language and Culture History* (Canberra: Australian National University, 2000)
Marcuse, Sibyl, *Musical Instruments: A comprehensive dictionary* (New York: W.W. Norton, 1975)
Marshall, Mac, Larry Gabriel & Joakim Manniwel Peter, 'Chuuk', in *The Garland Encyclopedia of World Music*, vol. 9, eds Adrienne L. Kaeppler & J.W. Love (New York, London: Garland Publishing, 1998), pp. 733–37
Marshall, William Barrett, *A Personal Narrative of Two Visits to New Zealand in His Majesty's Ship Alligator A.D. 1834* (London: Nisbet, 1836)
Marshall, Yvonne M., R.J. Scarlett & D.G. Sutton, *Bird Species Present on the Southwest Coast of Chatham Island in the 16th Century A.D.* (Auckland: Dept. of Anthropology, University of Auckland, 1987)
Martin, Mary, 'Maori music' (unpublished manuscript held in Alexander Turnbull Library, Wellington, MS-Papers-8544-32, n.d.)
Matthews, R.H., 'Reminiscences of Maori life fifty years ago', *Transactions of the New Zealand Institute*, vol. 43, 1910, pp. 598–605
Matisoo-Smith, Elizabeth, 'More than just old bones: On the contribition of biological anthropology to New Zealand archaeology', in *Change Through Time: 50 years of New Zealand archaeology*, eds Louise Furey & Simon Holdaway (Auckland: New Zealand Archaeological Association, 2004), pp. 235–49
——, 'Ancient DNA and the human settlement of the Pacific: A review', *Journal of Human Evolution*, vol. 79, 2014, pp. 93–104
——, 'The human landscape: Population origins, settlement and impact of human arrival in Aotearoa/New Zealand', in *Landscape and*

Quaternary Environmental Change in New Zealand, ed. J. Schulmeister (Paris: Atlantis Press, 2017), pp. 293–311

Matisoo-Smith, Elizabeth et al., 'Patterns of prehistoric human mobility indicated by mitochondrial DNA from the Pacific rat', *Proceedings of the National Academy of the Sciences*, vol. 95, no. 25, 1998, pp. 15145–50

Matisoo-Smith, Elizabeth et al., 'Prehistoric mobility in Polynesia: MtDNA variation in *Rattus exulans* from the Chatham and Kermadec Islands', *Asian Perspectives*, vol. 38, no. 2, 1999, pp. 186–99

Matisoo-Smith, Elizabeth & J.H. Robins, 'Origins and dispersals of Pacific peoples: Evidence from mtDNA phylogenies of the Pacific rat', *Proceedings of the National Academy of the Sciences*, vol. 101, no. 24, 2004, pp. 9167–72

——, 'Mitochondrial DNA evidence for the spread of Pacific rats throughout Oceania', *Biological Invasions*, vol. 11, 2008, pp. 1521–27

Maxwell, Justin, 'The Moriori: The integration of arboriculture and agroforestry in an East Polynesian society', PhD thesis, University of Otago, 2014

——, *Assessment and Suggested Management Actions for Kaingaroa Station Covenant, J.M. Barker (Hāpūpū) National Historic Reserve, Taia Historic Reserve and Kairae Reserve, Updated 2016* (Dunedin: University of Otago, 2016).

Maxwell, Justin & Ian Smith, 'A re-assessment of settlement patterns and subsistence at Point Durham, Chatham Island', *Archaeology in Oceania*, vol. 50, no. 3, 2015, pp. 162–74

Mayer, Raymond, 'Uvea and Futuna', in *The Garland Encyclopedia of World Music*, vol. 9, eds Adrienne L. Kaeppler & J.W. Love (New York; London: Garland Publishing, 1998), pp. 808–16

McAlister, Andrew, Peter Sheppard & Melinda S. Allen, 'The identification of a Marquesan adze in the Cook Islands', *Journal of the Polynesian Society*, vol. 122, no. 3, 2015, pp. 257–74

McCallum, Rua, *He Kete Taoka* (Dunedin: Komiti Taoka Tuku Iho & Hughes Lithographics Ltd, 2008)

McDonnell, Thomas, *A Maori History: Being a native account of the Pakeha–Maori wars in New Zealand* (Auckland: H. Brett, 1887)

McFadgen, Bruce G., 'Coastal stratigraphic evidence for human settlement', in *The Origins of the First New Zealanders*, ed. Douglas G. Sutton (Auckland: Auckland University Press, 1994), pp. 195–207

McFadgen, B.G., F.B. Knox & T.R.L. Cole, 'Radiocarbon calibration curve variations and their implications for the interpretation of New Zealand prehistory', *Radiocarbon*, vol. 36, no. 2, 1994, pp. 221–36

McGlone, Matt & Janet Wilmshurst, 'Dating initial Maori environmental impact in New Zealand', *Quaternary International*, vol. 59, 1999, pp. 5–16

McKinnon, Malcolm (ed.), *Bateman New Zealand Historical Atlas* (Auckland: David Bateman, 1997)

McLean, Mervyn, 'The N.Z. nose flute: Fact or fallacy?', *Working Papers in Anthropology, Archaeology, Linguistics, Maori Studies*, no. 18, Dept of Anthropology, University of Auckland, 1972

——, 'An investigation of the open tube Maori flute or kooauau', *Journal of the Polynesian Society*, vol. 77, no. 3, 1968, pp. 213–41

——, 'An analysis of 651 Maori scales', *Yearbook of the International Folk Music Council* 1, 1969, pp. 123–64

——, 'A chronological and geographical sequence of Maori flute scales', *Man*, vol. 17, 1982, pp. 123–57

——, *Maori Music* (Auckland: Auckland University Press, 1996)

——, *Weavers of Song: Polynesian music and dance* (Auckland: Auckland University Press / Honolulu: University of Hawai`i Press, 1999).

——, *Were Lapita Potters Ancestral to Polynesia?* (Auckland: Archive of Maori and Pacific Music, University of Auckland, 2008)

——, *Music, Dance and Polynesian Origins: The evidence from POc and PPn* (Auckland: Archive of Maori and Pacific Music, University of Auckland, 2010)

——, *Music, Lapita, and the Problem of Polynesian Origins* (Auckland: Mervyn McLean, 2014)

McLean, Mervyn & Margaret Orbell, *Traditional Songs of the Maori* (Auckland: Auckland University Press, 2004)

McNab, Robert, *Historical Records of New Zealand*, vol. 2 (Wellington: Government Printer, 1914)

Mead, Sidney Moko (ed.), *Te Maori: Maori art from New Zealand collections* (Auckland: Heinemann in association with the American Federation of Arts, 1984)

Mekalik, Sally, 'Te Mata Hapuka pukaea', in Richard Nunns (1993–1998) 'Research papers' (unpublished manuscript held in Alexander Turnbull Library, Wellington, MS-Papers-8544-33, 1996)

Melbourne, Hirini, *Toiapiapi: He huinga o ngā kura puoro a te Maori* (Wellington: Shearwater, 2016)

Millener, Philip, 'The history of the Chatham Islands' bird fauna of the last 7000 years – a chronicle of change and extinction', in *Avian Paleontology at the Close of the 20th Century: Proceedings of the 4th international meeting of the Society of Avian Palaeontology and Evolution, Washington, D.C., 4–7 June 1996*, ed. Storrs L. Olson (Washington D.C.: Smithsonian Institution Press, 1999), pp. 85–109

Miller, David, 'The insect people of the Maori', *Journal of the Polynesian Society*, vol. 61, 1952, pp. 1–61

Mills, Toby, 'Taonga puoro: A gift of sound', in *Toi Puoro: Taonga Puoro*, videos, slides, films, dir. Toby Mills (Wellington: Tawera Productions, 1994–1999)

Morrell, William P. (ed.), *Sir Joseph Banks in New Zealand: From his journal* (Wellington: A.H. & A.W. Reed, 1958)

Morrison, Scotty, *Origins*, three-part docuseries (Greenstone TV and Scottie Douglas Productions for TVNZ, 2020), www.tvnz.co.nz/shows/origins

Moser, Thomas, *Mahoe Leaves* (Whanganui: H.I. Jones & Son, 1888)

Moulin, Jane Freeman, *Music of the Southern Marquesas Islands* (Auckland: Archive of Maori and Pacific Music, 1994)

——, 'Gods and mortals: Understanding traditional function and usage in Marquesan musical instruments', *Journal of the Polynesian Society*, vol. 106, no. 3, 1997, pp. 250–83

——, 'Marquesas Islands', in *The Garland Encyclopedia of World Music*, vol. 9, eds Adrienne L. Kaeppler & J.W. Love (New York; London: Garland Publishing, 1998), pp. 889–96

——, 'Kapatuhe: Exploring word-based performance on Marquesan musical instruments', *The Galpin Society Journal*, vol. 55, 2002, pp. 130–60

Moyle, Richard, 'Samoan musical instruments', *Ethnomusicology*, vol. 18, no. 1, 1974, pp. 57–74

——, *Tongan Music* (Auckland: Auckland University Press, 1987)

——, *Traditional Samoan Music* (Auckland: Auckland University Press in association with the Institute for Polynesian Studies, 1988)

——, *The Sounds of Oceania: An illustrated catalogue of the sound producing instruments of Oceania in the Auckland Institute and Museum* (Auckland: Auckland Institute and Museum, 1989)

——, *Polynesian sound-producing instruments* (Princes Risborough: Shire Ethnography, 1990)

Mulrooney, Mara A. et al., 'High-precision dating of colonization and settlement in East Polynesia', *Proceedings of the National Academy of the Sciences*, vol. 108, no. 23, 2011, pp. 192–94

Museum of New Zealand Te Papa Tongarewa, *Icons: Ngā taonga* (Wellington: Te Papa Press, 2004)

Nachman, Steven R., 'Nissan Atoll', in *The Garland Encyclopedia of World Music*, vol. 9, eds Adrienne L. Kaeppler & J.W. Love (New York; London: Garland Publishing, 1998), pp. 632–40

Neumüller, M., A. Reichinger, F. Rist & C. Kern, '3D printing for cultural heritage: Preservation, accessibility, research and education', in *3D Research Challenges in Cultural Heritage*, eds M. Ioannides & E. Quak (Berlin, Heidelberg: Springer, 2014), pp. 119–34

Newman, Alfred K., 'On the musical notes and other features of the long Maori trumpet', *Transactions of the New Zealand Institute*, vol. 38, 1905, pp. 134–39

Ngata, A.T., 'The Io Cult – early migration – puzzle of the canoes', *Journal of the Polynesian Society*, vol. 59, no. 4, 1950, pp. 335–46

Ngata, Ronald Spencer, 'Understanding matakite: A kaupapa Māori study on the impact of matakite/intuitive experiences on wellbeing', PhD thesis, Massey University, 2014

Niles, Don, 'Mamose region of Papua New Guinea', in *The Garland Encyclopedia of World Music*, vol. 9, eds Adrienne L. Kaeppler & J.W. Love (New York; London: Garland Publishing, 1998), pp. 526–33

——, 'Papuan region of Papua New Guinea: Musical instruments', in *The Garland Encyclopedia of World Music*, vol. 9, eds Adrienne L. Kaeppler & J.W. Love (New York; London: Garland Publishing, 1998), pp. 489–90

Nunn, Patrick D. et al., 'Times of plenty, times of less: Last-millennium societal disruption in the Pacific Basin', *Human Ecology*, vol. 35, no. 4, 2007, pp. 385–401

Nunns, Richard, 'Te taonga pūoro: The traditional instruments of the Māori', in Hirini Melbourne, Richard Nunns with Aroha Yates Smith, *Te Hekenga ā Rangi*, CD and DVD (Rattle Records, 2003)

——, 'Maori flute series: The koauau', *Flute Focus*, vol. 4, October 2005, pp. 33–34

——, 'Poi (raupō, ipu kōrero, poi piu)', 'Tarakimere', 'Kazoo', 'Ororuarangi', 'Hoputea and whakai i tama', 'Pū hue', 'Poi āwhiowhio and tuarōria (with nīkau leaf)' and 'Rore/Tātara', *He Ara Pūoro*, RNZ, 2 February 2012, www.rnz.co.nz/audio/player?audio_id=2508857, www.rnz.co.nz/audio/player?audio_id=2508859, www.rnz.co.nz/audio/player?audio_id=2508882, www.rnz.co.nz/audio/player?audio_id=2508857, www.rnz.co.nz/audio/player?audio_id=2508867, www.rnz.co.nz/audio/player?audio_id=2508869, www.rnz.co.nz/audio/player?audio_id=2508846 and www.rnz.co.nz/audio/player?audio_id=2508993

——, 'Taonga puoro and Peka Mākarini's bugle', in *Kia Rōnaki: The Māori performing arts*, eds Rachael Ka`ai-Mahuta, Tania Ka`ai & John Moorfield (Auckland: Pearson, 2013), pp. 179–90

Nunns, Richard & Allan Thomas, 'The search for the sound of the pūtōrino: "Me te wai e utuutu ana"', *Yearbook for Traditional Music*, vol. 37, 2005, pp. 69–79

——, *Te Ara Puoro: A journey into the world of Māori music* (Nelson: Craig Potton Publishing, 2014)

Oldman, W.O., *Catalogue of Ethnographical Specimens* (London, 1908)

Olivares, Gabriela et al., 'Human mediated translocation of Pacific paper mulberry [*Broussonetia papyrifera* (L.) L'Hér. Ex Vent. (Moraceae)]: Genetic evidence of dispersal routes in Remote Oceania', *PloS ONE*, vol. 14, no. 6, 2019, p. e0217107, https://doi.org/10.1371/journal.pone.0217107

Oliver, Douglas L., *Ancient Tahitian Society* (Hawai`i: University of Hawai`i Press, 1974)

Ollivier, Isabel, *Extracts from the Journals of the Ships* Recherche, Espérance *and* Coquille *1793 and 1824* (Wellington: Alexander Turnbull Library Endowment Trust with Indosuez New Zealand, 1986)

Orbell, Margaret, *The Illustrated Encyclopedia of Māori Myth and Legend* (Christchurch: Canterbury University Press, 1995)

——, *A Concise Encyclopedia of Māori Myth and Legend* (Christchurch: Canterbury University Press, 1998)

Otago Museum, *Kāi Tahu Taoka: Treasures from the Otago Museum* (Auckland: Reed Books, 2006)

Paringatai, Karyn, 'Poia mai taku poi: Unearthing the knowledge of the past', MA thesis, University of Otago, 2004

Parker, H., '1833: Chatham Islands, with notes in an unknown hand' (unpublished manuscript held in Alexander Turnbull Library, Wellington, MS-Papers-3864, 1833)

Parkinson, Sydney, *A Journal of a Voyage to the South Seas, in his Majesty's Ship, the* Endeavour (London: Caliban Books, 1984)

Pearthree, Erik & Anne Di Piazza, 'An "archaic East Polynesian assemblage" from Phoenix and Line archipelagos', in *Pacific Archaeology, Assessments and Prospects: Proceedings of the international conference for the 50th anniversary of the first Lapita excavation, Koné-Nouméa, 2002*, ed. Christophe Sand (Nouméa, Nouvelle-Calédonie: Département Archéologie, Service des Musées et du Patrimoine de Nouvelle-Calédonie, 2003), pp. 327–36

Phillipps, W.J., 'Maori bird calls or whistles', *Ethnos*, vol. 15, nos 3–4, 1950, pp. 201–5

Phillips, Caroline, *Waihou Journeys* (Auckland: Auckland University Press, 2000)

Pietrusewsky, Michael, 'The physical anthropology of Polynesia: A review of some cranial and skeletal studies', in *Oceanic Culture History: Essays in honour of Roger Green*, eds Roger Green & Janet Davidson (Dunedin: New Zealand Journal of Archaeology Special Publication, 1996), pp. 343–53.

Polack, Joel Samuel, *Manners and Customs of the New Zealanders*, vol. 1 (London: Madden, 1840)

POLLEX-Online: The Polynesian Lexicon Project Online, database compilation overseen by Bruce Biggs and Ross Clark, first published online 2011: https://pollex.eva.mpg.de/

Pomare, Maui & James Cowan, *Legends of the Maori*, vol. 1 (Auckland: Southern Reprints, 1987)

Potts, Thomas H., *Out in the Open* (Christchurch: Lyttelton Times, 1882)

Prickett, Nigel, *Maori Origins: From Asia to Aotearoa* (Auckland: David Bateman & Auckland Museum, 2001)

Puketapu Hetet, Erenora, *Maori Weaving* (Auckland: Longman, 2000)

Ratawa, Wendy Margaret, 'Fijian vocal music and the Vanua: A field study from Lambasa, Vanua Levu', MA thesis, Deakin University, 1991

Reeves Lawrence, Helen, 'Northern Cook Islands', in *The Garland Encyclopedia of World Music*, vol. 9, eds Adrienne L. Kaeppler & J.W. Love (New York; London: Garland Publishing, 1998), pp. 903–7

Reigle, Robert, 'Madang Province', in *The Garland Encyclopedia of World Music*, vol. 9, eds Adrienne L. Kaeppler & J.W. Love (New York; London: Garland Publishing, 1998), pp. 561–66

Rewi, Tangiwai, *Ngā Taonga Pūoro Māori* (Te Wanganui-a-tara: Te Tāhuhu o te Mātauranga, 2019)

Richards, Eva C., *The Chatham Islands, Their Plants, Birds and People* (Christchurch: Simpson & Williams, 1952)

Richards, Rhys, 'An historical geography of Chatham Island', MA thesis, University of Canterbury, 1962

——, *Manu Moriori: Human and bird carvings on live kopi trees on the Chatham Islands* (Wellington: Paremata Press, 2007)

——, *Moriori: Origins, lifestyles and language* (Wellington: Paremata Press, 2018)

Richter, A.M. et al., 'Digital archaeological landscapes & replicated artifacts: Questions of analytical & phenomenological authenticity & ethical policies in cyberarchaeology', in *2013 Digital Heritage International Congress (DigitalHeritage)* (Marseille: IEEE, 2013), pp. 569–72

Riley, Murdoch, *Māori Love Legends – and other True Stories* (Paraparaumu: Viking Sevenseas, 2003)

Roberts, Helen H., *Ancient Hawaiian Music* (Hawaii`: Bernice P. Bishop Museum, 1926)

Robertson, John A., 'Chatham Islands (with a map)', *Proceedings and Transactions of the Queensland Branch of the Royal Geographical Society of Australasia*, vol. 5, 1890, pp. 72–92

Robinson, Samuel Timoti, *Tohunga: The revival: Ancient knowledge for the modern era* (Auckland: Reed Books, 2005)

Rolett, Barry V., 'Voyaging and interaction in ancient East Polynesia', *Asian Perspectives*, vol. 41, no. 2, 2002, pp. 182–94

Rollo, Te Manaaroha Pirihira, 'Mā te wai ka piki ake te hauora', *New Zealand Journal of Music Therapy*, vol. 11, 2013, pp. 51–80

Ross, Malcolm, Andrew Pawley & Meredith Osmond, *The Lexicon of Proto Oceanic: The Culture and Environment of Ancestral Oceanic Society*, vol. 1 (Canberra: Australian National University, 1998)

Rossen, Jane Mink, 'Bellona', in *The Garland Encyclopedia of World Music*, vol. 9, eds Adrienne L. Kaeppler & J.W. Love (New York; London: Garland Publishing, 1998), pp. 848–53

Roth, Henry Ling (trans.), *Crozet's Voyage to Tasmania, New Zealand … in the Years 1771–1772* (London: Truslove & Shirley, 1891)

Roullier, Caroline et al., 'Historical collections reveal patterns of diffusion of sweet potato in Oceania obscured by modern plant movements and recombination', *Proceedings of the National Academy of the Sciences*, vol. 110, no. 6, 2013, pp. 2205–10

Rout, Ettie, *Maori Symbolism* (New York: Harcourt, 1926)

Royal, Te Ahukaramū Charles, 'Te Whare Tapere: Towards a model for Māori performance art', PhD thesis, Victoria University, 1998

Salisbury, Kevin, 'Pukapuka', in *The Garland Encyclopedia of World Music*, vol. 9, eds Adrienne L. Kaeppler & J.W. Love (New York; London: Garland Publishing, 1998), pp. 909–13

Saumaiwai, Vula, 'Fijian *Meke*', in *Talking About Oral Traditions*, ed. Saimone Vatu (Suva: Fiji Museum Oral Tradition Series, 1976), pp. 35–44

Savage, John, *Some Account of New Zealand* (London: Murray & Constable, 1807)

Seelenfreund, D. Et al., 'Paper mulberry (*Broussonetia papyrifera*) as a commensal model for human mobility in Oceania: Anthropological, botanical and genetic considerations', *New Zealand Journal of Botany*, vol. 48, 2010, pp. 231–47

Shand, Alexander, 'Letters to S. Percy Smith, 1840–1910' (unpublished manuscript held in Alexander Turnbull Library, Wellington, qMS-1789)

——, 'The Moriori people of the Chatham Islands: Their traditions and history', *Journal of the Polynesian Society*, vol. 3, no. 2, 1894, pp. 76–92

——, 'The Moriori people of the Chatham Islands: Their traditions and history. Chapter VII: Ko Matangiao (continued)', *Journal of the Polynesian Society*, vol. 4, no. 4, 1895, pp. 209–25

——, 'The Moriori people of the Chatham Islands: Their traditions and history. Chapter VIII: Ko Hokorongo-tiringa', *Journal of the Polynesian Society*, vol. 5, no. 1, 1896, pp. 13–32

——, 'The Moriori people of the Chatham Islands: Their traditions and history. Chapter XIV: Tawhaki', *Journal of the Polynesian Society*, vol. 7, no. 2, 1898, pp. 73–88

——, 'The early history of the Morioris', *Transactions of the New Zealand Institute*, vol. 37, 1904, pp. 144–56

——, *The Moriori People of the Chatham Islands, their History and Traditions* (Wellington: Polynesian Society, 1911)

Shawcross, F.W. & J.E. Terrell, 'Paterangi and Oruarangi Swamp pas', *Journal of the Polynesian Society*, vol. 75, no. 4, 1966, pp. 404–29

Shawcross, Wilfred, 'The Cambridge University collection of Maori artefacts, made on Captain Cook's first voyage', *Journal of the Polynesian Society*, vol. 79, no. 3, 1970, pp. 305–48

——, 'Kauri Point swamp: The ethnographic interpretation of a prehistoric site', in *Problems in Economic and Social Archaeology*, eds Gale de G. Sieveking et al. (London: Duckworth, 1977), pp. 277–305

Shirres, M., *The Relationship of the Moriori Language to the Maori Language* (Auckland: Dept of Anthropology, University of Auckland, 1977)

Shortland, Edward, *Traditions and Superstitions of the New Zealanders* (London: Longman, Brown, Green & Longmans, 1856)

Simmons, D.R., 'The Moriori of the Chatham Islands', *Newsletter (New Zealand Archaeological Association)*, vol. 5, no. 4, 1962, pp. 238–44

——, *Craftsmanship in Polynesia* (Dunedin: Otago Museum Trust, 1963)

——, 'A preliminary report on an associated group of dendroglyphys in the Chatham Islands', *New Zealand Archaeological Association Newsletter*, vol. 8, no. 2, 1965, pp. 39–42

——, 'Suggested periods in South Island prehistory', *Records of the Auckland Institute and Museum*, vol. 10, 1973, pp. 1–58

——, *Whakairo: Maori tribal art* (Auckland: Oxford University Press, 1985)

Simpson, Frank A., *Chatham Exiles: Yesterday and to-day at the Chatham Islands* (Wellington: A.H. & A.W. Reed, 1950)

Sinoto, Yosihiko H., 'The Marquesas', in *The Prehistory of Polynesia*, ed. Jesse D. Jennings (Cambridge, Massachusetts: Harvard University Press, 1979), pp. 110–34

——, 'An analysis of Polynesian migrations based on the archaeological assessments', *Journal de la Sociéte des Océanistes*, vol. 39, no. 76, 1983, pp. 57–67

Skinner, Henry D., 'Archaeology of Canterbury: Moa-bone Point cave', *Records of the Canterbury Museum*, vol. 2, 1923, pp. 93–104

——, *The Morioris of Chatham Islands* (Honolulu: Bishop Museum, 1923)

——, 'A classification of the fish-hooks of Murihiku with notes on allied forms from other parts of Polynesia', *Journal of the Polynesian Society*, vol. 51, no. 4, 1942, pp. 256–86

——, *Comparatively Speaking: Studies in Pacific material culture 1921–1972* (Dunedin: University of Otago, 1974)

Skinner, Henry D. & William Baucke, *The Morioris* (Honolulu: Bishop Museum, 1928)

Skinner, Henry D. & W.J. Phillipps, 'Necklaces, pendants, and amulets from the Chatham Islands', *Journal of the Polynesian Society*, vol. 62, no. 2, 1953, pp. 169–95

Smith, Ailsa (from the writings of Te Kahui Kararehe of Rahotu, Taranaki), *Songs and Stories of Taranaki: He Tuhituhi Tai Hau-ā-uru* (Christchurch: Macmillan Brown Centre for Pacific Studies, University of Canterbury, 1993)

Smith, Barbara B., 'The music and dance of Micronesia: Musical instruments', in *The Garland Encyclopedia of World Music*, vol. 9, eds Adrienne L. Kaeppler & J.W. Love (New York; London: Garland Publishing, 1998), p. 716

Smith, S. Percy, 'Stone implements from the Chatham Islands', *Journal of the Polynesian Society*, vol. 1, no. 2, 1892, pp. 80–82

——, *Hawaiki: The original home of the Maori, with a sketch of Polynesian history* (Christchurch: Whitcombe & Tombs, 1904)

Söderstrom, Jan, *A. Sparrman's Ethnographical Collection from James Cook's Second Expedition (1772–1775)* (Stockholm: Ethnological Museum of Sweden, 1939)

Solly, Ruby, 'How to make an ukutangi', www.kauaeraro.com/matauranga/ukutangi

Sparrman, Anders, *A Voyage Round the World with Captain James Cook in H.M.S.* Resolution (UK: The Golden Cockerel Press, 1944)

Spearritt, Gordon Donald, 'Iatmul', in *The Garland Encyclopedia of World Music*, vol. 9, eds Adrienne L. Kaeppler & J.W. Love (New York; London: Garland Publishing, 1998), pp. 552–57

Stack, James West, *South Island Maoris: A sketch of their history and legendary lore* (Christchurch;

Wellington; Dunedin; Auckland: Whitcombe & Tombs, 1898)
Starzecka, D.C., Roger Neich & Mick Pendergrast, *The Māori Collections of the British Museum* (London: British Museum Press, 2010)
Stillman, Amy Ku`uleialoha, 'Hawai`i', in *The Garland Encyclopedia of World Music*, vol. 9, eds Adrienne L. Kaeppler & J.W. Love (New York; London: Garland Publishing, 1998), pp. 914–23
Stowell, H.M., 'Maori culture, language, history and waiata' (unpublished manuscript held in Alexander Turnbull Library, Wellington, MS-Papers-0062-45, 1920)
Striewski, Bernd et al., 'Multi-proxy evidence of late Holocene human-induced environmental changes at Lake Pupuke, Auckland (New Zealand)', *Quaternary International*, vol. 202, 2009, pp. 69–93
Sutton, Douglas G., 'Polynesian coastal hunters in the subantarctic zone: A case for the recognition of convergent cultural adaptation', PhD thesis, University of Otago, 1979
——, 'A culture history of the Chatham Islands', *Journal of the Polynesian Society*, vol. 89, no. 1, 1980, pp. 67–94
——, 'The Chatham Islands', in *The First Thousand Years*, ed. Nigel Prickett (Palmerston North: Dunmore, 1982), pp. 160–78
Sutton, Douglas G. (ed.), *The Origins of the First New Zealanders* (Auckland: Auckland University Press, 1994)
Sutton, Douglas et al., 'Towards the recognition of convergent cultural adaptation in the subantarctic zone [with comments and replies]', *Current Anthropology*, vol. 23, no. 1, 1982, pp. 77–97
Sutton, Douglas & H.J. Campbell, 'Patterns in the prehistoric distribution of stone resources in the Chatham Islands', in *Archaeological Studies of Pacific Stone Resources*, eds Foss Leach & Janet Davidson (Oxford: British Archaeological Reports, 1981), pp. 209–23
Sutton, Douglas & Y.M. Marshall, *Archaeological Bird Bone Assemblages from Chatham Island: An interpretation* (Dunedin: Dept of Anthropology, University of Otago, 1977)
Tamarapa, Awhina, 'The role of a museum (Te Papa) in the rejuvenation of taonga puoro', MA thesis, Massey University, 2015
Tamarapa, Awhina & Ariana Tikao, 'Mai te Pō, ki te Ao: The reclamation of taonga puoro as a living treasure', in *Searches for Tradition: Essays on New Zealand music, past and present*, eds Michael Brown & Samantha Owens (Wellington: Victoria University Press, 2017), pp. 139–57
Tapsell, Paul, *Māori Treasures of New Zealand* (Auckland: David Bateman, 2006)
Tau, Te Maire & Atholl Anderson (eds), *Ngāi Tahu: A migration history* (Wellington: Bridget Williams Books, 2008)
Taumoefolau, Melenaite, 'From *Sau 'Ariki to Hawaiki', *Journal of the Polynesian Society*, vol. 105, no. 4, 1996, pp. 385–410
Taylor, Richard, *Te Ika a Maui or New Zealand and its Inhabitants* (London: Wertheim & MacIntosh, 1855)
Taylor, R.M.S., 'Cause and effect in the wear of teeth', *Acta Anatomica*, vol. 53, 1963, pp. 99–157
Taylor, W.A., *Lore and History of the South Island Maori* (Christchurch: Bascands, n.d.)
Te Awekotuku, Ngahuia, 'Maori: People and Culture', in *Māori: Art and culture*, ed. D.C. Starzecka (London: British Museum Press, 1998), pp. 26–49
Teviotdale, David & Henry D. Skinner, 'Oruarangi Pa', *Journal of the Polynesian Society*, vol. 56, p. 4, 1947, pp. 340–56
Te Whetu, Karipa, 'Kame-tara and his ogre wife', *Journal of the Polynesian Society*, vol. 6, no. 3, 1897, pp. 97–106
Thacker, Murray, 'Excavations at Pa Bay, Banks Peninsula', *New Zealand Archaeological Association Newsletter*, vol. 4, no. 1, 1960, pp. 8–12
Thomas, Allan, 'Tokelau', in *The Garland Encyclopedia of World Music*, vol. 9, eds

Adrienne L. Kaeppler & J.W. Love (New York; London: Garland Publishing, 1998), pp. 823–28

——, 'West Futuna', in *The Garland Encyclopedia of World Music*, vol. 9, eds Adrienne L. Kaeppler & J.W. Love (New York; London: Garland Publishing, 1998), pp. 861–64

Thompson, Laura, *Southern Lau, Fiji: An ethnography* (Honolulu: Bernice P. Bishop Museum, 1940)

Thomson, Arthur S., *The Story of New Zealand: Past and present, savage and civilised* (London: Murray, 1859)

Thorne, Robert L., '(Re)constructing the Kōauau: Traditional and modern methods in the making of kōauau rākau', MA thesis, Massey University, 2012

Travers, Henry H., 'On the Chatham Islands', *Transactions and Proceedings of the New Zealand Institute*, vol. 1, 1868, pp. 173–80

Travers, W.T.L., 'Notes on the Chatham Islands, extracted from letters from Mr. H.H. Travers', *Transactions and Proceedings of the New Zealand Institute*, vol. 4, 1871, pp. 63–66

——, 'Notes of the traditions and manners and customs of the Mori-oris', *Transaction and Proceedings of the New Zealand Institute*, vol. 9, 1876, pp. 15–27

Tregear, Edward, 'The Moriori', *Transactions and Proceedings of the New Zealand Institute*, vol. 22, 1889, pp. 75–79

——, *The Maori Race* (Whanganui: A.D. Willis, 1904)

Trotter, M.M., 'Excavations at Katiki Point, North Otago', *Records of the Canterbury Museum*, vol. 8, no. 3, 1967, pp. 231–45

Underhill, Peter A. et al., 'Maori origins, Y-chromosome haplotypes and implications for human history in the Pacific', *Human Mutation*, vol. 17, 2001, pp. 271–80

Ure, John, *A Tour Round the World* (Glasgow: Robert Anderson, 1885)

Vayda, Andrew P., *Maori Warfare* (Wellington: Polynesian Society, 1960)

Wagner, Konrad, *The Craniology of the Oceanic Races* (Oslo: Jacob Dybwad, 1937)

Wagstaff, S.J. & M.I. Dawson, 'Classification, origin, and patterns of diversification of Corynocarpus (*Corynocarpaceae*) inferred from DNA sequences', *Systematic Botany*, vol. 25, no. 1, 2000, pp. 134–49

Waitangi Tribunal, *Ngai Tahu Land Report* (Wellington: Waitangi Tribunal, Dept of Justice, 1991), https://forms.justice.govt.nz/search/Documents/WT/wt_DOC_68476209/Wai27.pdf

Walter, Richard, 'The Cook Islands – New Zealand connection', in *The Origins of the First New Zealanders*, ed. Douglas G. Sutton (Auckland: Auckland University Press, 1994) pp. 220–29

Walter, Richard & Chris Jacomb, 'New Zealand', in *Encyclopedia of Archaeology*, ed. Deborah Pearsall (Sandiago, California: Elsevier/Academic Press, 2008), pp. 1738–47

Walter, Richard et al., 'Mass migration and the Polynesian settlement of New Zealand', *Journal of World Prehistory*, vol. 30, no. 4, 2017, pp. 351–76

Walter, Richard, Chris Jacomb & Sreymony Bowron-Muth, 'Colonisation, mobility and exchange in New Zealand prehistory', *Antiquity*, vol. 84, 2010, pp. 497–513

Walters, Muru, *An Examination of the Literary Evidence for the Existence of Discrete Groups of Moriori in the Chatham Islands in the 19th Century* (Dunedin: Dept of Anthropology, University of Otago, 1977)

Walworth, Mary, 'Eastern Polynesian: The linguistic evidence revisited', *Oceanic Linguistics*, vol. 53, no. 2, 2014, pp. 256–72

Weisler, Marshall, 'Introduction', in *Prehistoric Long-distance Interaction in Oceania: An interdisciplinary approach*, ed. Marshall Weisler (Auckland: New Zealand Archaeological Association, 1997), pp. 7–18

——, 'Hard evidence for prehistoric interaction in Polynesia', *Current Anthropology*, vol. 39, no. 4, 1998, pp. 521–32

Weisler, Marshall & Roger Green, 'Rethinking the chronology of colonization of southeast Polynesia', in *Polynesians in America: Pre-*

Colombian Contacts with the New World, eds Terry Jones et al. (Lanham, New York, Toronto, Plymouth, UK: Altamira, 2011), pp. 223–46

Weisler, Marshall et al., 'Cook Island artifact geochemistry demonstrates spatial and temporal extent of pre-European interarchipelago voyaging in East Polynesia', *Proceedings of the National Academy of the Sciences*, vol. 113, no. 29, 2016, pp. 8150–55

West, Katrina, 'Investigating patterns of prehistoric dispersal in Eastern Polynesia: A commensal approach using complete ancient and modern mitochondrial genomes of the Pacific rat, *Rattus exulans*', MSc thesis, University of Otago, Dunedin, 2016

White, John, *Maori Customs and Superstitions, being the Subject of Two Lectures Delivered at the Mechanics' Institute in Auckland, During the Year 1861* (Christchurch: Kiwi Publishers, 1999), pp. 132–83

——, *The Ancient History of the Maori, his Mythology and Traditions*, vol. 2 (Wellington: George Didsbury, 1887)

Williams, H.W., 'Some notes on the language of the Chatham Islands', *Transactions and Proceedings of the New Zealand Institute*, vol. 51, 1919, pp. 415–22

——, 'The Maruiwi myth', *Journal of the Polynesian Society*, vol. 46, no. 183, 1937, pp. 105–22

——, *A Dictionary of the Maori Language* (Wellington: Government Printer, 1971)

Williams, J.W., 'Notes on the Chatham Islands', *Journal of the Anthropological Institute of Great Britain and Ireland*, vol. 27, 1898, pp. 343–45

Williams, Thomas & J. Calvert, *Fiji and the Fijians* (London: Alexander Heylin, 1858)

Williams, William, *A Dictionary of the New-Zealand Language*, 7th edn (Paihia: Church Mission Press, 1844; Wellington, 1971)

Wilmshurst, Janet et al., 'Dating the late prehistoric dispersal of Polynesians to New Zealand using the commensal Pacific rat', *Proceedings of the National Academy of the Sciences*, vol. 105, no. 22, 2008, pp. 7676–80

Wilmhurst, Janet & Thomas Higham, 'Using rat-gnawed seeds to independently date the arrival of Pacific rats and humans in New Zealand', *Holocene*, vol. 14, 2004, pp. 801–6

Wilmshurst, Janet, Terry Hunt, Carl Lipo & Atholl Anderson, 'High-precision radiocarbon dating shows recent and rapid initial human colonisation of East Polynesia', *Proceedings of the National Academy of the Sciences*, vol. 108, no. 5, 2011, pp. 1815–20

Wilson, William H., 'Whence the East Polynesians? Further linguistic evidence for a Northern outlier source', *Oceanic Linguistics*, vol. 51, no. 2, 2012, pp. 289–359

Wood, John G., *The Natural History of Man*, vol. 2 (New York: Routledge, 1880)

Wood, J.R. et al., 'An extinct nestorid parrot (*Aves, Psittaciformes, Nestoridae*) from the Chatham Islands, New Zealand', *Zoological Journal of the Linnean Society*, vol. 172, no. 1, 2014, pp. 185–99

Wright, Duncan, '10,000 birds: Birding, nature, conservation, and the wide, wide world', www.10000birds.com/new-zealands-other-eagle.htm

Yate, William, *An Account of New Zealand* (London: Seeley & Burnside, 1835)

Ngā mihimihi

I acknowledge the deities the taonga pūoro trace their lineage to, and which are the source of their mana.

I thank the Royal Society of New Zealand Te Apārangi, whose Marsden grant funded the wider project this book is part of.

I'm indebted to all my teachers who have helped and continue to help guide and support my journey. In particular, I want to thank and acknowledge Maui Solomon and Susan Thorpe from the Hokotehi Moriori Trust for their incredible hospitality, generosity and tireless work to revive Moriori culture; fellow taonga pūoro practitioners James Webster and Alistair Fraser (as well as Jamie, Hinemoa and Shannon); Moriori musician Ajay Peni; archaeologist Ian Barber; research assistants Irene Hundleby and Maramena Tuna; Māori cultural advisors kaumātua Hata Temo and Louise Kewene-Doig; and Toby Mills and his team from Tawera Productions. Thanks to all the curators at the many museums visited both in Aotearoa and overseas for their passion, enthusiasm and help. To the school children and other community members of Rēkohu Chatham Islands who participated in workshops and came to our concerts, thanks so much for your energy and interest. I hope we helped fan a flame that will burn brightly in years to come. Thanks also to the fantastic editors, Imogen Coxhead, Gillian Tewsley and Anna Hodge, who've helped shape this book, and to Sue Wootton, Fiona Moffat, Mel Stevens and Meg Hamilton from Otago University Press for their tireless support and encouragement. Special thanks also go to Stephen Stedman for recording and mixing the audio samples that accompany this book. Heartfelt thanks go to Huata Holmes, whose beautiful foreword moved me to tears. Finally, I'd also like to mihi to all those who have been and continue to be responsible for ensuring the voices of these remarkable instruments are carried into the future.

Unuhia, unuhia
Unuhia ki te uru tapu nui
Kia wātea, kia māmā, te ngākau, te tinana, te wairua i te ara takatā
Koia rā e Rongo, whakairia ake ki runga
Kia tina! Tina! Hui e! Tāiki e!

Audio links

Listed by page number

Full playlist is available at: **oup.nz/efh-audio**

Index

*Page numbers in **bold** refer to images.*

Published by Otago University Press
533 Castle Street
Dunedin, New Zealand
university.press@otago.ac.nz
www.oup.nz

First published 2024

ISBN 978-1-99-004859-3

A catalogue record for this book is available from the National Library of New Zealand.

Published with the assistance of Creative New Zealand

Unless otherwise credited, photographs by Mel Stevens
Editors: Gillian Tewsley, Anna Hodge
Design and typesetting: Fiona Moffat
Index: Diane Lowther
Printed in China through Asia Pacific Offset